D1379410

Volume 2:
From A.D. 1500 to the Present

World History

Volume 2:
From A.D. 1500 to the Present

World History

Original and Secondary Source Readings

Charles A. Frazee, professor of history, California
State University, Fullerton, Book Editor

David L. Bender, Publisher
Bruno Leone, Executive Editor
Bonnie Szumski, Editorial Director
James Miller, Series Editor

Editorial Advisory Board
Michael Doyle, Ocean County College
Patrick Manning, Northeastern University
Richard Lewis, St. Cloud State University
Sara Tucker, Washburn University
Heidi Roupp, President, World History Association
Harry Wade, Texas A&M University

Perspectives
on History

GREENHAVEN PRESS, INC., SAN DIEGO, CA

RET
D
20
.W886
1999

Every effort has been made to trace the owners of copyrighted material. The articles in this volume may have been edited for content, length, and/or reading level. Those interested in locating the original source will find the complete citation on the first page of each article.

Library of Congress Cataloging-in-Publication Data

World history : original and secondary source readings / Charles A.
    Frazee, book editor.
        p.   cm. — (Perspectives on history)
    Includes bibliographical references and index.
    Contents: v. 2. From 1500 to the Present
    ISBN 1-56510-987-2 (lib. : alk. paper). — ISBN 1-56510-986-4
(pbk. : alk. paper)
    1. World history. 2. History—Sources. I. Frazee, Charles A.
II. Series.
D20.W886   1999   98-8852
909—dc21   CIP

Copyright © 1999 by Greenhaven Press, Inc.
P.O. Box 289009
San Diego, CA 92198-9009

Maps by Lineworks, Inc.

Printed in the USA

CONTENTS

To the Instructor   10

To the Student   11

Timeline   14

Unit 1
The Early Modern World

Chapter 1: European Discoveries: What Did the Explorers Find?   20
  The Portuguese in West Africa, J.D. Fage
  The Portuguese in India, Gaspar Correa
  October 12, 1492, Christopher Columbus
  Columbus, a Man of Contradictions, Felipe Fernández-Armesto
  The Dutch Overseas Empire, G.V. Scammell
  Living in New England, William Cronon

Chapter 2: Spanish America: How Was It Won and What Was
Its Culture?   32
  Cortés and Moctezuma, Bernal Díaz del Castillo
  The Fall of the Aztec Capital, anonymous
  In Defense of the Indians, Bartolomé de Las Casas
  Governing the Spanish Empire, Robert Ryal Miller
  Life in Colonial Lima, Josephe de Mugaburu
  The Columbian Exchange, Alfred W. Crosby

Chapter 3: The European Reformation: What Were the Issues?   42
  The Quest for Righteousness, Martin Luther
  Predestination, John Calvin
  The Reformers and Women, Jane Dempsey Douglass
  Reformation in England, Richard Rex
  Religious Women in the Americas, Asunción Lavrin
  Divine Love, Sister Juana Inés de la Cruz

Chapter 4: The Age of Absolutism: Does Sovereignty Have Limits?   53
  The Sun King, Pierre Goubert
  The Court of Versailles, Another View, Liselotte von der Pfalz
  James I and the Puritans, Arthur Wilson
  The King and Parliament, D. Harris Willson

Galileo and His Telescope, Galileo Galilei
Newton and the Laws of Motion, Isaac Newton

CHAPTER 5: The Eighteenth Century in Europe: How Enlightened Was It? 63
Religion Among the Christians: A Satire, Charles-Louis de Secondat
The Civil State, Jean-Jacques Rousseau
The Best of European Society—Paris, Voltaire
Catherine Seizes the Throne, John T. Alexander
A Criticism of Catherine the Great, M.M. Shcherbatov
Johann Sebastian Bach, Ronald Taylor

CHAPTER 6: The Ottoman Empire: Can Muslims and Christians Live
Together? 73
The Military Nature of the Ottoman State, Marshall G.S. Hodgson
Ottoman Christians, Charles Frazee
The Siege of Vienna, Antony Bridge
Problems of Government, Mustafa Ali
The Tale of a Warrior, The Book of Dede Korkut
Stories of Nasreddin Hoja, Barbara Walker and John Noonan

CHAPTER 7: Mughals and British: Who Shall Dominate India? 84
Rama Wins a Victory over Ravana, Tulsidas
Akbar's House of Worship, Muni Lal
The Economy of Mughal India, Rhoads Murphey
Wealth in Mughal India, François Bernier
Trade in India, James Mill
Cornwallis, Brian Gardner

CHAPTER 8: East Asian Traditions: Is There a Price for Isolation? 94
Chinese Nationalism, Susan Naquin and Evelyn S. Rawski
The Youth of the Wan Li Emperor, Ray Huang
Dinner in China, Matteo Ricci
Chinese Customs, Lord George Macartney
Riding Etiquette in Japan, Joâo Rodrigues
The Search for Identity in Japan, Marius B. Jansen

CHAPTER 9: Africa: How Did European Contact Affect Its People? 104
A Description of Benin, John Barbot
The Growth of the West African Kingdoms, Roland Oliver and J.D. Fage
Women of Dahomey, Archibald Dalzel
A Slave Remembers, Ayuba Suleiman Diallo
The Portuguese in East Africa, Zoë Marsh and G.W. Kingsnorth
The East African Coast, Duarte Barbosa

CHAPTER 10: The Americas: How Was Independence Achieved? 113
An Objection to Colonial Taxation, William Pitt
Common Sense, Thomas Paine
The Middle Class in America, Gordon Wood

The American Democracy, Alexis de Tocqueville
The Revolutions in South America, Tulio Halperín Donghi
Bolívar's Resignation, Simón Bolívar

UNIT 2
The Nineteenth Century

CHAPTER 11: The French Revolution and Napoleon: How Did They
Change the History of Europe?   126
    The Useless Nature of Nobility, Emmanuel Joseph Sieyès
    Women in the French Revolution, Olwen H. Hufton
    Violence Claims the Revolution, William Doyle
    A Critique of the Revolution, Edmund Burke
    Napoleon's Invasion of Russia, Jean Tulard
    Looking Back, Napoleon Bonaparte

CHAPTER 12: European Industrialization and Urbanization: What Were
the Consequences?   137
    Population Out of Control, Thomas Malthus
    Precious Metals as Wealth, Adam Smith
    The Working Class in Nineteenth-Century England, E.P. Thompson
    Bourgeoisie and Proletariat, Karl Marx and Friedrich Engels
    Railroads and Steamships, William Ashworth
    The Progress of Industrialization, W.O. Henderson

CHAPTER 13: Europe: How Did Nationalism Shape the Nineteenth
Century?   147
    Building a Nation, Anthony D. Smith
    Evils of the Revolutionary Spirit, Prince Klemens Metternich
    A Revolution on Trial, Documents on the French Revolution of 1848
    The Prussian Revolution, James J. Sheehan
    The Argument for an Independent Italy, Giuseppe Mazzini
    The Final Chapter for Garibaldi, Christopher Hibbert

CHAPTER 14: Asia and Africa: What Were the Challenges of the
Colonial Period?   156
    The Impact of Colonialism, E.J. Hobsbawm
    The Opium Trade, Lin Ze Xu
    The Attack on Delhi, N.A. Chick
    Great Britain and India, John R. McLane
    Africa in the Colonial Age, Michael Crowder
    Japan's Economy Under the Tokugawa Shoguns, W.G. Beasley

Unit 3
A Century of Change

CHAPTER 15: World War I: What Explains Its Tragedy?   169
The Last Chance for Peace, Barbara Tuchman
Germany's War Aims, Fritz Fischer
Intellectual Responsibility, Roland N. Stromberg
All Quiet on the Western Front, Erich Maria Remarque
The Home Front, Princess Evelyn Blücher
The Treaty of Versailles, Papers of the Paris Peace Conference

CHAPTER 16: The Russian Revolution: How Did Communism Affect
Russia?   179
The Bolshevik Revolution, Leon Trotsky
The Bolsheviks Take Power, John Thompson
The Significance of the Russian Revolution, Robert C. Tucker
Stalin vs. Trotsky, Isaac Deutscher
The Five-Year Plan, Joseph Stalin
Admission of Treason, Robert Conquest

CHAPTER 17: World War II: What Were Its Origins and Its Impact on
World Events?   189
Fundamentals of Fascism, Benito Mussolini
March to Totalitarianism, F.L. Carsten
A View of the German Future, Adolf Hitler
Hitler's War Plans, Raymond Aron
The Warsaw Deportation, Yisrael Gutman
Reflections on Pearl Harbor, Harry Wray

CHAPTER 18: The Cold War: What Explains the Conflict Between the
Communist Nations and the West After World War II?   199
The Novikov Telegram, Nikolay Novikov
Creating the Soviet Empire, Vojtech Mastny
A Prime Minister Forced from Office, Ferenc Nagy
A Soviet View of the Cold War, V.A. Zolotarev
The Chinese Revolution Defined, Mao Zedong
China's Social Revolution, Lucien Bianco

CHAPTER 19: Nationalism in Action: How Did It Cause the End of
Empire and the Creation of New Countries?   209
The Force of Passive Resistance, Mohandas K. Gandhi
A Woman of Accomplishment, Pupul Jayakar and Ved Mehta
Declaration for a New South Africa, African National Congress
South Africa Seeks a Way Out of Apartheid, Nelson Mandela

Creation of Israel, Israeli Knesset
Palestine, Jerome M. Segal

CHAPTER 20: The Collapse of Communism in the Soviet Union and
Eastern Europe and Its Survival in China: What Other Forces Now
Shape the Modern World?   221
    The Knock on the Door, Aleksandr Solzhenitsyn
    Obstacles to Soviet Reform, Mikhail Gorbachev
    Slogans in a Grocery Store, Václav Havel
    Communism in China, Craig Dietrich
    The Muslim Future, I.M. Lapidus
    The Democratic Ideal, Strobe Talbott

ACKNOWLEDGMENTS   231
INDEX   232

To the Instructor

This book of readings in world history examines various aspects of the human experience from approximately A.D. 1500 to the present. After that date the history of the world enters a new phase, with Europeans becoming the active element effecting change in a way that had not happened earlier. The world became much more interrelated.

The following selections cover politics, religion, economics, and culture, giving a comprehensive view of human life. Most deal with public events that made a difference in subsequent history. Readers should be reminded that historians know only those aspects of history that have been remembered, and this is only a small part of the total historical record.

I have taken the liberty, for the sake of easier reading, to make several changes in the original documents. These changes include breaking up long paragraphs, omitting some parenthetical phrases, and sometimes using American spelling and rules on capitalization. When possible, Chinese names have been put into pinyin orthography. Words and phrases in brackets are my editorial remarks, and are not a part of the text.

Charles A. Frazee

September 1, 1998

TO THE STUDENT

In beginning your world history course, you are embarking on an exciting voyage through time, one that will take you from A.D. 1500 to the present. You will meet a great variety of cultures and peoples; you will witness terrible tragedies and inspiring triumphs of the human spirit. You will encounter ideas that have changed the course of history and spoken profoundly of the human condition—ideas that people have believed worth dying for. Above all, you will encounter change, for that is what history is all about. How do people effect changes in their lives? How do they react to changes that are forced upon them? How do they interpret the changes that threaten familiar patterns of life? Do they welcome change, or flee from it? Explaining and interpreting change is what the historian does. You will encounter plenty of examples of change and interpretation as you move through this course; if your encounters help you understand changes that are happening in our own society, then the time you spend with world history will be a valuable lifetime investment.

This book is not a complete history of the world. The textbook that your instructor has probably assigned will provide you with a connected narrative of world history, and it is on that narrative, as well as on your instructor's lectures, that you should rely for the "big picture." This book has a different purpose: to take you closer to certain key events in world history. Taking these closer looks will give you two opportunities. First, you will hear actual participants in past events tell their stories. Second, you can benefit from the interpretations of these events that experts who have devoted their working lives to studying the past can share with you.

History does not write itself. It is written by historians who use evidence to construct an account of what happened. If there is no evidence, there can be no history. And whatever account the historian writes, remember that it is that historian's interpretation, based on the evidence that he or she has critically examined. New evidence is constantly turning up, sometimes causing historians to revise radically their understanding of the past. (Some of the most dramatic instances of such revisions occur in the case of very ancient cultures and civilizations, for which evidence is sparse; a single new discovery can overturn much of what historians have thought they knew.) More commonly, historical interpretations change subtly, as historians begin to ask other questions or to consider different kinds of evidence. For example, historians today are much more interested in the experiences of ordinary men and women of the past than they were a generation ago, when "history" mainly meant the doings of kings, generals, and other such leaders.

What is the evidence that historians use? Written documents, of course, reveal what someone said or did. But historians cannot accept such evidence at face value: Not only is forgery a possibility, but the trustworthiness of the source must be questioned. What motivated the person who wrote this report or recorded this list or ordered this inscription carved in marble? In asking such questions, the historian does the job that a good detective must do in investigating a case.

But there are far more varieties of historical evidence than written documents. Works of art and literature can reveal much about the values of past societies and cultures. Religious traditions, philosophical ideas, political attitudes, and all the complex patterns of thought and behavior that anthropologists call culture must come within the historian's field of vision. Oral traditions, passed by word of mouth through many generations who could not read or write, become important sources for understanding some cultures of the past.

Sometimes "material culture" provides the only direct evidence that has survived the ages. Did certain ruins result from a natural disaster, from abandonment of the site by its inhabitants, or from devastation by some enemy? Do scraps of broken pottery suggest who made them, and when, and how wealthy their society was, and who did the work? How was labor divided between men and women? What tools and weapons did these people use? How did they get their food? What did they eat?

Historians also rely on the evidence that experts in other disciplines can provide. Languages change, but according to patterns that can be scientifically analyzed; what does this tell us about how a certain ethnic group arose, and how it is related to other peoples? Scientific analyses of very old textiles, of ancient deposits of pollen in the soil, of glacial ice, or even of DNA and of the isotopes of fossils, can reveal surprisingly important information about the distant past.

All of what has been mentioned so far historians consider their primary sources. These are the fundamental building blocks of history, from which the historian hopes to extract reliable data. Included among these primary sources are historians' accounts written in the distant past, which can be useful for suggesting what past generations thought about their own historical traditions, or for narrating events. Obviously, however, the writings of, for example, ancient Greek, Roman, or Chinese historians, or of medieval Christian or Islamic chroniclers, have to be judged with the same highly critical eye that the historian casts upon an Egyptian pharaoh's boasts in his victory monuments of the enemies he has destroyed, or upon a thousand-year-old account of a visitor to a Japanese city.

In contrast to the primary sources of history are the writings that modern historians themselves produce, usually called "secondary sources." They are not primary sources because historians cannot use them as direct evidence of what happened. Instead, they are just what the working historian is trying to produce: an interpretation of the past. Historians build on the accomplishments of their colleagues and predecessors. Whatever they publish must withstand the critical scrutiny of other historians, both their contemporaries and those who will come later. New questions are continually asked, new interpretations advanced, and older interpretations either refined or rejected.

As you read the selections in the chapters that follow, keep in mind the nature of the source and keep your critical eyes open. If the text is a primary source, ask yourself how this evidence should be interpreted, both in light of other evidence available to you and from the perspective of historians' interpretations of this period. If it is a secondary source, ask yourself how persuasive is the modern historian's case. What kind of evidence has the historian considered? Has the historian even asked the right questions?

The readings in this book have been chosen to provide a useful and interesting collection of primary and secondary sources for the study of world history.

Timeline:
From A.D. 1500 to the Present

1492

Christopher Columbus makes first voyage to Western Hemisphere

1518–1521

Cortés conquers Mexico

1563

Council of Trent decrees reforms for Catholic Church

1600

Beginning of Tokugawa period in Japan

1643–1713

Reign of Louis XIV in France

1644

Ming Dynasty falls in China, replaced by Qing

ca. 1780

Industrial Revolution begins in Great Britain

1762–1796

Reign of Catherine the Great in Russia

1740–1786

Reign of Frederick the Great in Prussia

1775–1787

American Revolution

1500	1550	1600	1650	1700	1750	1800

1536

Parliament declares Henry VIII supreme head of Church of England

1526

Mughal Empire founded in India

1517

Martin Luther publishes the Ninety-Five Theses

1640–1660

English Revolution

1618–1648

Thirty Years' War in Germany

1607

English settlement of North America begins

1689–1715

Reign of Peter the Great in Russia

1688

Overthrow of James II in England initiates supremacy of Parliament

1683

Ottoman defeat at siege of Vienna

1763

Treaty of Paris, ending Seven Years' War, establishes British supremacy in North America and India

1789

French Revolution begins

1914

Outbreak of
World War I

1917

Russian
Revolution
begins

1989–1991

Fall of communism in
Soviet Union and Eastern
Europe; end of Cold War

1841–1842

Opium War
in China

1820–1822

Independence of
most Spanish
colonies in
Latin America
secured

1911–1912

Fall of the Qing in
China; proclamation of
Chinese Republic

1931

Japanese
invasion
of China

**1814–
1815**

Defeat of
Napoleon
ends era of
the French
Revolution

1884

Berlin
Conference
largely
completes
European
partition
of Africa

**1904–
1905**

Russo-
Japanese
War

1947

Cold War begins;
independence of
India

1948

Independence of
Israel; beginning
of Arab-Israeli
wars

| 1800 | 1850 | 1900 | 1950 | 2000 |

1848

Wave of revolutions
sweeps Europe

1918–1919

End of
World War I
and Treaty
of Versailles

1949

People's Republic
of China declared

1850–1864

Taiping Rebellion in China

1857–1858

Sepoy Revolt in India

1869

Opening of
Suez Canal

1929

Great
Depression
begins;
Stalin
consolidates
power and
begins
industrial-
ization drive

1939–1945

World War II, ending
in first use of nuclear
weapons

1989

Tiananmen
Square
demonstrations
for democracy
in China

1861–1865

Civil War in the
United States

1868

Meiji
Revolution
in Japan

1933

Hitler becomes
chancellor of
Germany

UNIT 1

The Early Modern World

CONTENTS

MAP   17

CHAPTER 1:
European Discoveries: What Did the Explorers Find?   20

CHAPTER 2:
Spanish America: How Was It Won and What Was Its Culture?   32

CHAPTER 3:
The European Reformation: What Were the Issues?   42

CHAPTER 4:
The Age of Absolutism: Does Sovereignty Have Limits?   53

CHAPTER 5:
The Eighteenth Century in Europe: How Enlightened Was It?   63

CHAPTER 6:
The Ottoman Empire: Can Muslims and Christians Live Together?   73

CHAPTER 7:
Mughals and British: Who Shall Dominate India?   84

CHAPTER 8:
East Asian Traditions: Is There a Price for Isolation?   94

CHAPTER 9:
Africa: How Did European Contact Affect Its People?   104

CHAPTER 10:
The Americas: How Was Independence Achieved?   113

The World in About 1500

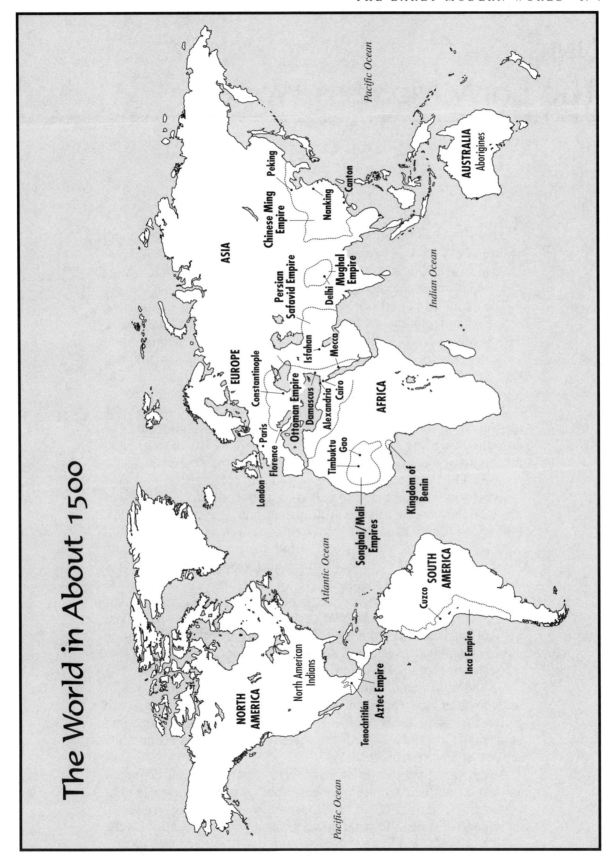

NORTH AMERICA

North American Indians

Tenochtitlán

Aztec Empire

Cuzco SOUTH AMERICA

Inca Empire

Pacific Ocean

Atlantic Ocean

London

Florence

Paris

Constantinople

EUROPE

Ottoman Empire

Damascus

Alexandria

Cairo

AFRICA

Timbuktu

Gao

Songhai/Mali Empires

Kingdom of Benin

Mecca

Isfahan

Persian Safavid Empire

Delhi

Mughal Empire

ASIA

Chinese Ming Empire

Peking

Nanking

Canton

Indian Ocean

Pacific Ocean

AUSTRALIA

Aborigines

UNIT 1
The Early Modern World

Historians label the three hundred years between A.D. 1500 and 1800 as early modern history. Selections that appear in this first unit are concerned with issues from this era. It was a time rich in events that helped shape the modern world.

The major event of this period of world history was the expansion of the Atlantic nations of Europe into the other parts of the world. This involved contacts between Europeans and native peoples on a scale never before experienced. In the Americas, the Spaniards and Portuguese arrived first, followed by the French, Dutch, and English. This meant new opportunities for the Europeans, but it proved disastrous for the Aztec and Inca Empires, which were themselves consolidating their control over neighboring peoples. Because the diseases carried by the Europeans, such as smallpox, measles, and tuberculosis, were unknown to the natives, a massive loss of life resulted when they came into contact with the foreigners.

Events in India, Africa, and east Asia also tended to cluster about the interaction between the Europeans and the native peoples. Portuguese, French, Dutch, and British merchants formed small colonies, or stations, on the coast of India and Africa. In China and Japan the rulers did their best to prevent European settlement, for their view of the world required nothing from outsiders. Their dense populations prevented large settlements of Westerners in their midst. Africa presented its own problems for Europeans, for here tropical sicknesses put them on the defensive. Most Westerners on this continent had a very low life expectancy, since they had none of the resistance to illnesses familiar to native Africans.

On the other hand Europeans found conditions right for major settlement in the American continents. During the early modern period their superiority in firearms, oceangoing sailing ships, and organizational skills enabled the western Europeans to become the active element in world history.

At the very time that Europeans were expanding their economy and exporting their culture overseas, their own continent was convulsed in a long period of religious and dynastic wars. However, these conflicts began to wind down in the eighteenth century as the

Enlightenment urged greater toleration of various religious beliefs.

The Ottoman Empire, in the southeast corner of Europe, was the major state during this era. Based on a centuries-long military tradition that had a strong element of religious fervor attached, the sultans in Istanbul proved to be remarkably successful in amassing territories through the seventeenth century. Then the lack of a strong central government and a merchant marine began to take its toll.

At the end of the eighteenth century the story of colonial independence movements in the Americas takes precedence. Completed in the thirteen British colonies by 1783, they required another generation to achieve the same result in South America.

CHAPTER 1
European Discoveries:
What Did the Explorers Find?

By 1500 European explorations had been in progress for over fifty years. The small country of Portugal took the lead; the Portuguese had first established bases on the North African coast, and from there they began sailing down the forbidding West African shoreline of modern Mauritania, where the Sahara Desert meets the Atlantic Ocean.

Prince Henry, called the Navigator because he sponsored these expeditions, collected the data brought back by his mariners. As governor of Ceuta, a port on the Moroccan coast, Henry, the third son of the Portuguese king, tapped into his resources to found a school for geographers at Sagres. Their purpose was to map the West African coast to enable Portuguese traders directly to reach the sources of gold, ivory, and slaves that Europeans had to buy from Muslim merchant middlemen in North Africa. In 1446 a Portuguese captain had reached the Sénégal River, and in 1473 Diogo Cão crossed the equator.

Besides trade, the Portuguese were also interested in bringing Catholic missionaries to the African kingdoms below the Sahara. If the Africans could be enlisted in the Christian camp, then the Muslims of North Africa would have enemies on two sides. The crusading ideal was still alive in western Europe.

SELECTION 1:

The Portuguese in West Africa

In the following selection, J.D. Fage, a professor of African history at the University of Birmingham, England, analyzes the Portuguese presence in Guinea, the West African region on the Atlantic, explaining why the goals of the Portuguese remained elusive. It may help to have a map of West Africa before you while you read this selection.

The Portuguese agents on the mainland were expected to assimilate the Africans to Portuguese and Christian ways, but this did not happen. The traders tended to settle down, marry African wives, and establish a mulatto society that was free from the more annoying restrictions of both European and African life. This society attracted to it a motley crowd of undesirable fugitives and exiles from Portugal and other European lands. It exerted no Christian influence on the Africans and when, during the sixteenth century, merchants from other European countries began to appear on the scene, it was quite prepared to forget the interests of Portugal and to provide agents for the trade of the foreigners. The Portuguese government tried to check this deterioration in Portuguese influence by revoking the mainland trading rights of the Cape Verde islanders in 1518, and by supporting the work of Catholic missionaries from Portugal, but they were too late. Except for the region around the Portuguese settlement of Cacheu, the coastal districts between the Senegal and Sierra Leone had become a happy hunting-ground for the more disreputable traders of many European nations.

The Portuguese had little contact with the Grain and Ivory Coasts principally because, since they lacked natural harbors, the strong offshore current and frequent storms of the region made it unsafe for sailing ships to venture close to them for any length of time. Consequently the peoples of this part of West Africa remained remarkably free from European influence right up to the nineteenth century.

On the other hand, the Gold Coast was the scene of the greatest Portuguese commercial activity in all Guinea. In addition to their headquarters at Elmina, the Portuguese built forts at Axim and Shama, which, like Elmina Castle can still be seen today, and also at Accra, though here the local Gã captured and destroyed their fort in 1576. By the early years of the sixteenth century, the officials and traders in these forts were sending to Portugal each year gold to the value of £100,000 or $400,000 in the money of the time (equivalent to one-tenth of the world's supply of gold), which they had received in return for imports of cloth, hardware, beads and slaves. (In view of what was to happen later, it may seem strange that the Portuguese were *importing* slaves into the Gold Coast. But this was undoubtedly the case in the sixteenth century, presumably because the upcountry merchants needed laborers for the mines and porters to carry back with them the much bulkier goods they had received in exchange for the gold-dust they had brought to the coast. The Portuguese brought the slaves from the area of Benin and the Niger delta.)

But though Portuguese trade with the Gold Coast was great, Portuguese influence there was limited. The attitude of the coastal states towards the Portuguese virtually restricted their power to within gun-shot of their forts and ships. The coastal peoples welcomed the Portuguese only for the trade they brought and the profits they

J.D. Fage, *A History of West Africa*, 4th ed. (Cambridge: Cambridge University Press, 1969), pp. 58–60.

themselves could make from this trade. They insisted that trade between the Portuguese and the inland countries, where most of the gold was mined, should pass through their hands, and they actively opposed Portuguese attempts to establish direct contact with the interior. They strongly objected to the Portuguese claim to a monopoly of their trade with Europeans, and particularly to the Portuguese habit of sending punitive expeditions against states who traded with other Europeans. They feared lest the Portuguese should use their forts as bases for the extension of their political and Christian influence into the country, so that they would become utterly under Portuguese control. They therefore insisted that the ground on which the forts were built belonged to them, and that the Portuguese rights were those of lessors only.

Nevertheless, the attractions of trade with the Portuguese were so great that an increasing number of Africans, from the inland as well as the coastal states, left home to work in new towns that began to grow up beneath the walls of the forts, Elmina in particular. These people were subject to the jurisdiction of no traditional African chief, the men of the Portuguese garrisons chose wives from among them, and in course of time communities developed which were almost as much European and Christian in character as they were African and animist, and which were governed according to a rough European pattern by chiefs of their own who were responsible to the Portuguese commanders of the forts.

The Portuguese did little trade between the Volta and Lagos. This part of Guinea offered no gold; consequently the Portuguese did not bother to solve the difficulties involved in establishing permanent contact with its peoples across the heavy surf and the lagoons characteristic of this part of the coast. The Portuguese were active, however, on the coast from Lagos (situated by the only permanent entrance to the lagoons) to the Niger delta and, initially, especially at Benin. There were a number of reasons for this. In the first place, this coast with its numerous creeks and rivers, was easily penetrable by, and offered safe anchorages for the Portuguese ships. Secondly, the Portuguese seem to have found an active local trade in progress—no doubt because this region formed part of the Yoruba trading system. Except in respect of peppers and ivory, there was no European demand for the principal commodities of this trade. But the Portuguese discovered that some of these, notably, it would seem, *akori* beads, cloth and slaves, were in demand on the Gold Coast. The Gold Coast peoples' interest in *akori* and in cloth from what is now Western Nigeria (and also, for that matter, in cloth and clothing which the Portuguese brought them from Morocco) suggests strongly, in fact, that at least some quantity of these commodities had been reaching the Gold Coast along established African trade routes before the Portuguese arrived on the scene. Since Portugal herself was not a great supplier of manufactured goods, the commodities she herself could offer on the Gold Coast were either little attractive to its exporters of gold or had to be purchased by her at a cost from other European countries. The Portuguese were therefore naturally attracted to the scheme of exchanging their European goods for Nigerian produce, and re-selling the latter on the Gold Coast, for in this way they gained two opportunities for profit instead of only one.

After reading this selection, consider these questions:
1. Why did the Portuguese attempt at assimilation fail?
2. What reasons hindered or accelerated Portuguese economic activity?
3. How did the African people react to the Portuguese presence?

SELECTION 2:

The Portuguese in India

The Portuguese were hardly content with their African finds; India, a much more attractive goal, lay beyond. No one in Portugal knew for sure if a sea route existed, but it certainly seemed worth the effort to find out.

One Portuguese captain, Bartolomeu Dias, sailed as far south as modern Namibia when a gale blew his ship out to sea. When he regained his course he saw that the coast was turning northward, for he had in fact rounded the Cape of Good Hope, the southern tip of Africa, which he called the Cape of Storms. His crew then demanded to go home, so Dias had to turn back, leaving the voyage to India for another discoverer.

In 1498 the sea route to India was finally discovered when Vasco da Gama sailed around Africa and into the Indian port of Calicut. In the following selection, Gaspar Correa, the historian of da Gama's voyages, recalls this first direct contact between the Portuguese and the Malabar kingdom. Correa calls the Arab Muslims of the city "Moors," the universal name the Portuguese gave to followers of Islam. Note how the Portuguese understood the caste system of India, speaking of the Brahmans, the highest class, as nairs. *He is accurate in explaining the progress of Islam in making converts from among the Indian population, especially from the lowest classes, for Muslims had no caste system.*

The city of Calicut, as it was the principal one of India, on account of its great trade since ancient times, was all inhabited by foreign and native Moors, the richest that there were in all India. There were Moors of Grand Cairo who brought large fleets of many ships with much trade of valuable goods, which they brought from Mecca, and they took back in return pepper and drugs, and all the other richest merchandise of India, with which they acquired great wealth; and the people who are natives of the country have no profit from it nor income, but only enough to sustain themselves with; this sustenance is of little cost. . . . As they are ill off for wealth they are much subject to the Moors who are so rich, and this especially in the seaports, in which they are

rich from the great resources which they draw from trade with the Moors. From this trade the Moors were very powerful, and had so established and ingratiated themselves in the countries of the seaports, that they were more influential and respected than the natives themselves, so that many of the heathen became Moors in such manner that they were more people than the natives. . . .

In this region of Malabar the race of gentlemen is called *nairs*, who are the people of war. They are people who are very refined in blood and customs, and separated from all other low people, and so much do they value themselves that no one of them ever turned Moor; only the low people turned Moors, who worked in the bush and in the fields. And these people are so accursed that they cannot go by any road without shouting, so that the nairs may not come up suddenly and meet them, because they kill them at once, for they always carry their arms, and these

Gaspar Correa, *The Three Voyages of Vasco da Gama,* in *Lendas da India,* trans. Henry E.J. Stanley (reprint, New York: Burt Franklin, n.d.), pp. 154–57.

low people may not carry arms to defend them-selves; and when they go along thus shouting if any nair shouts to them they at once get into the bush very far from the road.

The Moors, understanding that it was a good way to increase their sect, said to the king, and to the rulers of the places in which they traded, that they met with great difficulties with their mer-chandise, because they had not got laborers to cart it from one point to another, because the la-borers, being low people, could not go amongst other people, as the nairs would kill them when-ever they met them, and therefore they would es-teem it a favor if those of the low people who might turn Moors should be able to go freely wherever they pleased; since, being Moors, they would then be outside of the Malabar religion and usages, and that they might be able to touch all sorts of people; because if this was not agreed to they would not be able to transport their goods to sell them in their provinces. . . .

As these things were so, the Moors of Calicut, in which city there were many who were ac-quainted with the affairs of Christendom, per-ceived the great inconvenience and certain de-struction which would fall upon them and upon their trade, if the Portuguese should establish trade in Calicut, which they would immediately afterwards do throughout all the Indian countries. . . .With this design they spoke to the king's chief factor, who was the principal overseer of his ex-chequer [the treasury], also to the king's *gosil*, who is the minister of justice; and they spoke to him in secret, after the manner of true friends,

saying that they, as sincere friends of the king, for whose service they would spend their lives and property, told him, that they as persons so de-serving of credit would tell the king and warn him to take precautions and consideration as to what he did with the Portuguese, because, with-out any doubt, they were men who had got such wealth in their own country, that they did not un-dergo all this labor for trade, but only to conquer countries and acquire honors by arms.

First they had been sent to see and spy, in order later to come and take these countries; for which reason it might doubtless be believed that these who came in these ships did not come for anything else, except under the cloak of mer-chants who come to establish peace and trade, and bring presents and feigned pretenses only to see and spy, and afterwards come to conquer and plunder; and this was easily seen, since they came from so distant a country with two ships to trade and take cargo; therefore they (the Moors) had given information and warning to the King that he might look to what he should do with the Portuguese.

After reading this selection, consider these questions:

1. What prompted the Portuguese to sail to Malabar?
2. What advantages came to Indian con-verts to Islam?
3. Why were the Muslim traders anxious about the Portuguese presence?

SELECTION 3:

October 12, 1492

The Spanish sovereigns, Ferdinand and Isabella, had no intention of being left out of the world trade that the voyages of the Portuguese opened. However, it was only in the last decade of the fifteenth century, after they completed the conquest of Granada, that the Spanish monarchs could turn their attention to overseas expeditions. For a considerable time the royal court was aware that a Genoese seaman had been arguing the case for finding China and Japan by sailing westward. This was Christopher Columbus, whom the scholars of the day dismissed because they claimed (correctly) that he had underestimated the size of the world by about one-third. No one at that time dreamed there would be a whole new continent in the way of a voyage from Spain to east Asia.

Columbus was very fortunate that Queen Isabella agreed to outfit his expedition on the chance he might be right. In August 1492 he sailed out of Palos harbor. He kept a log of his trip that tells of that momentous day, October 12, when he landed on an island in the Bahamas and the Spaniards came ashore to meet the peaceful Arawak Indians. The sixteenth-century Spanish friar Bartolomé de Las Casas later incorporated Columbus's account into his history of Spain's discovery and—as he saw it—mistreatment of the "Indians."

Soon they saw naked people; and the Admiral went ashore in the armed launch, and Martín Alonso Pinzón and his brother Vicente Anes, who was captain of the *Niña*. The Admiral brought out the royal banner and the captains two flags with the green cross, which the Admiral carried on all the ships as a standard, with an F and a Y, and over each letter a crown, one on one side of the [cross] and the other on the other. Thus put ashore they saw very green trees and many ponds and fruits of various kinds.

The Admiral called to the two captains and to the others who had jumped ashore and to Rodrigo Descobedo, the *escrivano* [the royal notary] of the whole fleet, and to Rodrigo Sánchez de Segovia; and he said that they should be witnesses that, in the presence of all, he would take, as in fact he did take, possession of the said island for the king and for the queen his lords, making the declarations that were required, and which at more length are contained in the testimonials made there in writing. Soon many people of the island gathered there. What follows are the very words of the Admiral in his book about his first voyage to, and discovery of, these Indies.

I, he says, in order that they would be friendly to us—because I recognized that they were

people who would be better freed [from error] and converted to our Holy Faith by love than by force—to some of them I gave red caps, and glass beads which they put on their chests, and many other things of small value, in which they took so much pleasure and became so much our friends that it was a marvel. Later they came swimming to the ships' launches where we were and brought us parrots and cotton thread in balls and javelins and many other things, and they traded them to us for other things which we gave them, such as small glass beads and bells. In sum, they took everything and gave of what they had very willingly. But it seemed to me that they were a people very poor in everything.

All of them go around as naked as their mothers bore them; and the women also, although I did not see more than one quite young girl. And all those that I saw were young people, for none did I see of more than 30 years of age. They are very well formed, with handsome bodies and good faces. Their hair [is] coarse—almost like the tail of a horse—and short. They wear their hair down over their eyebrows except for a little in the back which they wear long and never cut. Some of them paint themselves with black, and they are of the color of the Canarians [people of the Canary Islands], neither black nor white; and some of them paint themselves with white, and some of them with red, and some of them with whatever they find. And some of them paint their faces, and some of them the whole body, and

The Diario *of Christopher Columbus's First Voyage to America 1492–1493,* abstracted by Fray Bartolomé de las Casas, trans. Oliver Dunn and James E. Kelley Jr. (Norman and London: University of Oklahoma Press, 1989), pp. 63–67.

some of them only the eyes, and some of them only the nose.

They do not carry arms nor are they acquainted with them, because I showed them swords and they took them by the edge and through ignorance cut themselves. They have no iron. Their javelins are shafts without iron and some of them have at the end a fish tooth and others of other things. All of them alike are of good-sized stature and carry themselves well. I saw some who had marks of wounds on their bodies and I made signs to them asking what they were; and they showed me how people from other islands nearby [the Caribs] came there and tried to take them, and how they defended themselves; and I believed and believe that they come here from *tierra firme* [the mainland] to take them captive.

After reading this selection, consider these questions:

1. How did the Indian people greet the Spaniards?
2. What were some differences between the Native Americans and the Spaniards?
3. What makes you think Columbus was disappointed in his discovery?

SELECTION 4:

Columbus, a Man of Contradictions

A *modern historian, Felipe Fernández-Armesto, offers an assessment of Columbus's discovery. It obviously makes a difference on how to judge 1492 if you happen to be a Native American or a European. The Arawak Indians are now extinct, demonstrating what the future had in store for them. Fernández-Armesto argues in the following selection that Columbus's title of explorer comes from the fact that he discovered a route to, not the place that was, the Americas.*

Despite nearly five hundred years of assiduous detraction, his prior role in the discovery of America remains the strongest part of Columbus's credentials as an explorer. But we should recall some of the supporting evidence too: his decoding of the Atlantic wind system; his discovery of magnetic variation in the Western hemisphere; his contributions to the mapping of the Atlantic and the New World; his epic crossings of the Caribbean; his demonstration of the conti-

nental nature of parts of South and Central America; his *aperçu* [perception] about the imperfect sphericity of the globe; his uncanny intuitive skill in navigation. Any of these would qualify an explorer for enduring fame; together they constitute an unequaled record of achievement.

Columbus was a self-avowed ignoramus who challenged the received wisdom of his day. His servility before old texts, combined with his paradoxical delight whenever he was able to correct them from experience, mark him at once as one of the last torchbearers of medieval cosmography, who carried their lights on the shoulders of

Felipe Fernández-Armesto, *Columbus* (Oxford and New York: Oxford University Press, 1991), pp. 191–93.

their predecessors, and one of the first beacons of the Scientific Revolution, whose glow was kindled from within by their preference for experiment over authority. The same sort of paradox enlivened every aspect of his character. His attraction towards fantasy and wishful thinking was ill accommodated in that hard head, half-full already with a sense of trade and profit. In his dealings with the Crown and his concern for his posterity, his mysticism was tempered by a materialism only slightly less intense—like the rich gurus who are equally familiar nowadays in spiritual retreats and business circles.

Though religion was a powerful influence in his life, its effects were strangely limited; his devotional bequests were few; his charity began and almost ended at home. The Indians he discovered he contemplated with evangelical zeal and treated with callous disregard. He was an inveterate practitioner of deception, a perennial victim of self-delusion, but he was rarely consciously mendacious. In dealing with subordinates, he was calculating and ingenuous by turns. He craved admirers, but could not keep friends. His anxiety for ennoblement, his self-confessed ambition for "status and wealth," did not prevent him from taking a certain pride in his modest origins and comparing the weaver-Admiral with the shepherd-King. He loved adventure, but could not bear adversity. Most paradoxically of all, beyond the islands and mainlands of the Ocean, Columbus explored involuntarily the marchlands between genius and insanity. Times of stress unhinged—sometimes, perhaps, actually deranged—him; in his last such sickness, he obsessively discarded his own most luminous ideas, and never recovered them.

It probably helped to be a visionary, with a flair for the fantastic, to achieve what he achieved. The task set himself—to cross the Ocean Sea directly from Europe to Asia—was literally beyond the capacity of any vessel of his day. The task he performed—to cross from Europe to a New World—was beyond the conception of many of his contemporaries. To have accomplished the highly improbable was insufficient for Columbus—he had wanted "the conquest of what appeared impossible." He died a magnificent failure: he had not reached the Orient. His failure enshrined what, in the long term, came to seem a greater success: the discovery of America.

One cannot do him justice without making allowances for the weakness that incapacitated him for ill fortune. He was too fearful of failure to face adverse reality—perhaps because he had too much riding on success: not only his personal pride, but also the claims to the material rewards on which his hopes for himself and his heirs rested. It is hard to believe, for instance, that his insistence on the continental nature of Cuba was other than perversely sustained in the face of inner conviction; or that he can really have felt, in his wild and self-contradictory calculations of the longitude of his discoveries, the confidence he claimed. The ambition that drove him was fatal to personal happiness. Almost anyone, it might be thought, would rest content with so much fame, so much wealth, so many discoveries, so dramatic a social rise. But not Columbus. His sights were always fixed on unmade discoveries, unfinished initiatives, imperfect gains, and frustrated crusades.

Instead of being satisfied with his achievements he was outraged by his wrongs. Unassuaged by acclaim, he was embittered by calumnies. This implacable character made him live strenuously and die miserably. Without it, he might have accomplished nothing; because of it, he could never rest on his laurels or enjoy his success. It was typical of him to abjure his achievement in discovering a new continent because he could not face failure in the attempt to reach an old one. He wanted to repeat his boast, "When I set out upon this enterprise, they all said it was impossible," without having to admit that "they" were right.

After reading this selection, consider these questions:

1. What claim does Columbus have to be considered one of the world's great explorers?
2. What were some of the contradictions in Columbus's character?
3. Do you think Columbus should be judged a success or failure?

SELECTION 5:
The Dutch Overseas Empire

The other Atlantic nations of Europe, seeing what the Portuguese and Spaniards were up to, also sought to tap into the wealth that was expected to follow contact with Asia, Africa, and the Americas. With the financial help of the monarchs of their countries, ships were dispatched to establish claims to overseas lands. Since the finding of precious metals was the object of most expeditions, there were many disappointments for the first generation of explorers. Neither Portugal nor Spain was strong enough to protect the vast lands that they claimed, so England, France, Sweden, and Denmark sent captains into the Atlantic and Indian Oceans to see what they could find.

However, it was the Netherlands' mariners that enjoyed the most success. Private businessmen formed the Dutch West India Company and the Dutch East India Company, providing the financing and sharing both risks and profits. A long tradition of seafaring, shipbuilding, and a taste for taking risks to make money served the Dutch captains well. They also recognized that the Portuguese were the weaker of the two Iberian nations and it was against their ports that they sailed. In time, they inherited the Portuguese empire in east Asia and many of its African stations. This selection written by G.V. Scammell considers the Dutch achievement.

The [Dutch] Republic was in the sixteenth and seventeenth centuries Europe's major shipowning and commercial power, and by the early 1600s possessed the continent's most advanced economy. Its merchants initially penetrated to the wider world to obtain goods and exploit opportunities denied them by Spanish policy, and its government saw attacks on the colonial commerce and possessions of the Hispano-Portuguese empire as a profitable way of deflecting Iberian energies away from the war for independence in the Low Countries. All this was to be achieved not by the state itself, nor by individuals or consortia, but by chartered joint-stock companies in which, however, state authority was to all intents paramount.

At the time of their foundation neither the East India Company (1602) nor the West India Com-

pany (1621) controlled any territory. The mercantile oligarchs who dominated the companies, and who were so influential in the government of the loosely federated United Provinces, were concerned with profit not conquest. The acquisition of colonies was regarded not only as expensive and irrelevant, but as dangerous. Such possessions might offer scope for the house of Orange, the Republic's only major aristocratic family, to acquire power and glory, thereby inflaming its ambitions to rule the Dutch state.

Such doubts, though never stilled, were not to prevail and empire was steadily amassed by the usual mixture of force and the manipulation of native rivalries. Nor was it limited to Asia, where it could at least be justified as the necessary defense of vital commercial interests. By the late seventeenth century the VOC [the Dutch East India Company] was not only exacting tribute from local peoples in South Africa, but, as their land

G.V. Scammell, *The First Imperial Age: European Overseas Expansion c. 1400–1715* (London: Unwin Hyman, 1989), pp. 155–56.

passed into Dutch hands, exercising sovereignty by regulating the succession of tribal chiefs. Its clients, like those of the Spaniards in the Indies, were invested with symbols of office and given some such grand name as Hercules or Hannibal.

Lands directly subject to the companies were ruled in equally familiar ways. The colony in Taiwan, while it lasted, had a governor, a council and a judiciary. Possessions in the East as a whole were subject to a governor-general who lived in opulent viceregal style in the cosmopolitan and bibulous capital at Batavia, aided by a council and a subordinate hierarchy of lesser officials. His rule was authoritarian, not to say absolute, with the city's "free burghers" denied, on company orders, any elected representation. The governor-general controlled that army of clerks and book-keepers an empire of commerce demanded and such small groups of colonists as VOC policies permitted.

The heads of the various Asian factories, commanders of forts and residents at the courts of local rulers bound to the Company by treaty were all supposedly under his authority. There was a central judiciary in Batavia and some effort was made, particularly in financial matters, to regulate the behavior of the Company's officers, with specially appointed functionaries, responsible to the VOC directors themselves, sent out from Holland to investigate (without much success) their misdeeds in the late 1600s. The selection and recruitment of the Company's servants destined for Asia left, as we have seen, much to be desired. There was little incentive for the able and ambitious to leave the prosperous and tolerant Netherlands.

There was even less to attract them to the East. The Republic cherished no such aspirations to rule and convert the indigenous masses as drew idealists and visionaries to the service of the Iberian crowns. The VOC's policies offered little for those of more mundane inclinations. Like the West India Company in North America it monopolized—at least in theory—the most lucrative opportunities, and given the modest amounts of territory it controlled there was small prospect of land and less of its successful exploitation in the face of vigorous indigenous competition. So the Company had to recruit who it could where it could. Many in its employment were aliens; many were refugees from misfortune or misdemeanors; and many, with the passage of time, were clients or relatives—usually the least able—of influential investors and directors.

No more than other Protestants were the Dutch greatly concerned to spread their faith in the wider world. Nevertheless the dispatch of Calvinist ministers to the lands under its jurisdiction was as closely regulated by the VOC as were the doings of the Catholic missions by the Iberian monarchies. But these *predikants*, such few as they were—with only five a year sent out on average—were usually chosen less for their zeal and piety than for their willingness to accept the Company's authority, and were to minister to the spiritual needs of its servants. However, like other Europeans established among unconquered and powerful civilizations, and without the backing of substantial white settlement, the VOC accepted that the imposition and exercise of its authority was in part dependent on the co-operation of local peoples. Hence the Chinese were involved in the government of Taiwan, Java was administered through native "regents" and in Batavia, whatever the godly might say, Company rule was remarkably tolerant.

After reading this selection, consider these questions:
1. What was unique about the sponsoring of Dutch colonial expeditions?
2. Why did the Dutch avoid occupying large foreign territories?
3. Why do you think that the two Dutch companies were so authoritarian in dealing with their overseas officials?

SELECTION 6:

Living in New England

The discovery of the Americas produced a great interchange of products between the New and Old World after Columbus's discovery. The result of this interchange is now the focus of much historical research, as is the life of European colonists in this new environment.

The selection below presents a modern American historian's account of the English colonists who came to New England. William Cronon makes it evident that many who crossed the Atlantic made little provision for the changes that their North American settlement required. The adjustment was not always easy, for the colonists arrived expecting that an ample supply of food would be awaiting them. They were victims of the accounts of earlier travelers who painted the New World in glowing terms as a land of plenty where little labor was required.

Cronon is a scholar of the New England settlers in their North American homes.

New England's seasonal cycles were little different from those of Europe. If anything, its summers were hotter and its winters colder. Colonists were prevented from realizing this only by their own high expectations of laborless wealth: many initially seemed to believe that strawberry time would last all year. Captain [Christopher]Levet wrote of one early attempt at settlement in which the colonists "neither applied themselves to planting of corn nor taking of fish, more than for their present use, but went about to build castles in the air, and making of forts, neglecting the plentiful time of fishing." They did so because their myths told them that the plentiful times would never end, but their refusal to lay up stores for the winter meant that many starved to death. The pattern occurred repeatedly, whether at Sagadahoc, Plymouth, or Massachusetts Bay: colonists came without adequate food supplies and died. At Plymouth alone, half the Pilgrims were dead before the first winter was over. Those

who had experienced the New England cold knew better, and warned that new arrivals who hoped to survive must bring provisions to last the year and a half before settlements could become self-sustaining. "Trust not too much on us for Corne at this time," wrote a spokesman for the Pilgrims, "for by reason of this last company that came, depending wholy upon us, we shall have little enough till harvest." This was hardly the advice one would send from a land of infinite plenty. The problem was perhaps stated most plaintively by the Massachusetts colonist John Pond, who in 1631 wrote his parents, "I pray you remember me as your child . . . we do not know how long we may subsist, for we cannot live here without provisions from ould eingland."

In New England, most colonists anticipated that they would be able to live much as they had done in England, in an artisanal and farming community with work rhythms, class relations, and a social order similar to the one they had left behind—the only difference being their own improved stature in society. There were many misconceptions involved in this vision, but the one most threatening to survival was the simple fact

William Cronon, *Changes in the Land: Indians, Colonists, and the Ecology of New England* (New York: Hill and Wang, 1983), pp. 35–37.

that establishing European relations of production in the New World was a far more complicated task than most colonists realized. Even to set up farms was a struggle. Once colonists had done this, adjusting to the New England ecosystem by re-creating the annual agricultural cycles which had sustained them in England, starving times became relatively rare. But for the first year or two, before European subsistence patterns had been reproduced, colonists found themselves forced to rely either on what little they had brought with them or on what New England's inhabitants—whether English or Indian—were willing to provide.

Few colonists expected that they would have to go abegging like this. At most, they contemplated supplementing their food stores by trading with the Indians; and as one promoter argued, should the Indians be reluctant to trade, it would be easy enough "to bring them all in subjection, and make this provision." Many colonists arrived believing that they could survive until their first harvest simply by living as the Indians supposedly did, off the unplanted bounties of nature.

Colonists were assured by some that Indian men got their livelihood with "small labour but great pleasure." Thomas Morton spoke of Indians for whom "the beasts of the forrest there doe serve to furnish them at any time when they please." If this were true, then surely Englishmen could do no worse. John Smith told his readers that, in New England, "Nature and liberty affoords us that freely which in *England* we want, or it costeth us deerly." The willingness of colonists to believe such arguments, and hazard their lives upon them, was testimony to how little they understood both the New England environment and the ways Indians actually lived in it.

After reading this selection, consider these questions:

1. What caused the English colonists to presume life would be so much better in New England?
2. Why was famine a serious problem in the early years of settlement?
3. Why could the colonists not adapt to the Indian way of life?

CHAPTER 2
Spanish America: How Was It Won and What Was Its Culture?

The American Indian population was not prepared for the invasion of the Spaniards in the sixteenth century. Isolated for thousands of years, the men and women on the western side of the Atlantic had been the sole creators of all that they had, without having the benefit of borrowing from other civilizations. Many of these inventions were dramatic: massive temple-pyramids, a sophisticated calendar, the Mayan alphabet, and the Incan road system, to mention but a few.

Mexico was the site of a succession of Indian civilizations beginning with the Olmec in the twelfth century B.C. to the Aztec in A.D. 1500. The Aztec capital, Tenochtitlán, may have held up to 200,000 people, then the largest city in the Americas. Its wealth could not help but attract Spanish explorers from the Caribbean Islands.

First to come, in 1519, was Hernando Cortés, eager to gain the wealth of the Aztec Empire for Spain. He had superior weapons, horses, and a brashness demonstrated by his burning his ships behind him to illustrate to his band of soldiers that there was no turning back.

Cortés was fortunate that the Aztecs had alienated many of the other Mexican Indians. Aztec religion required hundreds of human victims for their sacrifices—men and women usually obtained from raiding their neighbors. As a result, many other Indian peoples proved willing allies of the Spaniards.

SELECTION 1:

Cortés and Moctezuma

When Moctezuma, the Aztec emperor, learned of Cortés's arrival, he sent him gifts that he hoped would convince him to leave Mexico. Of course, this did not happen. Eventually Moctezuma decided on a personal meeting. Doña Marina, an Indian woman, served as a translator.

One of the soldiers with Cortés was Bernal Díaz del Castillo. In the following selection, he tells of this first meeting between Spanish captains and the Aztec emperor as the Spanish soldiers came in sight of Tenochtitlán.

Gazing on such wonderful sights, we did not know what to say, or whether what appeared before us was real, for on one side, on the land, there were great cities, and in the lake ever so many more, and the lake itself was crowded with canoes, and in the causeway were many bridges at intervals, and in front of us stood the great city of Mexico, and we—we did not even number four hundred soldiers! and we well remembered the words and warnings given us by the people of Huexotzingo and Tlaxcala, and the many other warnings that had been given that we should beware of entering Mexico, where they would kill us, as soon as they had us inside.

Let the curious readers consider whether there is not much to ponder over in this that I am writing. What men have there been in the world who have shown such daring? But let us get on, and march along the causeway. When we arrived where another small causeway branches off [leading to Coyoacan, another city] where there were some buildings like towers, which are their oratories, many more chieftains and caciques [the Aztec nobles] approached clad in very rich mantles, the brilliant liveries of one chieftain differing from those of another, and the causeways were crowded with them. The Great Moctezuma had sent these great caciques in advance to re-

Bernal Díaz del Castillo, *The Discovery and Conquest of Mexico, 1517–1521*, trans. A.P. Maudslay (New York: Farrar, Straus, and Cudahy, 1956), pp. 192–94.

ceive us, and when they came before Cortés they bade us welcome in their language, and as a sign of peace, they touched their hands against the ground, and kissed the ground with the hand.

There we halted for a good while, and Cacamatzín, the Lord of Texcoco, and the Lord of Iztapalapa and the Lord of Tacuba and the Lord of Coyoacan went on in advance to meet the Great Moctezuma, who was approaching in a rich litter accompanied by other great lords and caciques, who owned vassals. When we arrived near to Mexico, where there were some other small towers, the Great Moctezuma got down from his litter, and those great caciques supported him with their arms beneath a marvelously rich canopy of green colored feathers with much gold and silver embroidery and with pearls and chalchihuites suspended from a sort of bordering, which was wonderful to look at.

The Great Moctezuma was richly attired according to his usage, and he was shod with sandals, the soles were of gold and the upper part adorned with precious stones. The four chieftains who supported his arms were also richly clothed according to their usage, in garments which were apparently held ready for them on the road to enable them to accompany their prince, for they did not appear in such attire when they came to receive us. Besides these four chieftains, there were four other great caciques who supported the canopy over their heads, and many other lords who walked before the Great Moctezuma, sweeping the ground where he would tread and spreading cloths on it, so that he should not tread on the earth. Not one of these chieftains dared even to think of looking him in the face, but kept their eyes lowered with great reverence, except those four relations, his nephews, who supported him with their arms.

When Cortés was told that the Great Moctezuma was approaching, and he saw him coming, he dismounted from his horse, and when he was near Moctezuma, they simultaneously paid great reverence to one another. Moctezuma bade him welcome and our Cortés replied through Doña Marina wishing him very good health. And it seems to me that Cortés, through Doña Marina, offered him his right hand, and Moctezuma did not wish to take it, but he did give his hand to Cortés and then Cortés brought out a necklace which he had ready at hand, made of glass stones, which . . . are called *margaritas*, which have within them many patterns of diverse colors. These were strung on a cord of gold and with musk so that it should have a sweet scent, and he placed it round the neck of the Great Moctezuma and when he had so placed it he was going to embrace him, and those great princes who accompanied Moctezuma held back Cortés by the arm so that he should not embrace him, for they considered it an indignity.

Then Cortés through the mouth of Doña Marina told him that now his heart rejoiced at having seen such a great prince, and that he took it as a great honor that he had come in person to meet him and had frequently shown him such favor.

Then Moctezuma spoke other words of politeness to him, and told two of his nephews who supported his arms, the Lord of Texcoco and the Lord of Coyoacan, to go with us and show us to our quarters, and Moctezuma with his other two relations, the Lord of Cuitlahuac and the Lord of Tacuba who accompanied him, returned to the city, and all those grand companies of caciques and chieftains who had come with him returned in his train. As they turned back after their prince we stood watching them and observed how they all marched with their eyes fixed on the ground without looking at him, keeping close to the wall, following him with great reverence.

After reading this selection, consider these questions:
1. Why would Moctezuma want to meet Cortés?
2. What does Díaz think of the conversation between Moctezuma and Cortés?
3. How did the Aztec caciques demonstrate their reverence for Moctezuma?

SELECTION 2:

The Fall of the Aztec Capital

Eventually the Spaniards took Moctezuma hostage in order to assure their safety. He later died while trying to quell an uprising of the Aztecs against the Spaniards, after the caciques chose his brother Cuauhtémoc to succeed him. Although the Europeans suffered a setback and were almost destroyed, the victory was ultimately theirs.

In the following selection, an anonymous Aztec author describes the fate of Tenochtitlán as he saw it. Cuauhtémoc desperately, but in vain, sought to hold back the Spaniards.

And all these misfortunes befell us. We saw them and wondered at them; we suffered this unhappy fate.

Broken spears lie in the roads;
we have torn our hair in our grief.
The houses are roofless now, and their walls
are red with blood.

Worms are swarming in the streets and plazas,
and the walls are splattered with gore.
The water has turned red, as if it were dyed,
and when we drink it,
it has the taste of brine.

We have pounded our hands in despair
against the adobe walls,
for our inheritance, our city, is lost and dead.
The shields of our warriors were its defense,
but they could not save it.

We have chewed dry twigs and salt grasses;
we have filled our mouths with dust and bits of
  adobe;

Miguel Leon-Portilla, ed., *The Broken Spears: The Aztec Account of the Conquest of Mexico* (Boston: Beacon Press, 1962), pp. 137–38.

we have eaten lizards, rats and worms. . . .

When we had meat, we ate it almost raw. It was scarcely on the fire before we snatched it and gobbled it down.

They set a price on all of us: on the young men, the priests, the boys and girls. The price of a poor man was only two handfuls of corn, or ten cakes made from mosses or twenty cakes of salty couch-grass. Gold, jade, rich cloths, quetzal feathers—everything that once was precious was now considered worthless.

The captains delivered several prisoners of war to Cuauhtemoc to be sacrificed. He performed the sacrifices in person, cutting them open with a stone knife.

After reading this selection, consider these questions:

1. How did the siege of Tenochtitlán affect the Aztecs?
2. What did Cuauhtémoc do in hopes of holding back the Spaniards?
3. Why do you suppose the author speaks of a "price on all of us"?

SELECTION 3:

In Defense of the Indians

The Spaniards unwittingly brought with them illnesses to which their bodies had developed some immunity but for the Indians were devastating. Smallpox was the worst, but others were also present, killing more American Indians than ever died in battle.

Many of the Spanish emigrants regarded the Indians as free labor. In the Caribbean Islands those who survived disease were put to work as if they were slaves. Such a program was altogether contrary to the Spaniards' profession of wanting to convert the Indians to Christianity. The mute voice of the Indians found a spokesman in the bishop of Chiapas, Mexico, Bartolomé de Las Casas (in the selection below). His work in defense of the natives persuaded the Spanish court to forbid the enslavement of the American Indians.

They who teach, either in word or in writing, that the natives of the New World, whom we commonly call Indians, ought to be conquered and subjugated by war before the gospel is proclaimed and preached to them so that, after they have finally been subjugated, they may be instructed and hear the word of God, make two disgraceful mistakes.

First, in connection with divine and human law they abuse God's words and do violence to the Scriptures, to papal decrees, and to the teaching handed down from the holy fathers. And they go wrong again by quoting histories that are nothing but sheer fables and shameless nonsense. By means of these, men who are totally hostile to the poor Indians and who are their utterly deceitful enemies betray them. Second, they mistake the meaning of the decree or bull of the Supreme Pontiff Alexander VI, whose words they corrupt and twist in support of their opinions, as will be clear from all that follows.

Their error and ignorance are also convincingly substantiated by the fact that they draw conclusions on matters which concern a countless number of men and vast areas of extensive provinces. Since they do not fully understand all these things, it is the height of effrontery and rashness for them to attribute publicly to the Indians the gravest failings both of nature and conduct, condemning *en masse* so many thousands of people, while, as a matter of fact, the greater number of them are free from these faults. All this drags innumerable souls to ruin and blocks the service of spreading the Christian religion by closing the eyes of those who, crazed by blind ambition, bend all their energies of mind and body to the one purpose of gaining wealth, power, honors, and dignities. For the sake of these things they kill and destroy with inhuman cruelty people who are completely innocent, meek, harmless, temperate, and quite ready and willing to receive and embrace the word of God.

Who is there possessed of only a sound mind, not to say a little knowledge of theology, who has dared to pronounce a judgment and opinion so un-Christian that it spawns so many cruel wars, so many massacres, so many bereavements, and so many deplorable evils? Do we not have Christ's words: "See that you never despise any of these little ones," "Alas for the man who provides obstacles," "He who is not with me is against me; and he who does not gather with me scatters," and "Each day has trouble enough of its own"? Who is so godless that he would want to incite men who are savage, ambitious, proud, greedy, uncontrolled, and everlastingly lazy to pillage their brothers and destroy their souls as well as their possessions, even though war is never lawful except when it is waged because of unavoidable necessity?

And so what man of sound mind will approve a war against men who are harmless, ignorant, gentle, temperate, unarmed, and destitute of every human defense? For the results of such a war are very surely the loss of the souls of that people who perish without knowing God and without the support of the sacraments, and, for the survivors, hatred and loathing of the Christian religion. Hence the purpose God intends, and for the attainment of which he suffered so much, may be frustrated by the evil and cruelty that our men wreak on them with inhuman barbarity. What will these people think of Christ, the true God of the Christians, when they see Christians venting their rage against them with so many massacres, so much bloodshed without any just cause, at any rate without any just cause that they know of (nor can one even be imagined), and without any fault committed on their [the Indians] part against the Christians?

After reading this selection, consider these questions:

1. How did those Spaniards who warred against the Indians justify their actions?

2. What prompted Las Casas to become an advocate of the American Indians?

3. What kind of response do you suppose Las Casas received from his contemporaries?

Bartolomé de Las Casas, *In Defense of the Indians,* trans. and ed. Stafford Poole (DeKalb: Northern Illinois University Press, 1974), pp. 25–27.

SELECTION 4:

Governing the Spanish Empire

Tenochtitlán, once the Aztec capital, now became a Spanish town, which we know as Mexico City. Settlers from Spain crossed the Atlantic to settle Mexico, bringing with them their horses, cattle, and religion.

At the beginning the colonists were nearly all men, who took their wives from among the indigenous women. In time, families appeared in Mexico as husbands and wives sought to make a new life in the Americas. A colonial society developed that adapted Spanish customs to the Mexican world. These institutions are analyzed by a modern scholar in the following selection.

Life in colonial New Spain was complex—the dominant institutions and cultural patterns were Spanish in origin, but they were modified in their New World setting. Society was not static; evolution marked the political and religious systems; and change was a feature of the economic, social, and intellectual life. These adaptations generally mirrored developments in Europe, the source of basic decisions and control. During its three centuries as a colony, New Spain was kept subservient to the mother country in a number of ways, beginning with an enforced loyalty to the crown.

The government of the Spanish empire functioned through a massive bureaucracy, with the Spanish monarch at the peak of the administrative pyramid. Claiming divine appointment and espousing the political philosophy of absolutism, the monarch was a supreme earthly master to all his subjects. The reigning king or queen was responsible to God alone, and disobedience of royal edicts was considered both treason and sacrilege. Since the Indies technically did not belong to Spain but were the personal patrimony of the crown of Castile, they were not administered by the *Cortes* (the Spanish parliament) or traditional royal councils. Instead, two agencies were created in Spain to administer the overseas territories for the monarch.

Headquartered in Seville, the Council of the Indies was the principal governing body for Spain's crown colonies in the New World. First composed of seven members, the Council later added other officers including a cosmographer and historian. The personnel of the Council was composed of lawyers, clerics, treasurers, and high officials who had returned to Spain after service in the colonies. The councilors considered themselves to be advisors to the monarch, but in reality they regulated the Spanish Indies. They drafted royal laws, ordinances, and *cédulas* (decrees) and had the power of judicial review over local legislation enacted in the colonies.

A codification of all the laws and regulations of the Council was compiled and published several times as the *Recopilación de Leyes de los Reynos de las Indias*. It was a humane and comprehensive code for colonial government. By 1681 there were 6,377 laws indexed under various titles such as Bishops of New Spain, Universities, Treatment of Pirates, Fabrication of Gunpowder, and the Mail Service.

In addition to legislative duties, the Council of the Indies had administrative, ecclesiastical, and judicial powers. It acted as a supreme court for cases appealed from overseas, it granted permission for new expeditions, it supervised the treat-

---

Robert Ryal Miller, *Mexico: A History* (Norman: University of Oklahoma Press, 1985), pp. 124–26.

ment of Indians, it provided for military defense, it was a censorship board for printed matter bound for the Indies, it supervised the colonial treasury, and it organized *visitas* (inspections) and *residencias* (reviews) of retiring officials. One of the most important functions was to nominate for royal approval appointees for all overseas positions—civil, military, and religious—except those few selected by the colonists themselves. The Council's authority began to decline in the eighteenth century, but it was not abolished until 1834.

The *Casa de Contratación* (Board of Colonial Trade) was an agency in Spain charged with regulating New World commerce and emigration. Besides serving as a kind of passport office, it registered goods shipped between Spain and the Indies, making certain that the royal taxes were paid. Located first at Seville and later at Cadiz, the *Casa* maintained metropolitan Spain's trade monopoly, served as a commercial court, and was a clearinghouse for all traffic with the colonies. Its power declined in the eighteenth century, and the *Casa* was abolished in 1790, after Spain had been forced to liberalize its trading policies.

In New Spain itself the viceroy was the ranking officer and agent of royal absolutism. As a personal representative of the king he was armed with considerable authority and enjoyed high honors and deference. He received a handsome salary (twenty thousand pesos in the seventeenth century, triple that amount in the eighteenth), lived in a splendid palace surrounded by liveried servants, and maintained a court like a petty European monarch. During the colonial era there were sixty-one viceroys. Most of them belonged to the titled nobility or at least were of high birth; eleven were from the church hierarchy, and only three holders of this exalted office were *criollos* [Spaniards born in America], two of them being sons of viceroys.

The viceroy functioned as chief executive, captain-general of military forces, governor, supervisor of the royal treasury (*real hacienda*), and president of the *audiencia* (administrative court) of Mexico. He enforced royal laws and decrees, issued ordinances dealing with local matters, nominated minor colonial officials, distributed land and titles, promoted colonization and settlement, and protected the Indians. He was vice-patron of most religious endeavors, and his ecclesiastical powers included the right to determine boundaries of bishoprics and to nominate some church officers.

After reading this selection, consider these questions:
1. What were the major institutions set up to govern New Spain?
2. What were the powers of the viceroy?
3. Can you think of a better way for Spain to have governed its empire?

SELECTION 5:

Life in Colonial Lima

The Spaniards who settled in Peru after the expedition of Francisco Pizarro had brought down the Inca Empire tried to imitate the world of their Spanish homeland. Artisans and men and women skilled in crafts immigrated into the country, building towns like they remembered from Castile.

Fiestas were frequent, with colorful parades and floats to celebrate anniversaries of royalty and favorite saints' days. The Catholic Church calendar was full of occasions for such celebrations so that the expectation *of holidays was never too distant. From a diary kept by Josephe de Mugaburu it is possible to follow one such fiesta held in the winter of 1659 honoring Philip IV. It was a good thing that news traveled slowly to Peru, for in November of that year Spain had signed the Treaty of the Pyrenees transferring its frontier forts to France and beginning its decline as a major power in Europe.*

Tuesday, the 2nd of December of that year, the painters, sculptors, and carpenters held their celebration for [the birth of] our prince. There was a parade of floats, ludicrous and witty, with four carriages bearing the "four elements;" another three with very comic figures; [another with] figures of all the viceroys who had governed this kingdom; then eight costumed Incas; followed by a very large figure carrying the world on his shoulders and with veins of silver and gold, offering it all to the prince; and then [representations of] all the eminent artists that ever existed. Behind all this was another carriage which caused much admiration when seen; it was fourteen yards high, ten wide, and eighteen long, artistically made with large columns by Ascencio de Salas, great architect and sculptor. On top rode the prince, who was represented by the son of Don José González, and all who looked at him marveled that he moved along with such majesty. There were very brave bulls the rest of the afternoon, with which the day came to a close. Everyone was pleased to have seen such an extraordinary and majestic event.

On Friday, the 29th of December, the silversmiths, joined by other craftsmen, held their celebration in which they brought nine carriages [floats] out to the plaza. Each one represented a kingdom, offering the prince the treasures of each kingdom. All the grandees of Spain were represented, in their image, very well dressed and with much regalia; and also all the guard of His Majesty: Teutonic, German, and Spanish, with captains of the guard, all very splendid. There were bulls that same afternoon, and four who came out as grandees of Castile fought on horseback; a very merry afternoon with much to see.

On Tuesday, the 23rd of the month, the Indians held their *fiesta*, for which they built a fort in the plaza. The Inca king appeared and fought with two other kings until he conquered them and took over the fort. Then the three kings, with dignity, offered the keys to the [Spanish] prince who was portrayed on a float. Then [representatives of] all the Indians of this kingdom came out to the plaza, each in his native dress. There were more than two thousand. The plaza appeared to be covered with a variety of flowers as all the Indians were elaborately costumed and with much finery. There were bulls that afternoon, and the Indians came out to spear the bulls. It was a joyful *fiesta* for everyone, and it is said that they [the Indians] were the best of all, with which the celebrations ended.

After reading this selection, consider these questions:

1. What is in human nature that makes people enjoy parades?
2. What in this selection tells you that the people remembered life in the Spanish homeland?
3. What does the diary say about the relations between the Indians and the Spaniards?

Josephe de Mugaburu, *Chronicle of Colonial Lima*, trans. Robert Ryal Miller (Norman: University of Oklahoma Press, 1975), pp. 51–52.

SELECTION 6:

The Columbian Exchange

Historian Alfred W. Crosby has written one of the most important works on the results of the European arrival in the Americas. As has been noted, the most telling effect on the Indian population was the introduction of bacteria and viruses that until the Spanish conquest were unknown in the Americas. By 1622 demographers estimate that more than 90 percent of the native population had been carried off by imported diseases from Europe. Then a turnaround took place as immunities developed among the survivors and population growth once more commenced.

On a happier note, European food crops and cotton came into the Americas, opening up a new exchange of products that crossed the Atlantic. Because coffee drinking had become so popular, a huge demand for sugar resulted, for in Europe the taste of the population required that the brew be sweetened. The climate and soils of tropical America proved exceptionally suited for sugar cane production, and the temperate regions for the cultivation of corn (maize).

In terms of global significance the importation of the potato into Europe was equally important. At first kept as an ornamental plant or considered an aid to sexual satisfaction, potatoes were avoided by most people. However, in Europe's poorer regions men and women had no choice but to make them a staple of their diet. Crosby explains how this happened in the selection below.

The economic underpinnings of most of the important European settlements in the tropical and semitropical zones of America historically have been the raising of a certain few crops on large plantations for export to Europe. These plantation areas, with their fields of sugar, cotton, rice, indigo, have, at one time and another, stretched all the way from Virginia's tobacco fields to Brazil's coffee fields. Mining produced the most spectacular profits in the colonial New World, but the plantations employed more people and, in the end, produced greater wealth.

It all began in Española with sugar, which was already a profitable plantation crop in the Ca-

naries and Portugal's Atlantic islands in the fifteenth century. Columbus himself had shipped sugar from Madeira to Genoa in 1478, and the mother of his first wife owned a sugar estate on that island. He brought sugar cane with him to Española in 1493, and the cane grew well in American soil. But the growth of the sugar industry was painfully slow until Charles V intervened, ordering that sugar masters and mill technicians be recruited from the Canaries, and authorizing loans to build sugar mills on Española. There were thirty-four mills on the island by the late 1530s and sugar was one of the two staples of the island's economy (the other being cattle ranching) until the latter part of the sixteenth century.

One of the causes for this late sixteenth-century decline of the sugar industry in the Span-

Alfred W. Crosby Jr., *The Columbian Exchange: Biological and Cultural Consequences of 1492* (Westport, CT: Greenwood Publishing, 1972) pp. 68–69, 181–83.

ish Antilles was competition from the mainland. Wherever the sun was hot and the rainfall sufficient, the Spanish planted cane. It became a common crop early after the conquests of Mexico and Peru in the lowlands and deeper valleys of those regions. Sugar cane poked up its profitable shoots all over the Spanish empire, from the Gulf of Mexico to the Rio de la Plata. Asunción, for instance, boasted two hundred sugar mills in the early seventeenth century. The empire had a superabundance of sugar. Said Bernabe Cobo, "There must not be a region in all the universe where so much is consumed, and with all this many ships carry it to Spain."

Maize has had an important influence on population growth in southern Europe, but it cannot be credited with being one of the primary causes of the general European demographic expansion of the last two hundred years, which has had such awesome effects on world history. That population explosion is the result of many factors, not the least of which has been medical advance. Another factor of no minor significance has been Europe's love affair with the common American potato.

Sixteenth-century European documents mentioning the potato are of very little help to us because the same word was often used to indicate potatoes and/or sweet potatoes. This, however, is of no great significance because neither had any importance except as novelties and aphrodisiacs! Said Shakespeare's Falstaff in a moment of passion, "Let the sky rain potatoes." A few years later a lesser playwright put these words in the mouth of one of his characters: "I have fine potatoes, Ripe potatoes! Will your Lordship please to taste a fine potato? 'Twill advance your wither'd state, Fill your Honour full of noble itches."

For long after the initial century of acquaintance, the mass of Europeans looked upon the potato with fear and contempt. Many, for instance, were sure it caused leprosy. Others thought it a very dreary, plebeian sort of food. Diderot's *Encyclopedia*, that monumental production of the eighteenth-century avant-garde, declares that no matter how the potato is prepared, "this root is insipid and mealy. It cannot be classed among the agreeable food stuffs, but it furnishes abundant and rather wholesome nutrition to men who are content to be nourished. The potato is justly regarded as flatulent, but what are winds to the vigorous organs of peasants and laborers?"

Threats of rot and gas could not forever conceal from Europeans the significance of the fact that potatoes could produce more "wholesome nutrition" from the average piece of land in the northern half of Europe than any other crop. It was the Irish, of course, who first wholeheartedly adopted the potato. It came to their island sometime in the last years of the sixteenth century, and within a hundred years the Irish were known as "mighty lovers of potatoes." In 1724 Jonathan Swift, with typical bitterness, described his countrymen as "living in filth and nastiness upon buttermilk and potatoes." The moist, cool atmosphere and deep, friable soils of Ireland are perfect for the potato, and the Irish, condemned by foreign rule to the depths of poverty, could have asked God for no better gift than the potato. As the crop spread in Ireland, the population grew, which made further spread of the tuber almost compulsory, for no other plant could feed so many Irishmen on such small plots of earth. One-and-a-half acres, planted with potatoes, would provide enough food, with the addition of a bit of milk, to keep a family hearty for a year. It was not exceptional for an Irishman to consume ten pounds of potatoes a day and very little else. On this diet the Irish, without benefit of medical science, hygiene, industrialization, or decent government, increased from 3.2 million in 1754 to nearly 8.2 million in 1845, not counting the 1.75 million who emigrated before 1846. Then came the potato blight, the failure of the Irish staple, and one of the worst famines of modern times. The Irishmen who had lived by the potato died by the potato.

After reading this selection, consider these questions:

1. What was the connection between drinking coffee in Europe and the production of sugar in the Americas?
2. Why is population growth linked to food supply?
3. How was the history of Ireland affected by the growing of potatoes?

CHAPTER 3
The European Reformation:
What Were the Issues?

At the beginning of the sixteenth century there were two divisions in the European Christian churches. In eastern Europe the Orthodox community predominated, while in the West the Catholic Church was supreme. Except for Jews and Balkan Muslims, all Europeans belonged to one of these two churches that were separated much more by culture than doctrine. One hundred years later the unity of the Catholic Church in the West was shattered by the Reformation. There was no similar movement in the East.

The Reformers of the sixteenth century were a diverse group. Some were clergy, others laymen, and many came from academic backgrounds. Their followers were of equally diverse origin and accepted the Reformers more or less with enthusiasm. Theology is a discipline that is a specialty of teachers, not something that the general public finds of compelling interest. Therefore the doctrinal elements of the Reformation could not evoke much enthusiasm, but strong personalities such as Luther, Calvin, and Henry VIII could and did inspire millions of people to accept their visions of Christianity.

In the following selections we shall examine what happened in the sixteenth century by looking at the careers of these three men. First comes Martin Luther, for his thought opened the door for the others.

SELECTION 1:

The Quest for Righteousness

Luther taught that faith alone was the determining feature of Christian belief. In this selection, he tells of his spiritual journey in his own words.

Meanwhile, I had already during that year returned to interpret the Psalter anew. I had confidence in the fact that I was more skilful, after I had lectured in the university on St. Paul's epistles to the Romans, to the Galatians, and the one to the Hebrews. I had indeed been captivated with an extraordinary ardor for understanding Paul in the Epistle to the Romans. But up till then it was not the cold blood about the heart, but a single word in Chapter 1 [:17], "In it the righteousness of God is revealed," that had stood in my way. For I hated that word "righteousness of God," which, according to the use and custom of all the teachers, I had been taught to understand philosophically regarding the formal or active righteousness, as they called it, with which God is righteous and punishes the unrighteous sinner.

Though I lived as a monk without reproach, I felt that I was a sinner before God with an extremely disturbed conscience. I could not believe that he was placated by my satisfaction. I did not love, yes, I hated the righteous God who punishes sinners, and secretly, if not blasphemously, certainly murmuring greatly, I was angry with God, and said, "As if, indeed, it is not enough, that miserable sinners, eternally lost through original sin, are crushed by every kind of calamity by the law of the decalogue [the Ten Commandments], without having God add pain to pain by the gospel and also by the gospel threatening us with his righteousness and wrath!" Thus I raged with a fierce and troubled conscience. Nevertheless, I beat importunately upon Paul at

that place, most ardently desiring to know what St. Paul wanted.

At last, by the mercy of God, meditating day and night, I gave heed to the context of the words, namely, "In it the righteousness of God is revealed, as it is written, 'He who through faith is righteous shall live.'" There I began to understand that the righteousness of God is that by which the righteous lives by a gift of God, namely by faith. And this is the meaning: the righteousness of God is revealed by the gospel, namely, the passive righteousness with which merciful God justifies us by faith, as it is written, "He who through faith is righteous shall live."

Here I felt that I was altogether born again and had entered paradise itself through open gates. There a totally other face of the entire scripture showed itself to me. Thereupon I ran through the Scriptures from memory. I also found in other terms an analogy, as, the work of God, that is, what God does in us, the power of God, with which he makes us strong, the wisdom of God, with which he makes us wise, the strength of God, the salvation of God, the glory of God.

And I extolled my sweetest word with a love as great as the hatred with which I had before hated the word "righteousness of God." Thus that place in Paul was for me truly the gate to paradise. Later I read Augustine's *The Spirit and the Letter,* where contrary to hope I found that he, too, interpreted God's righteousness in a similar way, as the righteousness with which God clothes us when he justifies us. Although this was heretofore said imperfectly and he did not explain all things concerning imputation clearly, it nevertheless was pleasing that God's righteousness with which we are justified was taught.

Martin Luther, *Preface to Latin Writings,* in *Martin Luther,* ed. John Dillenberger (Chicago: Quadrangle Books, 1961), pp. 10–12.

After reading this selection, consider these questions:

1. Why did the term "righteousness of God" at first cause Luther a problem in St. Paul's epistles?
2. Does Luther believe a person can earn God's justification? Why or why not?
3. Do you consider the theological term of justification important enough to cause the Reformation? Why or why not?

SELECTION 2:

Predestination

Religious belief was not a private matter for the individual to decide in sixteenth-century Europe. It was very much a public concern, especially for Europe's princes, who regarded their subjects' beliefs with great interest. To reject the religion of the king or queen placed a man or woman into a potential state of treason.

For this reason, Holy Roman Emperor Charles V summoned Luther, his subject, to appear before an assembly of his counselors, called a Diet, in the city of Worms. For Luther it was a dangerous time, for to be declared a heretic was to risk imprisonment and possibly execution. He was fortunate that the elector of Saxony, Frederick the Wise, his own prince, was on his side.

John Calvin was in the second generation of Reformers. Making his headquarters in the Swiss city of Geneva, Calvin gained the support of followers throughout Europe, making inroads into Scotland, England, France, the Netherlands, and parts of eastern Europe. His work the Institutes of the Christian Religion *became the most important literary work of the Reformation era. It is a long work, in its final form over a thousand pages. The stress is on the transcendence of God, how everything depends on God's will. Therefore predestination was one part of Calvin's message: God has decided that some people will be rewarded in heaven, others will be rejected. This is spelled out in the following selection.*

As Scripture, then, clearly shows, we say that God once established by his eternal and unchangeable plan those whom he long before determined once for all to receive into salvation, and those whom, on the other hand, he would devote to destruction. We assert that, with respect to the elect, this plan was founded upon his freely given mercy, without regard to human worth; but by his just and irreprehensible but incomprehensible judgment he has barred the door of life to those whom he has given over to damnation. Now among the elect we regard the call as a testimony of election.

Then we hold justification another sign of its manifestation, until they come into the glory in

John Calvin, *Institutes of the Christian Religion*, iii, 21–22, ed. John T. McNeill and trans. Ford L. Battles (Library of the Christian Classics, 21) (Philadelphia: Westminster Press, 1960), vol. 2, pp. 931–32.

which the fulfillment of that election lies. But as the Lord seals his elect by call and justification, so, by shutting off the reprobate from knowledge of his name or from the sanctification of his Spirit, he, as it were, reveals by these marks what sort of judgment awaits them. Here I shall pass over many fictions that stupid men have invented to overthrow predestination. They need no refutation, for as soon as they are brought forth they abundantly prove their own falsity. I shall pause only over those which either are being argued by the learned or may raise difficulty for the simple, or which impiety speciously sets forth in order to assail God's righteousness. . . .

Many persons dispute all these positions which we have set forth, especially the free election of believers; nevertheless, this cannot be shaken. For generally these persons consider that God distinguishes among men according as he foresees what the merits of each will be. Therefore, he adopts as sons those whom he foreknows will not be unworthy of his grace; he appoints to the damnation of death those whose dispositions he discerns will be inclined to evil intention and ungodliness. By thus covering election with a veil of foreknowledge, they not only obscure it but feign that it has its origin elsewhere. And this commonly accepted notion is not confined to the common folk; important authors of all periods have held it. This I frankly confess so that no one may assume that if their names be quoted against us, our case will be greatly damaged. For God's truth is here too sure to be shaken, too clear to be overwhelmed by men's authority.

But others, not versed in Scripture, and deserving no approbation, so wickedly assail this sound doctrine that their insolence is intolerable. Because God chooses some, and passes over others according to his own decision, they bring an action against him. But if the fact itself is well known, what will it profit them to quarrel against God? We teach nothing not borne out by experience: that God has always been free to bestow his grace on whom he wills.

After reading this selection, consider these questions:

1. Why does Calvin insist that God must be free to reward some people and reject others?
2. Does the idea of predestination deny free will?
3. Do you see agreement between Calvin's doctrine of free will and Luther's view of justification?

SELECTION 3:

The Reformers and Women

A modern writer, Jane Dempsey Douglass, looks into the Reformation view that all people are called to the same vocation as Christians with no difference between clergy and laity. If this is the case, are women the equal of men in holding public roles in the church? In the following selection, she examines the positions of Calvin and Luther regarding women.

E xcept for Calvin, the mainstream Reformers seem to be unanimous that public leadership in worship or preaching is forbidden to women by

Jane Dempsey Douglass, *Women, Freedom, and Calvin* (Philadelphia: Westminster Press, 1985), pp. 88–89.

God. And we have seen that Calvin is ambivalent on this question. On the one hand, he knows of biblical women prophets; but on the other hand he expresses some puzzlement as to how, for example, the daughters of Philip had exercised their prophetic gifts in the early church without scandalizing the community. He thought they might have prophesied privately.

He clearly argues in both the *Institutes* and some commentaries that the injunction for women to be silent in church is in the realm of human law and could be adapted to changing cultures and needs of the church. On the other hand, he just as clearly communicates his conviction that the sight of a woman preaching in church with her head uncovered would be scandalous. It is uncertain to what extent it is the preaching and to what extent it is the uncovered head that is offensive. He also at times argues that it is improper for a woman who ought to be subject to men to exercise authority over them by preaching and teaching. So the priesthood of all believers did not for Calvin automatically free the church to call its women members to public leadership in the congregation.

Luther's commentary on 1 Timothy will give us a helpful point of comparison with Calvin. When Luther deals with 1 Timothy 2:11–14, where Paul tells women to learn in silence with submissiveness, he asks fewer questions about the way to interpret this passage than Calvin. He does show some awareness that women are treated differently in different cultures and asserts briefly that Paul was speaking against the Greek women, who have always been more "ingenious and clever" than others. And he mentions the problem that there have been apparent exceptions to this rule, biblical women skilled at management and with authority: Huldah, Deborah, Jael, the wise woman of Abel (2 Sam. 20:14–21), Philip's daughters, Queen Candace of Ethiopia (Acts 8:27). Luther dismisses the whole problem by saying that Paul is concerned that men be in authority when men are present, and that Huldah, Deborah, the woman of Abel, and the daughters of Philip are exceptional cases because they were unmarried. Since 1 Timothy 2:12 really means that wives should have no authority over their husbands, the problem is resolved, Luther thinks.

Since Huldah and Deborah had no husbands, they did not rule over husbands. It is not clear why Jael, the wife of Heber (Judg. 4:17), is brought in here by Luther, except perhaps simply as a clever manager. And it is certainly unclear why other unmarried women could not have authority over the community, since at the outset Luther explains that this passage is dealing with public matters, ministry in the public assembly of the church. Nonetheless Luther understands Paul to be protecting the biblical order that man must be the head of the woman, since Adam was created first, and that women are not permitted to speak in the assembly when men are present. For a woman to challenge a man's teaching would create disorder. "By divine and human law . . . Adam is the master of the woman." Still, at the end of the chapter Luther mystifies us further by adding, "If the Lord were to raise up a woman in order for us to listen to her, we would allow her to rule like Huldah." Then he moves on to the next section of the text.

In general we can observe that Luther seems much less aware of problems raised by the 1 Timothy passage than Calvin. The traditional cases of exceptional biblical women are cited, but the only explanation offered is their unmarried state. There is none of Calvin's preoccupation with the freedom of the Spirit to break through the normal order of creation. Luther simply accepts Paul's argument for male priority by Adam's creation before Eve in time as appropriate in divine, if not always in human, affairs, whereas Calvin finds that argument very weak, perhaps because of Renaissance criticisms of it. We also notice that Luther seems to be propounding an interpretation of Paul's second argument very similar to the one Calvin flatly rejects: Adam really was not deceived by the serpent; he just wanted to please his wife. He did not go astray himself but was deceived by Eve, the real cause of transgression. Finally, we notice that in 1 Timothy 2:15, the verse promising women salvation through bearing children if they continue in faith, there is a more direct focus on childbearing as punishment and as salutary than in Calvin. Luther has no admonitions here to husbands about their obligations in marriage and parenthood parallel to those of

Calvin in his sermon.

After reading this selection, consider these questions:

1. How would the doctrine of predestination affect the role of women in the church's ministry?

2. What was Luther's view of women's role in the church?

3. Do you find that the Reformation enhanced the position of women?

SELECTION 4:

Reformation in England

England's Reformation took a different course than that of the Continent's. Henry VIII, the second monarch of the Tudor dynasty, was very concerned that he should have a male heir lest his inheritance pass into another family. His queen was Catherine of Aragon, a Spanish princess, but of all her pregnancies only one child, Mary, survived.

Henry's fear of not having a son compelled him to pursue the possibility that God was punishing him for having married Catherine after she had been the wife of his brother Arthur. His father, after Arthur's premature death, had written to the pope for a dispensation from church law that forbade a man or woman to marry one of their in-laws. Pope Julius II had obliged, but Henry feared that the ban was of divine, not human, law; hence his predicament.

As years went by and Henry's case in Rome encountered delay after delay, the king took matters into his own hands. In 1534 Henry assumed, with Parliament's approval, the leadership of the church in England, and his appointee to Canterbury, the head churchman of the nation, granted the king a divorce so that he might marry again. All officials in England were required to take an oath to support the Act of Supremacy and the Act of Succession that forbade his daughter, Mary Tudor, from inheriting the throne. Henry wanted no change in doctrine as occurred on the Continent. His concern was the government of the church.

To prepare English men and women to accept a church governed by the king rather than the pope, the public was frequently reminded of the Fourth Commandment to honor one's father and mother. Henry's ministers and publicists extended the divine injunction to the king, emphasizing the role of the monarch as the "father" of his subjects. In the following selection, author Richard Rex follows the steps taken to ensure obedience to the new order.

Richard Rex, "The Crisis of Obedience" in *Historical Journal*, vol. 39, no. 4 (Decuember 1996), pp. 893–94.

In 1541, Henry explained why the injunctions of the 1530s had required an English Bible to be placed in every church, namely so that 'every

[one] of the king's majesty's minding to read therein, might be occasion thereof not only consider and perceive the great and ineffable omnipotent power, promise, justice, mercy, and goodness of Almighty God, but also to learn thereby to observe God's commandments, and to obey their sovereign lord and high powers, and to exercise godly charity'.

Of course it did not work out like that. That is why from 1539 Henry started to restrict the liberty of the Gospel that he had extended to his people. The problem was precisely what conservatives had always feared—the worse sort distorted the Gospel in favour of carnal liberty, which is to say that they deviated into unacceptable forms of protestantism such as sacramentarianism and anabaptism [forms of continental protestant practice]. The important point, however, is that the Bible was restricted for the same reason that it had initially been released—to foster obedience. The same objective was promoted by the publication of the other main genre in official vernacular religious literature—the *Primer*—and by the insistence from the 1536 injunctions onwards on memorising the Ten commandments in English. Henry's preface to the royal *Primer* of 1545 makes this perfectly clear. First among the good considerations which have caused him to publish the book, he says, is 'that the youth by divers persons are taught the Pater noster, the Ave Maria [Our Father and Hail Mary], the Creed and Ten commandments all in Latin, and not in English, by means whereof the same are not brought up in the knowledge of their faith, duty, and obedience'. His *Primer*, in contrast, will permit 'the better bringing up of youth in the knowledge of their duty towards God, their prince, and all other in their degree'.

In this one word, obedience, we have the essence of Henrician religion. It would not be going too far to say that Henry's Reformation turned, or began to turn, English religion into a distinctive and coherent version of Christianity, one in which obedience was the paramount virtue or value—as important as faith in Lutheranism or the real presence in catholicism. Of course, all churches, like all states, demand obedience of some kind. But this demand is secondary to the distinctive claims of the church or state in question. What is distinctive about the Henrician church-state is that obedience *was* its primary claim. The obsession with obedience evinced by the leading theologians and propagandists of that church-state arose out of the need to impose the newfound royal supremacy on a people accustomed to thinking of the Church of England as a body sovereign in its own right. Henry was not at any time talked by his advisers into following a straight catholic or protestant or Erasmian line. He could not be pushed around. But he could be worked on. And some at least of those around Henry realized that one way to win his support for a policy was to show how it would promote obedience, ideally by showing how it embodied and promulgated the word of God. Those around Henry were not necessarily pursuing his agenda, but they had to present their agenda in terms of his. From 1535 onwards, Henry's agenda was the preservation and promotion of his royal supremacy. We must look at his Reformation not, with whiggish [nineteenth-century Protestant] hindsight in the light of what came after, as the 'dawning of the Gospel'; nor, with excessive Revisionist zeal in the light of what had gone before, as 'catholicism without the pope'. We must look at it in its own terms, and try to make sense of it in its own context. What we find is a Reformation *sui generis* [one of its own kind]. It bequeathed much to the English protestant tradition: the royal supremacy, the English Bible, and the iconoclastic imperative. Yet these sat uncomfortably with transubstantiation, auricular confession, and masses for the dead. Perhaps in a world dividing ever more sharply between catholic and protestant, the Henrician settlement was never going to endure. But it was its own thing, folly to catholics and a stumbling-block to protestants. Its foundation was the royal supremacy. Its slogan was the word of God. Its keynote was obedience.

After reading this selection, consider these questions:

1. What was the cause of the Reformation in England?

2. How does the reform instituted by Henry VIII differ from that of Luther or Calvin?

3. Why would a church governed by a king differ from one headed by a pope?

SELECTION 5:

Religious Women in the Americas

The Catholic world, alerted to the challenge that Protestantism present-ed, responded with its own reformation. Assisted by new religious orders, such as the Jesuits, and a revival of spiritual commitment in older reli-gious communities, the church in southern Europe held its ground. Nowhere was Catholicism so ingrained into the lives of the people as in Spain. Here Teresa of Ávila led the way in inspiring a revitalized Carmelite community of nuns. Soon this religious enthusiasm passed to Spanish America.

The construction of large cathedrals, monasteries, and convents demonstrated the success of the Catholic Reformation in the New World. The lives of Spanish nuns in the Americas became a vital part of the re-gion's culture, as a modern historian demonstrates in the selection below.

Nuns were the most easily identifiable female group in Spanish American cities. They lived to-gether within the physical boundaries of an ar-chitectural unit, the convent, and were an impor-tant element in the hierarchical structure of one of the most influential institutions in colonial so-ciety, the Catholic church. The church lent them its own spiritual, social, and economic strength. No other group of women had the internal coher-ence, economic power, or social prestige that nuns enjoyed. Thus, despite their relatively small numbers within the total female population, they commanded both authority and respect in the cities and beyond their confines.

Unlike monasteries, which could be founded

in either city or countryside, nunneries were rarely built beyond city limits. They were strictly urban institutions, as it was considered undesir-able to have women living as hermits in rural areas exposed to physical risks and lacking the support services which could be provided only in an urban location, such as a supply of food, health services, and skilled craftsmen for building con-struction and maintenance. An urban location was also a necessity in order to remain close to the re-ligious authorities who regulated their spiritual lives and to their most likely sources of financial support, the urban rich and poor, whose alms and endowments sustained the hundreds of women who lived within the cloisters.

The foundation of nunneries in Spanish Amer-ica began in New Spain in the mid–sixteenth cen-tury, barely 30 years after the conquest, and con-tinued through the last years of the colonial period. In 1536, Fray Juan de Zumárraga, first

Asunción Lavrin, "Female Religious," in Louisa Schell Hoberman and Susan Migden Socolow, *Cities and Society in Colonial Latin America* (Albuquerque: University of New Mexico Press, 1986), pp. 165–67.

bishop of New Spain, requested the crown to send either *beatas* (pious lay women) or nuns to New Spain to establish the foundations of Christian life among the female Indian population. The concept of convents for Indians did not take hold, and the women who came from Spain soon joined the secular life. But despite these setbacks, the Conceptionist Order established its first convent, La Concepción, around 1550, for daughters of conquistadors and settlers. In Peru, the convent of La Encarnación, following the Rules of Saint Augustine, emerged in 1561 from a *recogimiento* (shelter) that had been established in 1558.

The appeal of religious life lasted for over 250 years, and only began to subside after independence. The immediate roots of such a consistent attraction are found in the religious spirit pervading the peninsula in the sixteenth century. Early in that century, after the political and religious unification of Spain, and prior to the Protestant Reformation, the Catholic church in Spain had initiated a process of internal reform aimed at regaining the spirit of the primitive Christian church. A new order for women, the Conceptionist, was approved by the pope in 1415, and eventually became extremely popular both in Spain and in its colonies. Equally important was the work of Santa Teresa de Jesús, who reformed the Carmelite Order, founded numerous convents in the peninsula, and through a process of stringent regulation restored respectability to female convent life.

By the sixteenth century, one of the most important spiritual forces within the Spanish church was that of recogimiento, the withdrawal of the self in order to reach God through mystical contemplation. This idea was readily accepted by religious as well as lay persons for observance in their lives. The word recogimiento was also eventually used to mean a place of shelter to which women could retreat in search of physical protection and spiritual development. Roman Catholicism after the Council of Trent (1545–63) stressed the cult of the Virgin Mary and the saints, works or "deeds" aimed toward perfection, and the acceptance of the church as an intermediary between God and humanity. A powerful religious drive prevailed in Spain and its colonies through the sixteenth and seventeenth centuries, and serves to explain the flowering of convent life among both men and women, and the strong spirituality characteristic of the age.

Religious life for women meant enclosure, a complete physical retreat from the world. This was certainly contrary to the goals of most male orders, which were mobilized for spiritual conquest. However, enclosure did not isolate these women from their world or their times. On the contrary, it helped them to become better defined as a group, perhaps elusive in presence, but with a strong and distinct character within colonial society. Bonds with the surrounding community were established through the acts of foundation and the patrons who sustained the convents; the social connections of the nuns; their relations with their ecclesiastical superiors; the economic interests of the convents as institutions; and the intellectual role the convents played in colonial cities.

After reading this selection, consider these questions:
1. Why were convents located in cities?
2. Why was the religious life so attractive to Spanish American women?
3. How did nuns relate to colonial society outside the convent?

SELECTION 6:

Divine Love

One of the nuns of seventeenth-century Mexico City, Sister Juana Inés de la Cruz, became the outstanding woman poet of colonial America. She recognizes in this poem the power of love directed to God. It contains the same combination of desire and pain that accompanies human love. The following is a sample of her poetry in translation.

There's something disturbing me,
so subtle, to be sure,
that though I feel it keenly,
it's not hard to endure.

It's love, but love, for once,
without a blindfold—whence
whoever sees his eyes,
feels torture the more intense.

It's not from their terminus a quo [their origin]
that my sufferings arise,
for their terminus is the Good;
it's in distance that suffering lies.

If this emotion of mine
is proper—indeed, is love's due—
why must I be chastised
for paying what I owe?

Oh, all the consideration,
the tenderness I have seen:
when love is placed in God,
nothing else can intervene.

From what is legitimate
it cannot deviate;
no risk of being forgotten
need it ever contemplate.

I recall—were it not so—
a time when the love I knew
went far beyond madness even,
reached excesses known to few,

but being a bastard love,
built on warring tensions,

it simply fell apart
from its own dissensions.

But oh, being now directed
to the goal true lovers know,
through virtue and reason alone
it must stronger and stronger grow.

Therefore one might inquire
why it is I still languish.
My troubled heart would reply:
what makes my joy makes my anguish.

Yes, from human weakness,
in the midst of purest affection,
we still remain a prey
to natural dejection.

To see our love returned
is so insistent a craving
that even when out of place,
we still find it enslaving.

It means nothing in this instance
that my love be reciprocated;
yet no matter how hard I try,
the need persists unabated.

If this is a sin, I confess it,
if a crime, I must avow it;
the one thing I cannot do
is repent and disallow it.

The one who has power to prove
the secrets of my breast,
has seen that I am the cause
of my suffering and distress.

Well he knows that I myself
have put my desires to death—
my worries smother them, their tomb is my own
    breast.

Juana Inés de la Cruz, "Divine Love," in *A Sor Juana Anthology*, trans. Alan S. Trueblood (Cambridge, MA: Harvard University Press, 1988), pp. 88–89.

I die (who would believe it?)
at the hands of what I love best.
What is it puts me to death?
The very love I profess.

Thus, with deadly poison
I keep my life alive:
the very death I live
is the life of which I die.

Still, take courage, heart:
when torture becomes so sweet,
whatever may be my lot,

from love I'll not retreat.

After reading this selection, consider these questions:

1. What would prompt a nun to write about love?
2. How does Sister Juana distinguish the qualities of love?
3. How does she see the love of God imitating human attraction?

CHAPTER 4
The Age of Absolutism: Does Sovereignty Have Limits?

The seventeenth century is known as the Age of Absolutism because of the claims of monarchs who contended that they had to answer to no one but God. Such an opinion put God's judgment to the test. Nevertheless most Europeans acted on the presumption that there was a natural order in society. God had chosen certain people to be rulers and obedience must be given them, even if what they did might sometimes seem folly.

The most absolute of sovereigns of the seventeenth century was the king of France, Louis XIV. His way had been paved by the very able Cardinal Armand-Jean du Plessis, known as Cardinal Richelieu, who served his father, Louis XIII. All over Europe other monarchs started speaking French and wearing wigs.

Louis XIV liked to be known as the Sun King. Just as the sun dominates the day and regulates people's conduct, everyone in France should look to the monarch. To demonstrate his importance, Louis commissioned a great palace at Versailles and there established a court renowned for its brilliance. Louis had visions of grandeur where his word would be absolute law. But two things stood in the way of royal absolutism: Huguenots—the French Calvinists—and the nobility, whose interests often clashed with the plans of the monarchy.

SELECTION 1:

The Sun King

In the following selection we learn of the rule of Louis XIV from the French historian Pierre Goubert.

As early as 1661, as he declared in his *Mémoires*, Louis meant to have sole command in every sphere and claimed full responsibility, before the world and all posterity, for everything that should happen in his reign. In spite of constant hard work, he soon found he had to entrust the actual running of certain departments, such as finance or commerce, to a few colleagues, although he still reserved the right to take major decisions himself. There were, however, some aspects of his *métier de roi* [profession] to which he clung absolutely and persistently, although his persistence was not invariably absolute. Consequently, it is permissible to single out a kind of personal sphere which the king reserved to himself throughout his reign, although this sphere might vary, while the rest still remained, as it were, under his eye.

As a young man, Louis had promised himself that his own time and posterity should ring with his exploits. If this had been no more than a simple wish, and not an inner certainty, it might be said to have been largely granted.

As a hot-headed young gallant, he flouted kings by his extravagant gestures and amazed them by the brilliance of his court, his entertainments, his tournaments and his mistresses. As a new Augustus he could claim, for a time, to have been his own Maecenas [the Roman adviser to Caesar Augustus]. Up to the year 1672, all Europe seems to have fallen under the spell of his various exploits and his youthful fame spread even as far as the 'barbarians' of Asia. For seven

or eight years after that, the armies of [François-Michel] Le Tellier and [Vicomte de] Turenne seemed almost invincible while [Jean-Baptiste] Colbert's youthful navy and its great admirals won glory off the coast of Sicily. Then, when Europe had pulled itself together, Louis still showed amazing powers of resistance and adaptability. Even when he seemed to be aging, slipping into pious isolation amid his courtiers, he retained the power to astonish with the splendours of his palace at Versailles, his opposition to the Pope and the will to make himself into a 'new Constantine', and later by allying himself with Rome to 'purify' the Catholic religion. When practically on his death bed, he could still impress the English ambassador who came to protest at the building of a new French port next door to the ruins of Dunkirk.

Dead, he became a kind of symbolic puppet for everyone to take over and dress up in his chosen finery. [French writer] Voltaire used him, in the name of 'his' age, as ammunition against Louis XV. On the other side, he long stood as the type of bloodthirsty warlike and intolerant despot. . . .

For precisely three centuries, Louis XIV has continued to dominate, fascinate and haunt men's minds. 'The universe and all time' have certainly remembered him, although not always in the way he would have wished. From this point of view, Louis' personal deeds have been a great success. Unfortunately, his memory has attracted a cloud of hatred and contempt as enduring as that which rises from the incense of his worshippers or the pious imitations of a later age.

In his personal desire to enlarge his kingdom, the king was successful. The lands in the north,

Pierre Goubert, *Louis XIV and Twenty Million Frenchmen*, trans. Anne Carter (New York: Pantheon Books, 1966), pp. 290–93.

Strasbourg, Franche-Comté and the 'iron belt' are clear evidence of success. In this way Paris was better protected from invasion. But all these gains had been made by 1681 and later events served only to confirm, rescue or reduce them. It has even been maintained that considering his strong position in 1661, surrounded by so many kings who were young, unsure of their thrones or simply incompetent, Louis might have hoped for greater things. He might have aimed at the annexation of the Spanish Netherlands, although Holland and England would always have managed to prevent him. Lorraine was vulnerable and Louis was less powerful there in 1715 than in 1661, while with a little shrewdness or cunning, there were Savoy and Nice to be had, to say nothing of the colonies which he tended to disregard, leaving them to traders, adventurers, priests and a few of his colleagues. He was satisfied with losing one West Indian island and the gateway to Canada while a handful of brave men were striving to win him an empire in America and another in India.

As absolute head of his diplomatic service and his armies, from beginning to end, he was well served while he relied on men who had been singled out by [Jules] Mazarin or Richelieu but he often made a fool of himself by selecting unworthy successors. He was no great warrior. His father and his grandfather had reveled in the reek of the camp and the heady excitement of battle. His preference was always for impressive maneuvers, parades and good safe sieges rather than the smoke of battle, and as age grew on him he retreated to desk strategy. Patient, secretive and subtle in constructing alliances, weaving intrigues and undoing coalitions, he marred all these gifts by ill-timed displays of arrogance, brutality and unprovoked aggression. In the last analysis, this born aggressor showed his greatness less in triumph than in adversity but there was never any doubt about his effect on his contemporaries whose feelings towards him were invariably violent and uncompromising. He was admired, feared, hated and secretly envied.

After reading this selection, consider these questions:

1. What were the ideas that motivated Louis XIV's kingship?
2. How did Louis's reign affect people outside of France?
3. How did the young Louis XIV differ from the old?

SELECTION 2:

The Court of Versailles, Another View

Elisabeth Charlotte, Duchess d'Orleans, lived at the court of Louis XIV for fifty years, married to his brother, Philippe d'Orleans. She wrote many intriguing letters, about forty a week to a variety of correspondents, giving a candid view of Louis and his mistresses, especially Madame de Maintenon, who dominated him in his later life. "Monsieur" is her husband; "the Dauphine" is Maria Anna Christine of Bavaria, wife of Louis, the Grand Dauphin, Louis XIV's only son. This letter was written August 11, 1686.

Our King is not well right now, and they say it might turn into a quartan fever. If that were true, God help us, for this is bound to make him a hundred times crankier than he already is. Truly, anyone who has nothing to do with this court would laugh himself half to death to see what is going on here. The King imagines that he is pious because he no longer sleeps with young women, and all his piety consists of being cranky, of having spies everywhere who bear false tales about everyone, of flattering his brother's favorites, and in general making everyone miserable.

The old woman, the Maintenon, gets her pleasure from making the King hate everyone in the royal house, except Monsieur; him she flatters with the King and sees to it that he is well liked and given whatever he desires. . . . Behind his back, however, this old woman worries that people might think that she esteems Monsieur, and therefore, whenever the courtiers speak to her, she says the very devil about him, calling him worthless, the most debauched person in the world, unable to keep a secret, false, and faith-

less. The Dauphine is quite unhappy, and although she does her best to please the King, she is treated very badly every day at the instigation of the old woman and must spend her life being bored and pregnant.

Her husband, Monsieur le Dauphin, does not care about anything in the world, seeks his own amusements and pleasures wherever he can find them, and is becoming dreadfully debauched. So is Monsieur, and the only thing to which he applies himself is to make trouble for me with the King and to show contempt for me, to recommend his favorites, . . . and to get extra favors for them from the King. But when it comes to promoting his children, he could not care less. As for me, I must therefore be constantly on the defense, for they are causing me new troubles every day, even though I am trying my very best to avoid them by my conduct.

After reading this selection, consider these questions:
1. What is the duchess's opinion of Louis XIV?
2. What is needed for royal absolutism to succeed?
3. Would you have enjoyed life at the French Court?

A Woman's Life in the Court of the Sun King: Letters of Liselotte von der Pfalz, 1652–1722, trans. Elborg Forster (Baltimore: Johns Hopkins Press, 1984), p. 52

SELECTION 3:

James I and the Puritans

Louis XIV may well have had in mind the attitude of King James I of England, who wrote a book on how to be a king. After the death of Queen Elizabeth, James inherited the English throne, for his mother, Mary Stuart, Queen of Scots, was Elizabeth's closest relative. Elizabeth had put Mary to death for she feared that the enemies of the Tudors in England could well promote Mary's cause since she was Catholic. James was another story; his upbringing was entirely Protestant.

When he arrived in England James discovered that he was not liked. English men and women regarded him a foreigner and the members of Parliament reacted strongly against James's views of what kingship demanded.

One of James's problems came from the Puritans, the English Calvinists. James had experienced Calvinism in the Presbyterian church of Scotland and had no intention of promoting its views in London. Ironically, the Puritan demand for a new translation of the Bible has attached King James's name to the most-read book in the English language. A contemporary source explains.

As the papist [Catholic] was different from the Protestant religion on one side, so was the Puritan (as they then called pious and good men) on the other. Both were active to attain their own ends; and the king had the command of himself, not bitterly to oppose, but gently to sweeten their hopes for his, thinking himself unsecure betwixt them. The latter were now solicitous for a more clear Reformation. This the bishops opposed, as trenching too much upon them, and the king listened to (having experienced of it in Scotland) how much it had encroached upon Him. For he thought their dissenting from the established government of the church was but to get that power into a great many men's hands, which was now but in one, and that one had dependence upon him, with whom he might better grapple.

The prelates distilling this maxim into the king, "No bishop, no monarch," so strengthening the miter by the same power that upholds the crown. Yet to satisfy the importunity, a conference is appointed at Hampton Court, where the bishops' opponents, Doctor Reynolds, Doctor Sparks, Mister Knewstubs, and Mr. Chadderton, men eminent in learning and piety, in themselves as well as in the opinion of the people, did desire in the name of the rest of their party, "that the doctrine of the church might be preserved in purity, that good and faithful pastors might be planted in all churches, that church government might be sincerely administered, that the Book of Common Prayer might be fitted to more increase of godliness."

Out of some of these particulars, they insisted upon the bishop's power of confirmation, which they would have every minister capable of in his own parish. They disputed against the cross in baptism, the ring in marriage, the surplice, the oath *ex officio* [the promise to support the king], and other things that stuck with them, which they hoped to get all purged away, because the king was of a northern constitution where no such things were practiced, not yet having felt the king's pulse, whom the southern air of the bishops' breaths had so wrought upon that he himself answers most of their demands.

Sometimes gently, applying lenitives where he found ingenuity (for he was learned and eloquent), other times corrosives, telling them these oppositions proceeded more from stubbornness in opinion than tenderness of conscience, and so betwixt his arguments, and kingly authority, menaced them to a conformity, which proved a way of silencing them for the present (and some of them were content to acquiesce for the future) and the king managed this discourse with such power (which they expected not from him, and therefore more daunted at) that Whitgift, Archbishop of Canterbury, (though a holy, grave, and pious man) highly pleased with it with a sugared bait (which princes are apt enough to swallow) said, he was verily persuaded, that the king spake by the spirit of God.

After reading this selection, consider these questions:

1. Why were the Anglican bishops concerned over the Puritans?
2. Why did James I side with the bishops?
3. What were some of the changes the Puritans wanted?

Arthur Wilson, *The History of Great Britain, Being the Life and Reign of King James the First* (London: Richard Lownds, 1653), pp. 7–8.

SELECTION 4:

The King and Parliament

James had nothing but trouble from the House of Commons in the London Parliament. His experience in Scotland, where the Parliament did not check the king's powers, gave him false hopes for life in England. James let his views be known in a work titled Trew Law of Free Monarchies, *which a modern historian discusses in the following selection.*

"The state of monarchy," James told the House of Commons, "is the supremest thing upon earth. For kings are not only God's lieutenants upon earth and sit upon God's throne, but even by God Himself they are called gods." Like God "They make and unmake their subjects. They have power of raising and casting down, of life and of death, judges over all, and yet accountable to none but God only. They have the power to exalt low things and abase high things and make of their subjects like men at the chess, a pawn to take a bishop or a knight, for to emperors or kings their subjects' bodies and goods are due for their defense and maintenance." With passages such as this, often quoted from memory from the *Trew Law of Free Monarchies*, the King sought to enlighten the English House of Commons. . . .

Parliament, then, was a court and an advisory council which could debate nothing but what the King propounded to it. It was not a place "for every rash and harebrained fellow to propose new laws of his own invention." A man wishing a new law, said James, should come with a halter round his neck, and if the law proved unacceptable the propounder should be hanged forthwith. The King would have no novelties, no laws to drive a wedge between prince and people, or to gratify private ends or personal grudges. Nor was Parliament a place for members to display their wit, to scoff at their prince, or to crack jests over each

other's heads. Let them do so in an ale-house but not in the King's Council. "Hold no Parliaments," James told his son, "but for necessity of new laws, which would be but seldom."

How abysmal was his ignorance of the English House of Commons! It was, he discovered, a formidable body that challenged his prerogative; but he never fathomed the sources of its strength, the growing effectiveness of its procedure and leadership, or the inevitability of its advance to power. . . .

Small wonder that James found himself opposed in Parliament. Yet he was always puzzled. In 1604 he told the Commons he was sure they did not mean to be seditious, but they were rash, curious and over-busy. They appeared (God forgive them!) to be suspicious of him. "In my government bypast in Scotland (where I ruled among men not of the best temper) I was heard not only as a King but, suppose I say it, as a counselor. Contrary, here nothing but curiosity from morning to evening to find fault with my propositions. There all things warranted that came from me. Here all things suspected."

As time went by his anger grew, but he was still perplexed. "We are sorry of our ill fortune in this country," he wrote bitterly in 1610. "We came out of Scotland with an unsullied reputation and without any grudge in the people's hearts but for want of us. Wherein we have misbehaved ourself here we know not, nor we can never yet learn. Yet our fame and actions have been tossed like tennis balls amongst them, and all that spite and malice might do to disgrace and

D. Harris Willson, *King James VI and I* (New York: Henry Holt, 1956), pp. 243–47.

infame us hath been used. To be short, this Lower House by their behavior have periled and annoyed our health, wounded our reputation, emboldened all ill-natured people, encroached upon many of our privileges and plagued our purse with their delays." Without a doubt he meant what he said.

The fissure between King and Commons may be seen in their divergent approach to grievances. James's government brought abuses which the Commons were not slow to point out, and redress of grievances became their constant theme. But grievances meant more than new abuses. Things that had been suffered under Elizabeth now appeared outmoded and intolerable, and the time seemed ripe for their reform. Often they involved a diminution of royal authority or revenue, and thus grievances merged with a demand for fundamental change, change that would shift power from Crown to Parliament.

To James the demand for redress of grievances was highly irritating. He was a pious King, the father of his people, willing to take great pains in hearing cases and in redressing wrongs. How could a kingdom with a King like James be such an unweeded garden? Hence he considered the furor about grievances as a personal affront, not to be attributed to flaws in government or in himself, but to the busy and turbulent nature of the Commons. In seeking redress, he informed them in 1610, they must not tell him how to govern, for that was his craft, and to meddle with that would be to lessen him. He had ruled in Scotland, he said, for thirty-six years and in England for seven more; he was an old King who must not be taught his office. Nor should the rights and powers he had received from his forebears be made into grievances. "All novelties are dangerous, and therefore I would be loath to be quarreled in my ancient rights and possessions, for that were to judge me unworthy of that which my predecessors left me."

The Commons' demand for redress of grievances, moreover, should not widen into attacks upon institutions established by law, such as the Court of High Commission, or, most reprehensible of all, upon the prerogative itself, for, as it was blasphemy to dispute what God might do, so it was sedition in subjects to debate what a king might do in the height of his power. The redress of grievances must be left wholly to the ruler. It angered James to find that the Commons asked for the same things over and over, though they had been denied already and were certain to be refused once more.

Yet upon himself he placed no restraint. He interfered constantly in the work of the Commons, sending them commands and instructions and making them far too many speeches. As a result he not only irritated them greatly but disturbed those avenues of influence that were still open to the Crown. It was [the earl of] Salisbury who had managed the government's business in Parliament during the last years of Elizabeth and who continued to do so in the reign of James, though his peerage removed him from the House of Commons. Versed in tactics and methods of influence, he was a skilful parliamentarian; but he was frustrated by the inept meddling of the King, by his tantrums and complaints, and by his misguided instructions, detailed and disturbing.

After reading this selection, consider these questions:

1. What were James's opinions on kingship?
2. How did Parliament react to James?
3. Why did "redress of grievances" become an issue between the king and Parliament?

SELECTION 5:

Galileo and His Telescope

The Age of Absolutism describes the political scene of seventeenth-century Europe, but there is another side to that period, for it was also the beginning of the Scientific Revolution. The greatest advances were in astronomy, as scholars sought to grasp that perhaps the earth was not the center of the universe around which the sun, moon, and stars circled in invisible celestial spheres. Two secular authorities buttressed this position: Aristotle, the Greek philosopher of the fourth century B.C., and Ptolemy, a second-century A.D. Greek geographer who worked in Alexandria, Egypt. Their books on the universe were the texts for centuries of scholars, most of whom believed that their views could not be challenged.

The second authority was the Bible, which universally was understood literally by Protestants, Catholics, and Orthodox Christians. Since biblical authors lived in a world that could be understood only from the perspective of what seemed to be reality, they never attempted a scientific approach to astronomy or physics. Therefore when the Polish scholar Copernicus (Nicolaus Kopernik) was convinced by his mathematical calculations that the motion of stars and planets could not be explained with the earth at the universe's center, he was hesitant to publish his results. It was only after his death in 1543 that his book circulated widely throughout Europe.

Other astronomers studied Copernicus, but visual confirmation of his findings awaited the invention of the telescope. This occurred in the Netherlands early in the seventeenth century. When the telescope came into the hands of an Italian physicist and mathematician at the University of Padua, Galileo Galilei, he not only improved on it but saw things that convinced him of Copernicus's accuracy. In 1613 he made his discoveries known in a work entitled The Sidereal Messenger, *from which the selection below is taken.*

Church authorities, concerned that Galileo's views ran counter to Revelation, requested that he keep his opinions to himself. However, nineteen years later he again published a work that brought him before a court of inquiry of Roman cardinals, who found him guilty of suspected heresy and sentenced him to house arrest for the remainder of his life. This famous trial set the stage for those who would argue that science and religion are not compatible, but the real issue concerned biblical interpretation. Does the Bible have only one literal interpretation?

The difference between the appearance of the planets and the fixed stars seems also deserving of notice. The planets present their discs perfectly round, just as if described with a pair of compasses, and appear as so many little moons, completely illuminated and of a globular shape; but the fixed stars do not look to the naked eye bounded by a circular circumference, but rather like blazes of light, shooting out beams on all sides and very sparkling, and with a telescope they appear of the same shape as when they are viewed by simply looking at them, but so much larger that a star of the fifth or sixth magnitude seems to equal Sirius, the largest of all the fixed stars. . . .

The next object which I have observed is the essence or substance of the Milky Way. By the aid of a telescope any one may behold this in a manner which so distinctly appeals to the senses that all the disputes which have tormented philosophers through so many ages are exploded at once by the irrefragable evidence of our eyes, and we are freed from wordy disputes upon this subject, for the Galaxy is nothing else but a mass of innumerable stars planted together in clusters. Upon whatever part of it you direct the telescope straightway a vast crowd of stars presents itself to view; many of them are tolerably large and extremely bright, but the number of small ones is quite beyond determination.

And whereas that milky brightness, like the brightness of a white cloud, is not only to be seen in the Milky Way, but several spots of a similar color shine faintly here and there in the heavens, if you turn the telescope upon any of them you will find a cluster of stars packed close together. Further—and you will be more surprised at this, —the stars which have been called by every one of the astronomers up to this day *nebulous*, are groups of small stars set thick together in a wonderful way, and although each one of them on account of its smallness, or its immense distance from us, escapes our sight, from the commingling of their rays there arises that brightness which has hitherto been believed to be the denser part of the heavens, able to reflect the rays of the stars or the Sun.

After reading this selection, consider these questions:
1. Why did the Scientific Revolution depend on better instrumentation?
2. What new finds did Galileo make with his telescope?
3. Is Galileo's description of the Milky Way still a valid one?

Galileo Galilei, *The Sidereal Messenger*, trans. Edward Stafford Carlos (London: Dawsons of Pall Mall, n.d.), pp. 40–43.

SELECTION 6:

Newton and the Laws of Motion

In the very year that Galileo died, 1642, the greatest scientist of the seventeenth century, Isaac Newton, was born in England. Astronomers and physicists who continued Galileo's work had improved upon it, but as yet there was still no synthesis to tie everything together. This task remained for Newton, a man of such talent in mathematics and physics that his list of accomplishments is a very long one. The most important of them all ap-

peared in the book The Mathematical Principles of Natural Philosophy. *In this work Newton explained that gravity was the answer to all questions involving motion in the heavens and on the earth. The same laws were acting when a pin dropped to the floor or the sun circled the earth. Newton's breakthrough enabled scientists to finally have a workable proposition to make further advances. The laws of physics so ably demonstrated in the* Principles *remained unchallenged until Albert Einstein extended them with his theory of relativity in the early twentieth century.*

In this selection, taken from the Principles, *Newton puts forward his thesis.*

Law I   *Every body continues in its state of rest or of uniform motion in a right line unless it is compelled to change that state by forces impressed upon it.*

Projectiles continue in their motions, so far as they are not retarded by the resistance of the air or impelled downward by the force of gravity. A top, whose parts by their cohesion are continually drawn aside from rectilinear motions, does not cease its rotation otherwise than as it is retarded by the air. The greater bodies of the planets and comets, meeting with less resistance in freer spaces, preserve their motions both progressive and circular for a much longer time.

Law II   *The change of motion is proportional to the motive force impressed and is made in the direction of the right line in which that force is impressed.*

If any force generates a motion, a double force will generate double the motion, a triple force triple the motion, whether that force be impressed altogether and at once or gradually and successively. And this motion (being always directed the same way with the generating force), if the body moved before, is added to or subtracted from the former motion, according as they directly conspire with or are directly contrary to each other; or obliquely joined, when they are oblique, so as to produce a new motion compounded from the determination of both.

Law III   *To every action there is always op-*

posed an equal reaction; or, the mutual actions of two bodies upon each other are always equal and directed to contrary parts.

Whatever draws or presses another is as much drawn or pressed by that other. If you press a stone with your finger, the finger is also pressed by the stone. If a horse draws a stone tied to a rope, the horse (if I may so say) will be equally drawn back toward the stone; for the distended rope, by the same endeavor to relax or unbend itself, will draw the horse as much toward the stone as it does the stone toward the horse and will obstruct the progress of the one as much as it advances that of the other. If a body impinge upon another and by its force change the motion of the other, that body also (because of the equality of the mutual pressure) will undergo an equal change in its own motion, toward the contrary part. The changes made by these actions are equal, not in the velocities but in the motions of bodies; that is to say, if the bodies are not hindered by any other impediments. For, because the motions are equally changed, the changes of the velocities made toward contrary parts are inversely proportional to the bodies.

After reading this selection, consider these questions:

1. What does Newton say about the motion of bodies?
2. How does gravity provide an equilibrium between bodies?
3. What other laws of physics are put forward in this passage?

Newton's Philosophy of Nature: Selections from his writings, ed. H.S. Thayer (New York: Hafner, 1953), pp. 25–26.

CHAPTER 5
The Eighteenth Century in Europe: How Enlightened Was It?

The Enlightenment is the name often given to eighteenth-century Europe. It receives its title from the large number of writers who appeared at this time espousing a new way to look at government and society. No longer, they said, should people quote authority in order to prove a point; instead, conclusions should be based on reason.

Another strand of the Enlightenment was an appeal to nature. What was natural was good. The problems with human history, according to the thinkers of the Enlightenment, flowed from men and women attempting to set up institutions that ignored or perverted nature. This was made most evident in the way the government and the church, the two major institutions of eighteenth-century Europe, set up laws for people that were based upon only their own views of reality.

The representatives of the Enlightenment were mostly western Europeans who resented the arbitrary decisions made by kings and their officials. They professed a belief in equality for all men, if not yet women, and urged significant political reform.

SELECTION 1:

Religion Among the Christians: A Satire

One of the "enlightened" authors was Charles-Louis de Secondat, the baron de Montesquieu, a French lawyer of Bordeaux. He was well acquainted with other writers who argued for reform, especially those who were British. Montesquieu was also concerned with tolerance, a virtue in short supply throughout European history. To promote this concept, Montesquieu composed a fictitious account about two Persian travelers on a visit to France who regularly write to their friends in their homeland telling of the strange customs they encounter. Since religion and politics provided much of the fuel for argument, Montesquieu directed many of the Persians' comments on those subjects. This passage from Persian Letters *recounts a view on religion in France.*

I have not found among the Christians that lively persuasion of their religion which is observable in the Mussulmans [Muslims]: there is a great difference here between profession and belief, between belief and conviction, between conviction and practice. Religion is not a cause of holiness but of contention, in which every body engages: courtiers, soldiers, nay the very women stand up against the clergy, calling upon them to prove what they are resolved not to believe. Not that they have taken this their resolution upon reason, or have given themselves the trouble to examine the truth or the falsehood of the religion which they reject: their rebellious necks have just felt the yoke and they have shook it off without knowing what it was. Neither are they more fixed in their incredulity than in their faith; they live in a constant flux and reflux, which is perpetually driving them from one to the other.

One day one of them plainly told me: I believe the immortality of the soul by fits; my opinions absolutely depend upon the constitution of my body; according as I have more or fewer animal spirits; as my stomach digests well or ill; as the air I breathe is subtle or gross; as the meats I feed on are light or heavy; I am Spinosist, Socinian, a Catholic, an atheist, or a bigot. [Spinoza was a Jewish philosopher, Socinus, a Unitarian who denied the Christian doctrine of the Trinity]. When the physician is at my bedside, my confessor has me at an advantage. I take care not to let religion afflict me when I am in health; but I allow it to comfort me when I am sick. When I have nothing more to hope for on the side of this world, religion steps in and wins me with her promises of the next. I am e'en willing to give myself over to her then, and to die in hope.

A long while ago the Christian princes set free all the slaves in their dominions, saying that Christianity renders all men equal. It is true, indeed, this act of devotion was of great service to them in their secular concerns, as it humbled the lords by withdrawing the common people from their obedience. Afterwards they made conquests in countries, where they found it convenient to have slaves; then they allowed the buying and selling of them, forgetting that principle of religion which before had touched them so close.

Charles de Secondat, Baron de Montesquieu, *Persian Letters*, trans. John Ozell, 2 vols. (New York: Garland, 1972), vol. 2 pp. 8–11.

What shall we call this? Truth at one time, error at another. Why do not we act like these Christians? We are very silly to refuse fine settlements and easy conquests in happy climates, because they have not water pure enough for us to wash in according to the principles of the holy Alcoran [Koran].

After reading this selection, consider these questions:

1. What do the Persian travelers observe about religious conviction in France?
2. After so many years of conflict between Catholics and Protestants in Europe, how do you suppose Montesquieu's readers responded to this jibe at current practice?
3. Do you think the author presents a true assessment of European views on slavery?

SELECTION 2:

The Civil State

A major contributor to enlightened thought was the Frenchman Jean-Jacques Rousseau. In 1762, after he had published a number of musical works, essays, and a novel, he took up the questions surrounding good government in his essay The Social Contract, *from which this selection is excerpted. Here he argues that republican government, based upon the general will, is the best form of government, provided that the general will is correctly formed. The work had a profound effect on the founders of the United States.*

The passage from the state of nature to the civil state produces a very remarkable change in man, by substituting justice for instinct in his conduct, and giving his actions the morality they had formerly lacked. Then only, when the voice of duty takes the place of physical impulses and right of appetite, does man, who so far had considered only himself, find that he is forced to act on different principles, and to consult his reason before listening to his inclinations. Although, in this state, he deprives himself of some advantages which he got from nature, he gains in return others so great. His faculties are so stimulated and developed, his ideas so extended, his feelings so ennobled, and his whole soul so uplifted, that, did

not the abuses of this new condition often degrade him below that which he left, he would be bound to bless continually the happy moment which took him from it forever. . . .

Let us draw up the whole account in terms easily commensurable. What man loses by the social contract is his natural liberty and an unlimited right to everything he tries to get and succeeds in getting; what he gains is civil liberty and the proprietorship of all he possesses. If we are to avoid mistake in weighing one against the other, we must clearly distinguish natural liberty, which is bounded only by the strength of the individual, from civil liberty, which is limited by the general will; and possession, which is merely the effect of force or the right of the first occupier, from property, which can be founded only on a positive title.

We might, over and above all this, add, to what man acquires in the civil state, moral liberty,

Jean-Jacques Rousseau, *The Social Contract* (New York: Carlton House, n.d.), pp. 14–15, 29.

which alone makes him truly master of himself; for the mere impulse of appetite is slavery, while obedience to a law which we prescribe to ourselves is liberty. . . .

Laws are, properly speaking, only the conditions of civil association. The people, being subject to the laws, ought to be their author: the conditions of the society ought to be regulated solely by those who come together to form it. But how are they to regulate them? Is it to be by common agreement, by a sudden inspiration? Has the body politic an organ to declare its will? Who can give it the foresight to formulate and announce its acts in advance? Or how is it to announce them in the hour of need? How can a blind multitude, which often does not know what it wills, because it rarely knows what is good for it, carry out for itself so great and difficult an enterprise as a system of legislation? Of itself the people wills always the good, but of itself it by no means always sees it. The general will is always in the right, but the judgment which guides it is not always enlightened.

After reading this selection, consider these questions:
1. What does Rousseau think are the advantages of living in a civil state?
2. What is the essence of the social contract?
3. Who does Rousseau want to make the laws of the state?

SELECTION 3:

The Best of European Society—Paris

The most honored of the "enlightened" authors was François-Marie Arouet, who called himself Voltaire. His writings cover a multitude of subjects, filling over a hundred volumes. Witty and charming, his correspondents included the kings and queens of Europe.

A little-known side to Voltaire was his pride in Paris and his French nationality—even to the point of a willingness to pay taxes in order to benefit from its society. These are points he makes in a letter sent to the comptroller-general of France, Jean Baptiste Machault d'Arnouville, in May 1749. Voltaire is speaking of a conversation he had with a bad-tempered man.

It was then remarked that what makes Paris the most flourishing city in the world is not so much the number of magnificent townhouses in which opulence is displayed with some luxury, as the prodigious number of private houses in which there is led a life of comfort unknown to our fathers, and to which other nations have not yet attained. In fact, let us compare Paris with London, which is its rival in size, but which is assuredly very far from being so in splendor, in taste, in sumptuousness, in rare commodities, in pleasure, in the fine arts, and above all in the social arts. I certainly do not think that I am mistaken in as-

Select Letters of Voltaire, ed. and trans. Theodore Besterman (London: Thomas Nelson and Sons, 1963), pp. 98–99, 102.

serting that five hundred times as much silver-ware is owned by the citizens of Paris as by those of London. Your notary, your attorney, your linen-merchant are much better lodged, better furnished, better served than a magistrate of the first city of England.

In a single evening more poultry and game is eaten in Paris than in a week in London. Perhaps a thousand times as many wax-candles are burnt, for in London, except in the neighborhood of the Court, only tallow-candles are known. I say nothing of the other capitals. Amsterdam, the most highly populated after London, is the home of parsimony. Vienna and Madrid are only mediocre towns. Rome is hardly more populated than Lyons, and I very much doubt whether it is as wealthy. In making these reflections we enjoyed the pleasure of recording our happiness; and if Rome has finer buildings, London more numerous ships, Amsterdam bigger shops, we agreed that there is no city on earth in which so great a number of citizens enjoy so much abundance, so much comfort, and so delightful a life. . . .

[Taxation, or tribute, as Voltaire calls it, is the price a person pays for living in France, in this prosperous land.]

The nation as a whole, in paying tribute to itself, is exactly like a farmer who sows in order to reap. I possess an estate on which I pay dues to the state; these dues serve to make me receive punctually my interests and my pensions, and to enable me to sell advantageously the produce of my land. The small farmer is in the same position. If he pays a tenth of his harvest, he sells the rest one tenth dearer. The taxed artisan sells his work in proportion to his tax. A state is as well governed as human weakness permits when tributes are levied to scale, when one estate of the nation is not favored at the expense of another, when the individual contributes to public expenses not according to his standing but in proportion to his income; and that is the result achieved by such a tribute as that of the twentieth of all one's possessions. If this arrangement is not accepted it must necessarily be replaced by an equivalent, for we must begin by paying our debts.

A nation is not weakened by taxes but by the manner in which they are collected or the bad use made of them. But if the King uses the money to settle his debts, to establish a navy, to beautify his capital, to complete the Louvre, to perfect his main roads which are the admiration of foreigners, to help manufactures and the fine arts, in a word, to encourage industry in every way, it must be admitted that such a tax, which appears an evil to some, would have produced a great good for all. The happiest people is that which pays the most and works the most, when it pays and works for itself.

After reading this selection, consider these questions:

1. Why does Voltaire favor Paris over other European cities?
2. In Voltaire's view, why do people pay taxes?
3. Would Voltaire favor an income or sales tax?

SELECTION 4:

Catherine Seizes the Throne

The thought of the Enlightenment spilled over into the royal courts of Europe. Monarchs wanted to appear "enlightened" as long as their own positions were not challenged. Prominent among these were Frederick II of Prussia and Catherine II of Russia. History has called them both "the

Great" because of their accomplishments as enlightened rulers who held an honest concern for their citizens. However, as monarchs, they were absolutely convinced that they alone knew what was best for their subjects.

Catherine the Great was actually a German princess, born Sophia Augusta of Anhalt-Zerbst, a tiny state of the Holy Roman Empire. Court officials in St. Petersburg chose her to be the wife of Tsar Peter III, also a German born in Holstein. Peter had no use for his wife, now known as Catherine, and took every opportunity to humiliate her. That had its risks, for Catherine was a very able woman, who built up friendships with the officers of the Imperial Guard, the Preobrazhenskii Regiment. Once she was sure of their allegiance, Catherine was ready to make her move against her husband.

In the following selection you will see how she came to power.

A second letter, handwritten in pencil, arrived from Peter imploring forgiveness, renouncing the throne, and requesting permission to leave for Holstein with Vorontsova [the tsar's mistress] and General Gudovich [his aide]. This time Catherine must have smiled, all the more so when the messenger, General Izmailov, offered to deliver Peter to her after he freely signed a formal abdication. The document was drafted on the spot and dispatched at once with General Izmailov, accompanied by Vice-Chancellor Golitsyn and Grigorii Orlov. Peter signed immediately. Shortly afterwards he entered his carriage, with Vorontsova, Gudovich, and Izmailov, and rode glumly over to Peterhof [one of the imperial palaces] with a convoy of jubilant hussars and horse-guards. Throngs of troops greeted the ex-emperor with shouts of "Long live Catherine the Second!"

In a virtual trance Peter stepped out of the carriage and handed over his sword and his ribbon of St. Andrew. Vorontsova and Gudovich were led away under arrest. Taken to the room where he had frequently resided while visiting Peterhof, the ex-emperor had to surrender his Preobrazhenskii Guards uniform. Nikita Panin visited Peter there and long remembered the pathetic sight, "the greatest misfortune of my life." So disoriented was Peter that he begged only not to be separated from his "Fraülein," Vorontsova. He did not even request a meeting with Catherine,

who discreetly avoided witnessing her husband's humiliation.

Later that afternoon a select guard led by Aleksei Orlov, Captain Passek, whose arrest had triggered the start of the coup, Prince Fedor Bariatinskii, and Lieutenant Baskakov supervised Peter's transfer to Ropsha, an estate some thirty kilometers inland that Empress Elizabeth had granted him as grand duke. A large coach pulled by more than six horses, the side curtains drawn shut and with armed guards on the running boards, spirited the former sovereign into temporary captivity at Ropsha, until permanent accommodations could be readied at Schlüsselburg. . . .

Peter's abdication completed the coup's formalities, so Catherine left Peterhof that evening in a carriage convoyed by horse-guards. Halfway back to Petersburg, the Empress halted at Prince Kurakin's dacha where she crumpled into bed completely exhausted—the first sleep she had savored in more than forty hours. In barely two days her prospects had completely changed. From a threatened, neglected, and powerless consort, Catherine had abruptly wrested command of the entire political arena and re-entered St. Petersburg in triumph on the morning of Sunday, 30 June [1762]. On horseback once again, the Empress rode into the capital at the head of the Preobrazhenskii Regiment along with the other Guards regiments, artillery, and three line regiments. The city turned out to see her grand entry, so unlike the one she had made two days before, as the clergy blessed her with holy water, churchbells pealed, and martial music rippled the sum-

John T. Alexander, *Catherine the Great* (New York and Oxford: Oxford University Press, 1989), pp. 12–13.

mer air. Crowds lined the streets and speckled the rooftops. At noon Catherine pulled up before the Summer Palace, where Grand Duke Paul welcomed his mother amid rank upon rank of government and church officials. Constantly solicitous of Russian religious sentiments, the Empress proceeded directly to the court chapel for prayers.

Sunday in Russia is also the traditional time for tippling. The raucous drinking, which began the day of the coup and resulted in some looting while Catherine was away at Peterhof, now redoubled in volume, led by delirious Guardsmen and abetted by police inaction or complicity. Shouting, singing, fighting resounded through the city far into the luminous night. Suddenly some drunken hussar started bellowing about a threat to Catherine's safety—30,000 Prussians were allegedly coming "to kidnap our Little Mother!" Others joined the tumult and refused to calm down even at the urging of Aleksei and Grigorii Orlov.

Though the exhausted Empress had already retired for the night, Captain Passek awakened her in alarm and accompanied her carriage on a visit to the Izmailovskii Guards past midnight. "I told them that I was completely healthy," the Empress later recalled, "that they should go to sleep and leave me in peace, that I had not slept for three nights and had just fallen asleep; I expressed my desire that henceforth they obey their officers. They replied that the damned Prussians had alarmed them but that they were ready to die for me. I told them: 'Well, fine, thanks; but now go to sleep.' They wished me a good night, good health, and dispersed like lambs, all looking back at my carriage." The role of mediator and peacemaker appealed to the new autocratrix.

Early the next morning all drinking establishments were ordered to close. Pickets of troops with loaded cannon and lighted linstocks were arrayed along all bridges, public squares, and street crossings. In the face of such measures and in the natural course of things the celebration/agitation quickly subsided. Within a week the tav-

erns could reopen. The troops ringing the capital were withdrawn; commercial and postal communications were restored. On Sunday, 7 July, the public parks were reopened to persons of all classes and both sexes, clean and neatly dressed, except for those wearing bast footwear (i.e., peasants) or Prussian clothes. That same day, with life in the capital having returned to normal, Catherine's government issued a lengthy "detailed" manifesto justifying her accession. Presumably Catherine herself dictated the basic ideas, which her state secretaries then carefully reworked and rephrased into the slightly archaic Russian used in official pronouncements.

Addressed to "All Our loyal subjects ecclesiastical, military, and civil," Catherine's manifesto amounted to a full-scale indictment of Peter III, who was charged with manifold crimes and criminal designs against Catherine and Paul, church and state, the army and the Guards in particular. Indeed, the manifesto maintained that the Emperor, after provoking universal discontent, had blamed it on Catherine and planned "to destroy Us completely and to deprive Us of life." He was also branded as unfit to rule, tyrannical, and ungrateful; for he had supposedly planned to exclude Paul from the succession instituted by Empress Elizabeth, whose pious memory he had repeatedly insulted. It was the threat to Catherine and the country, the manifesto insisted, that had caused "loyal subjects selected from the people" to rush to her defense and save the Empire from enslavement or bloody rebellion.

After reading this selection, consider these questions:

1. What leads you to think that Peter III had little support to hold on to his throne?
2. What shows Catherine's skills in rallying people to her cause?
3. What steps did Catherine take to assure her rise to power would not be challenged?

SELECTION 5:

A Criticism of Catherine the Great

Catherine soon went to work to reform the administration and the law code of Russia. She personally drew up the instructions that jurists were to follow to guide them in the reforms. Despite many efforts to improve the government, Catherine did not see fit to challenge the most serious problem besetting the country, serfdom.

While most applauded her reforms, there were also dissenters, even among the nobles, who received most of Catherine's benefits. One of these was Prince M.M. Shcherbatov, who wrote a tract, On the Corruption of Morals in Russia, *excerpted in the following selection. His work was published only one hundred years after his death.*

A woman not born of the blood of our sovereigns, who deposed her husband by an armed insurrection, she received, in return for so virtuous a deed, the crown and scepter of Russia, together with the title of "Devout Sovereign," in the words of the prayer recited in church on behalf of our monarchs.

It cannot be said that she is unqualified to rule so great an Empire, if indeed a woman can support this yoke, and if human qualities alone are sufficient for this supreme office. She is endowed with considerable beauty, clever, affable, magnanimous and compassionate on principle. She loves glory, and is assiduous in her pursuit of it. She is prudent, enterprising, and quite well-read. However, her moral outlook is based on the modern philosophers, that is to say, it is not fixed on the firm rock of God's Law; and hence, being based on arbitrary worldly principles, it is liable to change with them.

In addition, her faults are as follows: she is licentious; and trusts herself entirely to her favorites; she is full of ostentation in all things, infinitely selfish, and incapable of forcing herself to attend to any matters which may bore her. She takes everything on herself and takes no care to see it carried out, and finally she is so capricious, that she rarely keeps the same system of government even for a month.

For all that, once on the throne, she refrained from taking cruel vengeance on those who had previously vexed her. She had with her her favorite, Grigory Grigor'evich Orlov, who had helped her to accede to the throne. He was a man who had grown up in alehouses and houses of ill-repute. He had no education, and had hitherto led the life of a young reprobate, though he was kind and good-hearted.

This was the man who reached the highest step which it is possible for a subject to attain. Amid boxing-matches, wrestling, card-games, hunting and other noisy pastimes, he had picked up and adopted certain rules useful to the state. His brothers did likewise.

These rules were: to take vengeance on no one, to banish flatterers, to leave each person and government-organ in the uninterrupted execution of their duties, not to flatter the monarch, to seek out worthy men and not make promotions except

M.M Shcherbatov, *On the Corruption of Morals in Russia*, trans. A. Lentin (Cambridge: Cambridge University Press, 1969), pp. 235–37.

on grounds of merit, and finally, to avoid luxury. These rules were kept by Grigory Grigor'evich Orlov (later Count and finally Prince) to the day he died. . . .

The whole reign of this monarch has been marked by events relating to her love of glory. The many institutions founded by her apparently exist for the good of the nation. In fact they are simply symbols of her love of glory, for if she really had the nation's interest at heart, she would, after founding them, have also paid attention to their progress. But she has been content simply with their establishment and with the assurance that she will be eternally revered by posterity as their founder; she has cared nothing for their progress, and though she sees their abuses she has not put a stop to them.

This is attested by the establishment of the Foundlings' Home, the Convent for the Education of Young Ladies of the Nobility, the reorganization of the Cadet Corps, and so on. In the first of these, a large number of infants have died, and even today, after over twenty years, few or hardly any artisans have emerged. In the second, the young ladies have emerged with neither learning nor morals, apart from what nature has provided them with, and their education has consisted in acting comedies rather than in the improvement of their hearts, morals and reason. From the third, the pupils have emerged with little knowledge and with an absolute aversion to all discipline. . . .

Measures have been drawn up which men are not ashamed to call laws, and the new provincial governorships have been filled indiscriminately, to the ruin of all that went before, to the detriment of society, to the increase of sharp practice and the ruin of the people; and no watch is kept over these governors to see whether they carry out their instructions exactly.

After reading this selection, consider these questions:

1. Why does Prince Shcherbatov think Catherine's moral sense lacking?
2. Do you think Prince Shcherbatov believes the tsarina has some qualities that make her an able ruler?
3. What does Shcherbatov find unacceptable in Catherine's behavior?

SELECTION 6:

Johann Sebastian Bach

While government and politics might have been the concern of many Germans in the eighteenth century, others could turn to the arts. Music, above all, was favored with great composers, among them surely one of the world's best, Johann Sebastian Bach, who lived from 1685 to 1750. Frederick the Great knew of his talent, and in the following selection you will read of their meeting.

Johann Sebastian Bach . . . stands at the summit

Ronald Taylor, "German Music," in *Germany: A Companion to German Studies*, ed. Malcolm Pasley (London: Methuen, 1972), pp. 620–22.

of a German—indeed, a specifically North German, Protestant—tradition, while holding, in his Olympian stature, a position so much more than that of just the consummator of a tradition.

Apart from the occasional incidents, a chronicle of the external events of Bach's life amounts to little more than a list of his employers. He never left Germany, and the farthest he ever traveled from his native Thuringia was Lübeck—and that only for a brief period as a chorister and organ scholar. From 1723 onwards he was cantor at St. Thomas's Church in Leipzig in succession to Johann Kuhnau (1660–1722), the interesting composer of a set of so-called "Biblical Sonatas" for harpsichord, one of the earliest-known examples of extended program music. Very little of Bach's music was published during his lifetime, and what reputation he had was as an organist and as an improviser at the keyboard. It was for his fame in the latter capacity that Frederick the Great invited him to Potsdam in 1747, setting him themes on which to exercise his skill in canon, fugue and other contrapuntal techniques. On one such theme of the king's invention Bach built the work—one of his last, and one of the very few to be published in his lifetime—known as *The Musical Offering.* . . .

[Bach] had an extensive knowledge of French and especially Italian music. Vivaldi in particular provided him with many starting-points for his own compositions, and certain of Bach's instrumental works are straight recastings, for different combinations of instruments, of pieces by Vivaldi. But, unlike Handel, these cases are not numerous, and the influence is peripheral. The great works with which the name of Bach is synonymous—the *Mass in B minor,* the *St. Matthew Passion,* the *Brandenburg Concertos,* the organ preludes and fugues, *The Well-Tempered Clavier, The Art of Fugue* and the rest—present a massive, monolithic personality whose power to command emotional and intellectual reverence, to inspire the mind and to enrich the spirit, is as individual as it is irresistible.

Yet alongside the lofty language that seems appropriate to the description of such lofty works of art must be ranged the sober realization that Bach was a practical musician. He was not given to theorizing about his own or anyone else's music, and his only surviving theoretical works consist of two sets of thorough-bass rules, based on a current textbook, which he used for teaching his pupils. Also, he had the practitioner's view of what constituted good organ design, and had his instruments modified to meet his requirements. . . .

Throughout his career, Bach was required by his various employers to produce works, religious and secular, to order, and his view of music as a craft as much as an art lay very much in the tradition of the whole Bach family. Of his 200 or so church cantatas, for example, the majority owe their existence to the blunt necessity of providing music for Sunday worship, and one would not expect the level of inspiration behind them to remain constant. The miracle is that so many of such occasional pieces, vocal, choral and instrumental, should occupy unassailable positions in the ranks of the world's greatest music.

Our modern, "moral" distinction between secular and religious in music has no relevance to the world of Bach. That Bach himself was a deeply religious person is apparent from the spirit of his music alone, but this is not contradicted by such knowledge as that seventeen numbers of the *Christmas Oratorio* are borrowings from secular cantatas written by Bach for earlier and entirely worldly occasions.

After reading this selection, consider these questions:
1. Why do you suppose Bach's life was so outwardly uneventful?
2. How did Bach have a connection with Frederick the Great?
3. What prompted Bach's compositions?

CHAPTER 6
The Ottoman Empire: Can Muslims and Christians Live Together?

One of the greatest empires of the east Mediterranean was created by the Ottoman sultans. Beginning as only one tribal people among many, in the fourteenth century those Turks under the leader Osman established themselves in the northwestern part of Anatolia.

Their inheritance came from several sources. First, they followed the Seljuk Turks who had preceded them into Anatolia. The Mongols had devastated the Seljuks, allowing the Ottomans to become the predominant power in Anatolia. A second factor was a conversion to Islam. Their conversion was wholehearted, and to become a *ghazi* (a warrior for the faith) was the highest calling a man could follow. Finally, the Ottomans were influenced by the Byzantine Empire. In 1453 the Turkish conquest of Constantinople permitted the sultans to lay claim to the legacy to the Christian emperors that for so long had dominated the east Mediterranean.

SELECTION 1:

The Military Nature of the Ottoman State

A *modern historian of the Islamic world, Marshall G.S. Hodgson, sets the stage for an understanding of the Ottoman political structure in the following selection.*

The original Ottoman state had been military, indeed, but far from an absolute monarchy of any kind. But the character of the military base of the state had been transformed and absolutism gradually was imposed on the ghazi warriors' descendants. When the Ottoman military activities had come to be channeled in major campaigns, whose distance required great central organization, the former more or less irregular ghazi troops had tended gradually to recede into the general herding and peasant population, while their leaders became prosperous landlords, holding systematic military land grants. With their changed social position, their attitudes changed; well established themselves, they were less ready to look for a heroic chief, more ready to accept an established monarch. At the same time, their power was diluted.

The military traditions of the frontier ghazis persisted. The troops still regarded their destiny as the subjugation of the infidel—and perhaps, now, of the heretic Shi'is of the Safavi empire. But their personnel had gradually ceased to be drawn from Muslim adventurers and hereditary frontiersmen. The military had come to be composed of two contrary and rival groups. The old ghazi families, with the expansion of the empire, had come to form a landed Turkic aristocracy increasingly independent of their chief and contented with results already achieved. Under the

forms of a common monarchy, they would have been glad to rule each his own domain in private.

To maintain a central government at all, Mehmed II had leaned on the alternative sources of power which the Ottoman state had been able to build up in its sudden victories. These included partly the old families of the Balkan nobility, who had served even as Christians but in the sixteenth century were becoming Muslim. More important was the new element brought to the fore by the use of gunpowder. With the development of gunpowder weapons, the infantry became a crucial arm.

From the time of Mehmed II through that of Süleyman (1520–66), the number and variety of infantry corps, variously recruited, increased. Among them, one of the most highly trained infantry corps, the Janissaries, formed the heart of the army. As in the case of the Safavis [the Persians], these and other infantrymen were outsiders (largely lower-class Christians by birth), standing apart from the powerful classes of society. Paid from the treasury, they were at the disposal of the monarch without reservation, in contrast to the holders of military land grants, with their far-ramifying connections. With a well-supported dynasty solidly established in Istanbul, then, something of the Byzantine political idea reasserted itself: the same strategic opportunities and problems were reproduced. But the political idea had been reasserted in a thoroughly Islamicate form.

Byzantium had indeed been an absolute monarchy, and not only imperial strategy but the forms

Marshall G.S. Hodgson, *The Venture of Islam*, 3 vols. (Chicago and London: University of Chicago Press, 1974), vol. 3, pp. 99–101.

of absolutism owed something to it. Mehmed II had developed an elaborate courtly ceremonial in place of the comradely simplicity of his ancestors; relying on the diverse elements of the state other than the descendants of ghazis, he had not only reduced the almost independent power of the grandees of the state, but did much to organize it centrally and hierarchically. But though his models in ceremonial may often have been Byzantine, his basic political ideals were molded by the stories of the great Muslim states. . . .

When Selim enlarged the empire, then, the most important segments of the central power structure were organized as a single army, with the emperor, the *padishah*, at its head; within this army, not only soldiers but many kinds of administrators held military rank and were compensated either by a military land grant or, increasingly, on the military payroll. The rewards of power were frankly conceived in military terms; the revenues of the whole empire were allotted to members of the Ottoman ruling class according to their military contributions: a conception originally appropriate to ghazis, indeed, but, with the dominance of the figure of the emperor, the padishah, recast in military patronage form. . . . The seat of government, accordingly, was wherever the padishah and his army happened to be. The chief officials of the usual capital city, responsible for policing and for justice in its various quarters, and even the chief men responsible for keeping the central financial accounts, were expected to go on campaign with the padishah whenever he set out with the armed forces.

After reading this selection, consider these questions:
1. Why does Hodgson call the Ottomans a military state?
2. How did the Janissaries differ from the *ghazis*?
3. What were the powers of the sultan?

SELECTION 2:

Ottoman Christians

Balkan peoples had no choice but to accept Ottoman rule, which destroyed the Christian kings and nobles who lived in that part of Europe. After Mehmed II's conquest of Constantinople, Christians and Muslims entered a new arrangement. The most difficult aspect of life for Balkan Christians was the practice of recruiting their sons in the devshirme. *About every four years units of the Ottoman army went through the Balkan villages taking the most promising boys from their families for service in the Janissary Corps or in the sultan's civil service, as this selection—a modern historian's account—relates.*

Balkan Christians were governed in accordance with the *sheriat*—the religious code of the

Ottomans—and a variety of other legal precedents. These laws dictated that, in general, Christian *zimmi* should be permitted to worship freely, to hold on to their properties, and to manage their internal affairs. Mehmed reserved the right to appoint George Scholarios, who had taken Gennadios for his monastic name, patriarch of the Or-

Charles Frazee, "Christianity and Islam in Southeastern Europe," *East European Studies Occasional Paper,* no. 47 (Washington, DC: Woodrow Wilson International Center for Scholars, 1997) pp. 11–13.

thodox church. Contrary to legend, Mehmed probably did not personally invest Gennadios in his office, but there is little doubt that even if an episcopal synod, the usual canonical electoral body for choosing a patriarch, had been convened, it would have had no choice but to oblige Mehmed. The notion that Mehmed at once set up the *Millet-i Rum*—the Greek (Roman) nation—has also been seriously questioned. It seems much more likely that Mehmed, like his predecessors, was content to deal with his Orthodox subjects as circumstances demanded.

The basic division of society within the early Ottoman state was between those who belonged to the ruling class and those who did not. The former paid no taxes. The latter, known by the collective term *reaya,* did. Since *reaya* means "flock" it has often been judged a contemptuous name for Christians and Jews. But it was also used to describe Muslims, if they belonged to the class of taxpayers. The term *askeri* was given to military and civil personnel who served the state. In the fifteenth and sixteenth centuries, Christians as well as Muslims were members of the *askeri* because service to the ruler, not religion, was the determining factor in judging personal status.

The major tax that the *reaya* were obligated to pay was the head tax known as the *cizye* or, more commonly, the *haraj*. The *cizye* fell upon every Christian male of military age. Theoretically, the tax was in lieu of army service, since Christians were not supposed to bear arms. Orthodox Christian clergy, at first exempt, were later taxed along with everyone else. The *zimmi* found this tax extremely burdensome because it was often set in an arbitrary manner. Both Muslim and Christian peasants also paid a land tax to the central government. A major concern of Ottoman officials, if not their most important consideration, was to make sure that all revenues owed the state were collected, and churchmen were expected to work toward that end. In the early centuries of the Ottoman Conquest, taxes gathered by the Istanbul government were judged to be fair, but as the years passed, local officials tended to circumvent the sultan's bureaucracy. They raised the obligations of the peasantry to such an extent that the majority of the farming population found it diffi-

cult to survive. In some locations, tax farmers, greedy beyond imagination, fleeced the Christian *zimmi* at every opportunity. Christian peasants suffered from too little, not too much, government from Istanbul. . . .

Turkish records show that in the sixteenth century Christians outnumbered Muslims in twenty-four of the twenty-eight *kazas* of the Balkans. Only four *kazas*: Vize, Silistria, Chirmen, and Gallipoli, had a Muslim majority. Some cities, such as Athens, were nearly all Christian. Ethnic Turks and Christians who were converts preferred to make their homes in the larger Balkan towns because a full Muslim life could only be lived in an urban setting. It was in cities that the Ottomans located their administration, courts, and *medresses* [Muslim schools] and built their mosques or refitted Christian churches for Islamic worship. Christians also lived in these towns, often working alongside Muslims in public life, but rarely in private. Each community lived in its own section of town—the *mahalle*—where homes were built and families reared. Christian women and children very seldom left the *mahalle*. Both Muslims and Christians adhered to a strictly patriarchal structure in their homes.

The *mahalle* sought to manage its own affairs as much as possible. Houses of both Christians and Muslims were one-story, squat wooden structures where people sat on divans rather than chairs. The streets of the town were not paved and became nearly impassable when it rained or snowed. Members of the *mahalle* had their own baths, shops, and warehouses conveniently located within their quarter's boundaries. In the downtown area, there were a few stone structures. These were the mosques, churches, and public buildings. Unlike West European cities, Balkan towns had no walls because the government wanted to be sure of easy access in case of trouble. Since most Muslims found the city's amenities so much better, they were quite content to leave rural life to Christians.

The cities that grew in Muslim population were those along the major trade arteries and those that were administrative centers. By 1530 Sarajevo was almost completely Muslim. Other towns with large Islamic populations included

Edirne, Skopje, Sofia, Larissa, and Monastir. Their numbers grew as more immigrants arrived from Anatolia and the number of converts from the indigenous population increased. Turkish tax records of 1553–54 show the following numbers for the Balkan part of the empire: Christians 832,707; Muslims 194,958; and Jews 4,134. Only taxable hearths were counted, so not every household was included. Nevertheless, these statistics show that, despite conversions, a century after the Ottoman Conquest about 80 percent of the Balkan population was Christian and less than 20 percent was Muslim.

After reading this selection, consider these questions:
1. What were the basic divisions in Ottoman society?
2. What was the *devshirme*?
3. What motivated some Christians to convert to Islam?

SELECTION 3:

The Siege of Vienna

One of the most important padishahs, *or sultans (as Westerners call them), was Süleyman the Magnificent. As his predecessors had done before him, he made yearly campaigns to expand his territories against Christian states in Europe or to war against Shi'ite enemies in eastern Anatolia. For Süleyman the Shi'ites were heretics deserving of destruction.*

Antony Bridge has written a biography of this man, a contemporary of Martin Luther and Henry VIII, who had his own plans for changing Europe. In the following selection he narrates the events surrounding Süleyman's attack on Vienna, Austria, in 1529. This was to be the farthest penetration of Europe ever made by the Turks. It failed thanks to the courage of the defenders and the approach of cold weather, for the Ottoman army did not have sufficient supplies to withstand the winter.

The first sign which the people of Vienna had of the approach of the enemy was the sight of a few thin black columns of smoke rising lazily into the sky in the far distance as villages were set on fire by the marauding *akinji* [the Ottoman irregular troops]; and as the Turks approached nearer to the city, so they grew in number and proximity until they rose like a forest all round the city from horizon to horizon. At the same time refugees from the countryside began to arrive in the capital to the terrifying accompaniment of the slow ringing of "Turkbells," as the church bells were tolled from every nearby tower and steeple until the air was filled with their sonorous alarm. On 23 September the Turkish horsemen reached the walls of Vienna with their pikes lifted high, each with an Austrian head on the end of it, and as the silent men on the battlements watched them arrive the Turks whooped and screamed in defiance. Four days later on the eve of St. Wenceslas's Day, 27 September, Süleyman joined them with the main body of the army. He pitched his tent at a safe distance from the city near the village of Simmering, and the Janissaries camped

Antony Bridge, *Suleiman the Magnificent, Scourge of Heaven* (New York: Franklin Watts, 1983), pp. 115–17.

round his headquarters while the rest of his men spread out round the city. The siege of Vienna had begun.

With a few exceptions, historians have seen the battle which followed as the most crucial challenge to western Christendom since the battle of Tours eight centuries previously, when a Moslem army of Moors was defeated by Charles Martel. Ferdinand [the Austrian ruler] himself was not in the city; he was trying to raise more troops in Germany, having given command of the garrison to Count Nicholas von Salm, a veteran of Pavia and many other battles and a highly competent soldier. When Süleyman heard from some prisoners taken by his cavalry that neither the Archduke nor his brother, the Emperor Charles, was in the city, he told them angrily that he intended to chase Ferdinand and chastise him wherever he might be; then he sent them into the city to tell the defenders and citizens that if they submitted their lives would be spared, but that if they did not surrender at once, they and their city would be utterly destroyed.

His army was so enormous and the garrison of the place so small by comparison, being outnumbered by at least ten to one, that it is surprising that the idea of accepting the Sultan's offer occurred to no one; they were few in number, and their means of defending themselves were meager with only seventy-two cannon in the city, but their morale was high and their hatred of the Turks intense; indeed, even more intense than it had ever been, for everyone had heard the stories of atrocities committed by the approaching Turks on the women and children of the outlying villages, recounted by the refugees who had sought safety in Vienna. Moreover, they had made their preparations well; the suburbs had been burnt to the ground so that the invaders should not be able to use the houses there as cover, the garrison was on full alert, and every able-bodied citizen of the place had been mobilized and was ready to help in the coming struggle. When they received Süleyman's ultimatum, their answer was delivered by a task force of 2,500 men, who made a sortie from the Carinthian Gate and killed 200 Turks under the Sultan's very eyes, as his tent was being pitched at Simmering.

Without heavy artillery the Turkish bombardment, which began at once, did little damage to the fortifications of Vienna, old-fashioned as they were, and von Salm felt safe enough at the top of the tall spire of St. Stephen's Church, from which vantage point he could watch every movement of the enemy outside the city walls; if a stray ball hit the spire, it was too small and spent to do much harm, and the Count spent most of his time there. The Turks realized that they would never breach the walls by using their artillery alone, and they began mining operations early in the siege, driving shafts beneath the Carinthian Gate and the monastery of St. Clare; but some prisoners taken during another sortie on 6 October gave away the secret of these mines, and counter-mines were begun immediately by some German sappers and blown successfully a few days later. Frustrated by the failure of their attempt to blow up the Carinthian Gate, the Turkish gunners subjected it to a furious bombardment, and early in October scaling ladders were prepared and great bundles of faggots were bound together in bundles with which to fill the moat at the foot of the city wall in preparation for an assault. In order to forestall this attack, the Austrians made a dawn sortie from the city, hoping to surprise the Turks, but the Janissaries were waiting for them, and 500 of them were killed while others were taken prisoner; almost certainly their plan of attack had been betrayed to the enemy by an informer.

Although this was a disaster, which the defenders could ill afford, it might have been worse; for as the survivors fled back to the safety of the city walls they were so hotly pursued by the Turkish infantry that for a moment it looked as if Süleyman's men would carry one of the city gates before it could be shut against them. Fortunately for the Viennese, they just failed to do so, and when they tried to scale the walls beside the gate which had been slammed in their faces, they were beaten back by the Austrians, who killed and wounded many of them in the process. Honors were not exactly even, for the Turks could afford their casualties much better than the Austrians, but if the Christian forces had not won a spectacular victory at least they had not suffered an irreversible defeat; and time was on their side. Indeed, their most powerful ally was fast approaching, and the longer the defenders could hold out, the more surely could they rely on this imminent support. That ally, of course, was winter.

After reading this selection, consider these questions:

1. Why has so much importance been attached to the siege of Vienna?
2. What encouraged the Austrians to hold out against the Ottomans?
3. Why did the Turkish attack fail?

SELECTION 4:

Problems of Government

Although Vienna was never captured, Süleyman had enough victories to be remembered for a long time. Unfortunately, after his reign the quality of the sultans began to decline. The dynasty, which had produced ten remarkably able men in succession, now seemed to have run out of ability. The men preferred life in the harem to the battlefield. This caused an evaluation to be made in 1581 by Mustafa Ali, an official who served in a minor position in Aleppo, Syria. Ali was especially upset that the viziers, the sultan's prime ministers, had obtained so much power. In his opinion, provided in the following selection, Sultan Murad III was much too isolated to know the true state of affairs in his empire.

Without any doubt, it is in every respect the duty of the honorable sultans and majestic pillars [of the Faith] to march on the road of justice and to grant the [high] offices to those who qualify, so that the prominent and conspicuous persons excel over the low-bred persons. However, the King of the World, the Sovereign of Sublime Rank, the Chosen One among the rulers mighty as Destiny, the praised one of the House of Osman, [namely] Sultan Murad, the son of Sultan Selim—may God confirm his reign until the end of time!—has recommended the investigation of the conditions of the people and the examination of the events of months and years to his statesmen, as it had already been the practice

with his great and noble ancestors, his eminent predecessors. Since it had become difficult for them themselves to mix with their soldiers, as numerous as drops in the ocean, and contrary to good practice personally to take care of the affairs of the people, the orientation toward the path of justice had become an indicator of righteousness only in respect to the viziers. . . .

To appoint ignorants when there are wise men available, to choose those who excel in flattery and eulogy rather than those who are truthful and just, is not only equal to condoning the oppression of the people but also a shining example of the maxim: "He who delegates an act to a person betrays God and His Prophet and His community, the true believers." To condone the darkness of tyranny is equal to causing the eclipse of the sun of justice. To hand over the Treasure of the True Believers, that trust of the Creator of the Universe, to undeserving men is a terrible sin, and it

Andreas Tietze, ed. and trans., *Mustafa Ali's Counsel for Sultans of 1581*, 2 vols. (Vienna: Verlag der Osterreichischen Akademie der Wissenschaften, 1979), vol. 1, pp. 18–20.

is also quite evident that to let it go to unqualified persons is a real disaster. In this matter ignorance is by no means an excuse; unawareness of the situation of the viziers will not count as a valid defense on the Day of Judgment. . . .

To sum up, [I], this humble slave, watching carefully, have [always] seen the viziers in pleasure and luxury, enjoying themselves no end in their palaces and gardens, and the other members of the Imperial council occupied with the acquisition of money and property, always going along with the viziers, should they even order the abrogation of justice. Likewise have I found those that were closest to the king and occupied high offices, with the king's favors and bounties being showered upon them, to be silent vis-à-vis this problem. Aghast they would exclaim: "God forbid! The Creator's world needs no reform!"

Under these circumstances His Royalty the World-Conqueror has no helper nor assistant in managing the affairs of state. As he is isolated behind the curtain and respectable people assert the contrary of what is happening, every disorder is—so I have become aware—a hidden secret kept away from his noble knowledge. However,

on the Day of Judgment he himself will be asked to answer for it and it will become evident that his excuse that the viziers had not told him will not be accepted. Then why does he not long for an upright servant time and again to discuss with him the affairs of the world, so as to be able to examine the order of things, viewing everything to its very depth? Provided, however, that this thus favored person be of an exquisite mind, a man of zeal and education, and that, when he goes in and out in the viziers' offices, his testimony is not influenced by their wishes (he himself having certain wishes from them), in short, that he be a man of rectitude that has nothing to fear from anybody, loyal to the bread and salt of the king but not taking notice of anybody else.

After reading this selection, consider these questions:

1. What does Mustafa Ali see as a major weakness in Ottoman government?
2. Can you imagine what caused Mustafa Ali to criticize the government?
3. Why is the isolation of a ruler always a serious problem?

SELECTION 5:

The Tale of a Warrior

The Ottoman world produced some of the world's finest literature, much of it filled with stories of soldiers' heroism. Such a tale from The Book of Dede Korkut *depicts Seghrek, son of Ushun Koja. Note the values put on life in a Turkish community. (The Ottomans were earlier known as Oghuz when they lived in Turkmenistan in Inner Asia.)*

During the time of the Oghuz, there was a man by the name of Ushun Koja who had two sons. The

Faruk Sumer, Ahmet Uysal and Warren Walker, trans., *The Book of Dede Korkut* (Austin and London: University of Texas Press, 1972), pp. 145–47.

elder son, who was called Eghrek, was a brave, reckless, and fine young man. He used to attend Bayindir Khan's meetings whenever he wished. The doors of the council of Kazan Bey, the bey of beys, were always open to him. He used to step over the beys and sit right in front of Kazan. He did not care about the rules of precedence.

One day, when, as usual, he stepped over the beys and sat in front, a man of the Oghuz who was called Ters Uzamish said to him: "O son of Ushun Koja, each one of these beys sitting here has earned his place with his sword and bread. What have you ever done? Have you cut off heads, shed blood, fed the hungry, or dressed the naked?"

To this, Eghrek replied, "Ho, you, Ters Uzamish, do you think cutting off heads and shedding blood are acts of great skill?"

"Indeed they are," replied Ters Uzamish.

To these words of Ters Uzamish, Eghrek could not say anything. A few minutes later, he stood up and asked Kazan Bey's permission to make a raid. The permission was granted. He announced this fact and began to raise men for the raid. Three hundred men with straight spears gathered round him.

There was eating and drinking in the tavern for five full days. After this, Eghrek raided the territory between the tip of Shiro-guven and the Gokche Sea. Much booty was taken. On the way back, he stopped by Alinja Castle. Kara Tekur had set aside a grove there that was stocked with all kinds of game, such as geese, hens, deer, and hares. This place was a trap set up for the Oghuz. One day the son of Ushun Koja stopped at the grove and entered it by tearing down its gate. He and his friends hunted fat deer, geese, and hens there. They ate and drank, unsaddled their horses, and took their harnesses off.

Kara Tekur had spies there who saw them and who reported to Tekur, saying: "A company of Oghuz horsemen came, broke the gate of the grove, and have now taken the saddles and harnesses off their horses. Hasten!" Six hundred black-clad infidels attacked them there, killing the Oghuz warriors and capturing Eghrek, whom they put in the dungeon of Alinja Castle.

The news crossed the dark mountains and bloody rivers until it reached the country of the strong Oghuz. Grief broke loose in front of Ushun Koja's house. His gooselike daughter took off her white clothing and put on black. Ushun Koja and his white-faced wife cried, "Son, Son."

Whoever has sides and ribs grows. Ushun Koja's younger son Seghrek grew to be a brave, gallant, and reckless young man. One day he happened to go to a meeting, where he ate and drank and became drunk. When he stepped outside . . . he saw there an orphan beating another boy. Saying, "Here! What is going on?" he slapped both of them.

The worm in an old mulberry and the tongue of an orphan both have a bitter taste. The orphan boy said: "Why do you hit me? Is it not bad enough that I am an orphan? If you think you are so mighty, go and rescue your brother from Alinja Castle, where he is imprisoned."

"What is the name of my brother?" asked Seghrek.

"His name is Eghrek," replied the boy.

Seghrek said, "*Eghrek* goes well with *Seghrek*. Oh, that my brother should be alive and I should not care for him! Is it ever possible? I shall remain no longer in Oghuz territory without a brother." He then wept, saying, "My brother, the light of my dark eyes." He returned to the meeting inside, took leave of the beys, and said, "May you remain in peace."

They brought his horse, which he mounted at once and rode to his mother's house. There he dismounted and went to learn the truth of the matter from his mother's mouth. Let us see what he said to her.

> "My mother, I stood up from where I sat,
> And, mounted on my black-maned Kazi-
> lik horse,
> I reached the foot of yonder Ala Moun-
> tain.
> There was a meeting in the bloody
> Oghuz land;
> To this I went. There, as we ate and
> drank,
> A messenger rode up astride a gray-
> white horse.
> He spoke about a young man they call
> Eghrek,
> Who has been captive now for many
> years.
> With permission of Almighty Allah,
> He left that prison to go home again.
> The old, the young, and everyone gave
> welcome to that man.

Should I go, too, my mother? Speak to
me!"

His mother replied as follows:

"Let me die for the mouth that brought
such words, my son.
Let me die for the tongue that uttered
them, my son.
If the mountain that lies out yonder, so
dark,
Once fell, now it rises again.
If the beautiful swift-running stream
Once dried up, now it rushes again.

If the branches of the large spreading tree
Withered once, it grows green once
again."

After reading this selection, consider these
questions:

1. What values of Ottoman society are
   found in this story?
2. What makes his imprisoned brother
   such a concern to Seghrek?
3. Why did his mother not want Segrekh
   to learn of his brother's fate?

SELECTION 6:

Stories of Nasreddin Hoja

*A much different kind of literature in Ottoman society was storytelling,
as exemplified by the following selection about a folk hero, Nasreddin
Hoja. (Hoja is a term of respect.) Nasreddin is always outwitting those
who would get the better of him. These stories were a favorite of Ottoman
villagers as they were passed on from generation to generation.*

One Friday as Nasreddin Hoja was getting
ready to go to the mosque to read the lesson from
the Koran to the congregation, he heard a *Tak!
Tak! Tak!* at his door. As he opened the door, he
found all the boys from his school standing in the
courtyard. "What is this!" he exclaimed.

"Well, Hoja Effendi, we decided to go with
you to the service today," said one. And the others agreed that this was so.

"I'll be happy to have you attend the service,"
said the Hoja, "but I'm not quite ready yet to
leave. Just wait out there, and I'll be along in a
minute or so."

The Hoja shut the door and quickly put on his
long coat and his ample turban. Then he hurried

to the door, opened it, slipped into his shoes beside the doorstep, and rushed across the courtyard to mount his little donkey. But in his haste,
he mounted his donkey backward!

The boys began to grin and to nudge one another, wondering what the Hoja would find to say
about his ridiculous mistake. As for the Hoja, he
was wondering, too, but he kept a firm grasp on
his wits as he glanced from one boy to another.

"I suppose you are all wondering," he said,
"why I have seated myself backward on my donkey, but *I have my reasons.* If I were to seat myself forward on my donkey and ride ahead of you,
I could not keep my eye on you. On the other
hand, if I were to sit forward on the donkey and
ride behind you so that I could watch you, that
would be improper, for I am your master. Therefore, I am riding ahead of you *and* keeping my
eye on you!"

Barbara K. Walker, *The Art of the Turkish Tale* (Lubbock: Texas Tech
University Press, 1990), pp. 98–99; John Noonan, "Tales of the
Hoja," *Aramco World*, vol. 48, no. 5 (September/October 1997), p. 33.

[Another example of the Hoja's cleverness appears in this story:]

Nasreddin Hoja had journeyed long on his donkey to reach the town where an Ottoman official had invited him to dinner. Stiffly, he dismounted and knocked on the imposing front door. When it was opened, he saw that the feast was already in progress. But before he could introduce himself, his host, looking at his travel-stained clothes, told him curtly that beggars were not welcome—and shut the door in the startled Hoja's face.

Undismayed, Nassredin Hoja went to the saddlebag on his donkey and unhurriedly changed into his finest attire: a magnificent silk robe trimmed with fur, and a vast silk turban. Thus arrayed, he returned to the front door and knocked again.

This time, his host welcomed him warmly and with many courtesies, and conducted him to the main table. Servants placed dishes of delicacies before him. Nassredin Hoja poured a bowl of soup into one pocket of his robe. To the astonishment of the other guests, he tucked pieces of roast meat into the folds of his turban. Then, before his horrified host, he pushed the fur facing of his robe into a plate of *pilav*, murmuring, "Eat, fur, eat!"

"What's the meaning of this?" demanded the host.

"My dear sir," replied the Hoja, "I am feeding my clothes. To judge by your treatment of me half an hour ago, it is clearly they, and not myself, which are the objects of your hospitality!"

After reading this selection, consider these questions:

1. Why would storytelling become so popular among the Turkish people?
2. Why is Nasreddin Hoja a hero in these stories?
3. What lessons are to be learned from these tales?

CHAPTER 7
Mughals and British: Who Shall Dominate India?

The Indian subcontinent was from ancient times a major center of civilization. Located in a tropical area of the world, Indian agriculture depended on monsoons coming out of the ocean to provide the water for its crops. India was the place of origin for cotton, always a major export of the region.

Political unification in India has always been difficult because of its large variety of peoples and languages. As different invasions of India occurred, the newcomers kept their own culture as much as possible. This was especially true about 1500 B.C. after the great move of Indo-European–speaking Aryans into northern India.

In order to avoid assimilation, for the Aryans were a minority, over time a system of social classes developed that rigidly placed every man and woman into a caste. The caste system, based principally upon occupation, developed the lines beyond which people were not allowed to pass. It determined which partners were to be chosen for marriage and with whom one could eat or even strike up an acquaintance. The highest caste was that of the Brahmans, the priests of the Aryan religion, the only ones allowed to learn the sacred texts and offer sacrifices of their religion that guaranteed prosperity. (See chapter 1, selection 2.) The religion of the Brahmans developed into what is now known as Hinduism, a religion today followed by four out of five Indians. For the past two millennia, its beliefs and values have determined India's culture.

Despite the formation of two empires, the Mauryan and Gupta, in earlier times, there was always a tendency for local Indian maharajas (rulers) to reject strong central government. Therefore after the eighth century they proved unable to resist the inroads of Islamic invaders. The Muslims became a ruling elite in much of northern India and the Hindus a subject people. Conversions took place, especially from the lower castes and the *dasas*, men and women of no caste.

SELECTION 1:

Rama Wins a Victory over Ravana

The following selection gives a taste of the rich literature of Hinduism in the early modern period. The author is Tulsidas, who lived from 1532 to 1623 and is the best-known poet and holy man of the age. In his work The Mighty Acts of Lord Rama, *he tells one of India's favorite epics concerning Rama, an incarnation of the god Vishnu. In his climactic battle with Ravana, a ten-headed demon god, Rama's allies are bears and monkeys, among them Humayun, king of the monkeys. Rama fights Ravana to regain his kidnapped wife, Sita, in this vivid description. Vibhishan is Ravana's brother, who had warned him against kidnapping Sita. In modern India, millions of people celebrate Rama's victory, one of Hinduism's most important holidays.*

The huge monkeys and formidable bears rushed on carrying mountains in their hands. They attacked with the utmost fury and the demons fled before their onslaught. Having routed the army, the mighty monkeys then surrounded Ravana and, buffeting him on every side and tearing his body with their claws, utterly confounded him.

When he saw the overwhelming strength of the monkeys, Ravana took thought and, becoming invisible in a moment, shed abroad an illusion. When he exercised his magic power, awful beings came into view, vampires, ghosts, and goblins with bows and arrows in their hands; witches, grasping swords in one hand and in the other human skulls, drank draughts of fresh blood as they danced and sang their many songs. "Seize and kill!" they shrieked, and their cries reechoed all around; with open mouths they rushed on to devour and the monkeys took flight. Whenever the monkeys fled, they saw fire blazing, and they and the bears were at a loss; and next, there

fell on them a shower of sand.

Having thus on all sides robbed the monkeys of their courage, Ravana roared again, and all the brave monkeys, with Lakshman and their king, lost consciousness. "Alas, O Rama!" cried the warriors and wrung their hands. Having thus broken down all their strength, Ravana created a new phantasm. He made appear a number of Hanumans, who rushed forward with rocks in their hands and surrounded Rama in a dense throng on every side. They gnashed their teeth and raised their tails aloft and cried, "Kill him! Seize him! Don't let him go!" Their tails encircled him, and in their midst stood the king of Kosala.

In their midst the beauteous, dark-hued body of Rama shone glorious as a loft *tamala* [a flowering tree] fenced in by countless gleaming rainbows. The gods looked on the Lord with mingled feelings of pleasure and pain, uttering cries of "Victory! Victory! Victory!" Rama angrily dispelled the illusion with one arrow in the twinkling of an eye. The monkeys and the bears were delighted at the disappearance of the phantoms, and all grasped trees and hills and returned to the assault. Rama let fly a volley of arrows and Ravana's arms and heads once more fell to the

Tulsidas, *The Mighty Acts of Lord Rama*, trans. W.D.P. Hill, in *Sources of Indian Tradition*, ed. Ainslie T. Embree, 2nd ed., 2 vols., (New York: Columbia University Press, 1988), vol. 1, pp. 355–57.

ground. Though his heads and arms were severed time and again, the warrior king of Lanka did not die. The Lord was making sport, but gods, adepts, and sages were dismayed at the sight of his suffering.

No sooner were the demon's heads severed than multitudes sprang up anew, as avarice increases with every gain. In spite of all endeavor the enemy would not die. Then Rama looked toward Vibhishan, that Lord, in obedience to whose will Death himself would die, tested the devotion of his servant. "Hearken," said Vibhishan, "O omniscient Lord of all creation, protector of the suppliant, delight of gods and sages! In the hollow of Ravana's navel there lies a pool of nectar, and by its virtue, Lord, his life is preserved."

When he heard what Vibhishan said, the gracious Lord was glad and grasped his dreadful arrows. Then appeared all manner of evil omens; numbers of asses, jackals, and dogs began to howl; birds cried, predicting universal woe, and comets were seen all over the sky. Blazing fires broke out in every quarter, and though there was no new moon, the sun was eclipsed.

Images wept, thunderbolts fell from heaven, a violent wind sprang up, earth reeled, clouds rained down blood and hair and dust—who can describe all the inauspicious omens? Beholding these innumerable portents, the gods in heaven cried anxiously for victory; and perceiving that the gods were terrified, the gracious Rama fitted arrows to his bow. He drew the string to his ear and shot forth thirty-one arrows, and the arrows sped forth like great serpents of doom.

One arrow dried up the depths of Ravana's navel; the others furiously smote his heads and arms and carried them away with them. The headless, armless trunk danced upon the ground. The earth sank down, but the trunk rushed violently on. Then the Lord struck it with an arrow and cut it in two. Even as he died, he roared aloud

with a great terrible yell, "Where is Rama, that I may challenge him and slay him in combat?" Earth shook as the Ten-headed [Ravana] fell; the sea, the rivers, the mountains, and the elephants of the quarters were troubled. Spreading abroad the two halves of his body, he fell to the ground, crushing beneath him crowds of bears and monkeys. The arrows laid the arms and the heads before Mandodari [wife of Ravana] and returned to the Lord of the world; they all came back and entered his quiver.

The gods saw it and beat their drums. His spirit entered the Lord's mouth; Shiva and Brahma saw it and were glad. The universe was filled with cries of triumph: "Victory to Rama, mighty of arm!" Companies of gods and sages rained down flowers, crying, "Victory to the Lord of mercy! Victory, victory to Lord Vishnu, the all-merciful destroyer of the pairs, the Lord who delights his suppliants and scatters miscreant hosts, First Cause, the pitiful, ever supreme!" Full of joy, the gods rained down flowers and loud throbbed the drums.

There on the field of battle Rama's limbs were beautiful with the beauty of many loves. The crown of knotted hair on Rama's head, with flowers intertwined, was very lovely, as when among the lightning-flashes stars glitter on the Purple Hills.

After reading this selection, consider these questions:

1. How does this epic demonstrate the close relationship between humans and animals in Hindu thought?

2. What symbols for good and evil are found in the account of Rama's victory?

3. Why would Shiva and Brahma, the other two major divinities of Hinduism, rejoice in Rama's victory?

SELECTION 2:

Akbar's House of Worship

In 1526 a new Muslim invasion struck India from the north, when Zahīr-ud-Dīn Muhammad, known as Babur (the Lion), charged into India. Babur had an army of mixed Turkic-Mongol units and he himself was a distant relative of the famous conqueror Timur Lenk. Like the dynasty he replaced, he made Delhi his capital, initiating the period of Indian history known as Mughal.

Babur's grandson, Akbar, was one of the better Mughal rulers, ruling from 1556 to 1605. Unlike his predecessors, Akbar became known for his toleration and interest in other faiths. The following selection, a modern historian's account, demonstrates his inquiring mind.

On a Friday when he was engaged in exchange of views with the head of the Jama Masjid [mosque], there came to Akbar the idea of convening a conference of the learned men of the empire; the purpose was to sift evidence for and against the belief that at the turn of the millennium, i.e., one thousand years of the existence of Islam, there would emerge a Mahdi, a religious leader who would recast Islam and reinterpret its tenets in the light of the changing circumstances. A hint had been thrown a couple of years earlier by Sheikh Mubarak, father of Abul Fazl and Faizi, that perhaps Akbar himself was destined to don the robes of the promised Mahdi. This suggestion seemed to have taken root in the Emperor's mind; and gradually it flowered into a conviction that God had chosen him to be both secular and religious head. But doubts still haunted him. He wanted to be certain that he had not fallen a prey to auto-suggestion. To that end, a conference was called.

Accordingly, a conference hall—the House of Worship—was ordered to be built. Here the professors and priests of Islam would meet occasionally and engage themselves in debates on

specific issues. It was in February 1575—a month after his return to Fateh-pur-Sikri from the eastern provinces—that the construction of the Ibadatkhana started; the site chosen was close to the palace and near the dwelling of Sheikh Salim.

The hermitage of the Miyan (Sheikh Abdullah Niazi of Sirhind) was the center around which a grand edifice went up. The Miyan, a well-known ascetic, was at one time a disciple of Sheikh Salim, but later left for his native Sirhind. The dilapidated hermitage was rebuilt, and on all four sides of it a hall was built for accommodation of invitees. No trace of the building remains, nor is its exact location known. Perhaps religious fanatics razed it to the ground after the death of Akbar; there were many in Delhi and Agra who took strong exception to the Emperor's liberalism; they went to the length of even denying him a burial according to Muslim rites.

The first conference was in the nature of an experiment, a dress rehearsal for the real things that came later. The invitees were first confined to Muslims of four classes, viz., Sheikhs, Saiyads, Ulema and Amirs. Later the lists were enlarged to include representatives of other religions, viz., Hinduism, Jainism, Buddhism, Zoroastrianism, and Christianity. The Emperor himself acted as the chairman or moderator. He moved about freely from one sector of the hall to another, con-

Muni Lal, *Akbar* (New Delhi: Vikas Publishing House, 1980), pp. 198–99.

versing with his guests on points discussed or remaining to be debated. Akbar was in his element at these gatherings. Tempers at times rose high, but whatever the provocation the Emperor invariably kept his calm. Not unoften these conferences, which started on Thursday evenings, went on without a break till late hours on Friday. Scribes kept records of the proceedings. Akbar spent hours listening to these records; very often he could point to an omission here or a faulty emphasis there and get the account changed accordingly. His memory was photographic; at times he astounded his guests by repeating verbatim what each one of them had expounded.

The Ibadatkhana was a bold innovation; it gave Akbar a platform to propound the equality of all religions, a subject which became an obsession with him after the conquest of Bengal. His empire now stretched from the Arabian sea to the Bay of Bengal. Consolidation of this vast land was a task which, he reckoned, necessitated a close look at the causes which led to the breakup of kingdoms in the past. Akbar was in search of a formula to unite different segments of his domains into a well-knit, cohesive state. He felt that religious intolerance and economic exploitation were the two social evils whose ill effects could not be overstressed. His approach was revolutionary; the Islamic priesthood and the hereditary jagirdars [nobles holding tax-free estates] ranged themselves against him. Akbar was, however, determined to level up the two inequalities which seemed to him to be the most pernicious.

The House of Worship became a regular rendezvous for the political and religious elite. Not by authority and royal persuasion, but by hard logic Akbar convinced a majority of them of the inequities of the past, and obtained their support for the reforms he intended to carry out. The objectors, whose number was considerable, were left alone to wallow in the mud of their own prejudices.

After reading this selection, consider these questions:

1. What prompted Akbar's convening a religious conference?
2. What made Akbar's decision unpopular with some people?
3. Can you think of examples of religious intolerance in the present world?

SELECTION 3:
The Economy of Mughal India

India presented a challenge to west European merchants intent upon expanding both imports and exports. The Indians themselves had a large commercial network with a community of traders as far away as Moscow and port cities of China. Their trade was in diamonds, spices, cotton, and silk textiles.

India and China were prosperous enough that few imports came into their countries, while, in contrast, Europe needed or at least wanted many of the products of the Orient. After the Portuguese came the Dutch, French, and English to tap into the Indian economy. In the following selection, a modern historian looks at the entrance of Europeans into Mughal India.

India at the beginning of the Western presence was far from being economically or even politically underdeveloped, let alone culturally. It was at least productive enough to be self-sufficient, to generate some external as well as internal trade, to support large and often magnificent cities, temples, palaces, and imperial grandeur, and to maintain a population probably many times the size of contemporary Europe's, if not of China's. There was both absolute and individual wealth, but it was grossly maldistributed among groups within the population and spatially over the country. There was also a considerable trade, and a relatively sophisticated set of merchant groups and commercial techniques. But most trade goods came from a multitude of small-scale and spatially scattered producers. Western traders complained chronically that they could never obtain adequate amounts of the goods they sought (especially textiles) and for which they had external markets. . . .

Local marketing systems with a radius of a few miles, which exchanged primarily local agricultural products mainly through barter, appear to have dominated the commercial sector in India to a greater extent than in China or in Europe. Long-distance marketing was also hampered by the intricate Indian mosaic of separate languages and cultures; it was above all else a centrifugal rather than centripetal pattern, in trade, in culture, and in social and political systems.

The units of which it was composed were both relatively small for the most part and relatively unused to mutual interaction except on a minor and superficial plane, for example, the trade in a few high-value commodities. The Indian trade which was important to each European country engaged in it and which did have much impact on European economies was of relatively negligible importance or had little impact in the far larger mass of India as a whole or even of those areas where trade was proportionately more important, such as Gujerat or Bengal, themselves almost cer-

tainly more populous than any European country. The largest groups of skilled artisans were attached as virtual slaves to the Mughal court and its workshops, or to provincial governors, where they produced luxuries for the elite. Sophisticated hand craftsmanship even for more utilitarian goods, such as textiles, was no substitute for and was indeed inimical to high productivity. . . .

The Indian climate with its precarious water balance reflecting very high evaporation rates restricted vegetation cover and inhibited its recovery so that it could contribute relatively little, by European or even East Asian standards, to fuel needs. Metal and metal tools seem to have been scarce and expensive in comparison with Europe or East Asia, perhaps in part reflecting the fuel problem but also a shortage of known workable ores until later nineteenth-century discoveries. This too must have contributed to low agricultural and industrial productivity.

Areas of higher productivity in agriculture or handicrafts and those which had a surplus for export to other areas or abroad were widely scattered, separated by extensive tracts of marginal subsistence agriculture. Communication was difficult, expensive, and frequently dangerous. India was very poorly supplied with usable internal waterways in particular contrast to China. The best of the river systems, the Ganges, was indifferently navigable at best in its lower reaches by shallow-draft boats within the delta, but could not carry much more than barge traffic farther inland. The Indus and its tributaries were no better. The advent of steam did make somewhat more use possible of these two streams, but never on a significant scale relative to the area and population to be served. The other Indian rivers were even less navigable, their heavily braided deltas choked with silt brought down by the spates of the monsoon, and their upper courses drying up to near-trickles during the long dry period between monsoons; these problems were evident also in the two master streams of the north, the Ganges and the Indus.

India was too large and physically and culturally diverse to be effectively integrated by preindustrial land transport alone, but roads were in any case relatively few (again in comparison with

Rhoads Murphey, *The Outsiders: The Western Experience in India and China* (Ann Arbor: University of Michigan Press, 1977), pp. 47–49.

either China or Europe) and were apparently chronically bad for the most part. This was a reflection of the relative weakness of the politico-administrative system; the Mughals did make some effort at road building, albeit for primarily military reasons, but the network was inadequate in scope and was not well maintained. Here again the Indian climate was a factor; the violence of monsoonal rainfall imposed special needs for road construction and maintenance which in practice were rarely met; most roads were literally impassable for many months each year. Coastal shipping links between west and east, around the tip of the subcontinent, were too long and too exposed to piracy to offer an adequate alternative even for the littoral areas, let alone the vast inland bulk of the country. Finally, the acute shortage of adequate harbors along the whole of the east coast and large stretches of the west above Malabar further discouraged coastal shipping.

After reading this selection, consider these questions:

1. Why was the Indian economy so decentralized?
2. What made transportation so difficult in Mughal India?
3. What was the work of the artisan class in India?

SELECTION 4:

Wealth in Mughal India

A seventeenth-century French traveler to India, who lived in the country for many years, François Bernier wrote several works on his experiences, including the following to Louis XIV's finance minister, Jean-Baptiste Colbert.

Thus, although the *Great Mogol* [the Mughal emperor] be in the receipt of an immense revenue, his expenditure being much in the same proportion, he cannot possess the vast surplus of wealth that most people seem to imagine. I admit that his income exceeds probably the joint revenues of the *Grand Seignior* [the Ottoman sultan] and of the King of Persia; but if I were to call him a wealthy monarch, it would be in the sense that a treasurer is to be considered wealthy who pays with one hand the large sums which he receives with the other.

I should call that King effectively rich who, without oppressing or impoverishing his people, possessed revenues sufficient to support the expenses of a numerous and magnificent court—to erect grand and useful edifices—to indulge a liberal and kind disposition—to maintain a military force for the defense of his dominions—and, besides all this, to reserve an accumulating fund that would provide against any unforeseen rupture with his neighbors, although it should prove of some years' duration. The Sovereign of the *Indies* is doubtless possessed of many of these advantages, but not to the degree generally supposed. What I have said on the subject of the great expenses to which he is unavoidably exposed, has perhaps inclined you to this opinion; and . . . [what] I am about to relate, of which I had an opportunity to ascertain the correctness, will convince your lordship that the pecuniary resources

François Bernier, *Travels in the Mogul Empire, A.D. 1656–1668*, ed. Archibald Constable, 2nd ed. (New Delhi: S. Chand, 1968), pp. 222–24.

of the *Great Mogol* himself may be exaggerated.

Before I conclude, I wish to explain how it happens that, although this Empire of the *Mogol* is such an abyss for gold and silver, as I said before, these precious metals are not in greater plenty here than elsewhere; on the contrary, the inhabitants have less the appearance of a moneyed people than those of many other parts of the globe.

In the first place, a large quantity is melted, re-melted, and wasted, in fabricating women's bracelets, both for the hands and feet, chains, earrings, nose and finger rings, and a still larger quantity is consumed in manufacturing embroideries; *alachas,* or striped silken stuffs; *touras,* or fringes of gold lace, worn on turbans; gold and silver cloths; scarves, turbans, and brocades. The quantity of these articles made in *India* is incred-

ible. All the troops, from the *Omrah* [the army generals] to the man in the ranks, will wear gilt ornaments; nor will a private soldier refuse them to his wife and children, though the whole family should die of hunger; which indeed is a common occurrence.

After reading this selection, consider these questions:
1. What, according to the French traveler, are the expenses that a rich king should be able to afford?
2. What happens to the gold and silver that come into Mughal India?
3. Why does the French traveler think that reports of the Mughal emperor's wealth may be exaggerated?

SELECTION 5:
Trade in India

The British slowly but surely began the process of pushing out other European merchants from India. By 1720 the Mughal Empire was breaking up. The British, without much resistance, convinced the maharajas to join their side rather than that of the emperors. The agent of this expansion was the British East India Company, a private concern that merchants in London formed to trade in India. In the following selection, an eighteenth-century author, James Mill, describes the working of the company.

That part of the business of the Company which was situated in India, was distinguished by several features which the peculiar circumstances of the country forced it to assume. The sale indeed of the commodities imported from Europe, they transacted in the simplest and easiest of all possible ways; namely, by auction, the mode in which they disposed of Indian goods in England. At the

beginning of this trade, the English, as well as other European adventurers, used to carry their commodities to the interior towns and markets, transporting them in the hackeries of the country, and established factories or warehouses, where the goods were exposed to sale. During the confusion, however, which prevailed, while the empire of the Moghuls was in the progress of dissolution, the security which had formerly existed, imperfect as it was, became greatly impaired. . . .

The powers exercised by the Governor or President and Council, were, in the first place, those of masters in regard to servants over all the

James Mill, *The History of British India*, ed. William Thomas, rev. ed. (Chicago and London: University of Chicago Press, 1975), pp. 341, 346–47.

persons who were in the employment of the Company; and as the Company were the sole master, without fellow or competitor, and those under them had adopted their service as the business of their lives, the power of the master, in reality, and in the majority of cases, extended to almost every thing valuable to man. With regard to such of their countrymen, as were not in their service, the Company were armed with powers to seize them, to keep them in confinement, and send them to England, an extent of authority which amounted to confiscation of goods, to imprisonment, and what to a European constitution is the natural effect of any long confinement under an Indian climate, actual death. At an early period of the Company's history, it had been deemed necessary to intrust them with the powers of martial law, for the government of the troops which they maintained in defense of their factories and presidencies; and by a charter of Charles II, granted them in 1661, the Presidents and Councils in their factories were empowered to exercise civil and criminal jurisdiction according to the laws of England. Under this sanction they had exercised judicial powers, during all the changes which their affairs had undergone; but at last it appeared desirable that so important an article of their authority should rest on a better foundation. In the year 1726 a charter was granted, by which the Company were permitted to establish a Mayor's Court at each of their three presidencies, Bombay, Madras, and Calcutta; consisting of a mayor and nine aldermen, empowered to decide in civil cases of all descriptions. From this jurisdiction, the President and Council were erected into a Court of Appeal.

After reading this selection, consider these questions:
1. What method did the East India Company use to dispose of its goods?
2. What authority did the governor of the East India Council hold?
3. Does it appear that the Indians profited from the presence of the East India Company?

SELECTION 6:

Cornwallis

*I*t *became obvious to many in Great Britain that by the late eighteenth century corruption and decay had entered the ranks of the personnel of the East India Company. As a result a new system was to be tried—a governor-general would go to India to try to improve conditions there. The third of these was Lord Charles Cornwallis (who earlier led the British army in its losing war against the Americans). Before he left for India he demanded complete freedom to make decisions in India with company officials having no way to veto them. The following selection is a modern account of his stay in India.*

Lord Cornwallis, a tubby, rather sleepy-looking man with a squint, forty-eight years old, was not a likely choice for such a demanding post. He had no experience of India. He had recently been employed as a major-general in America, where he had had a mixed record against the rebel

Brian Gardner, *The East India Company* (London: Rupert Hart-Davis, 1971), pp. 124–27.

colonists, culminating in the capitulation of his force at Yorktown (his position there had been so "precarious" that he had nobly recommended against help being sent him). He was, however, a good friend of the King, and [Prime Minister William] Pitt thought well of him. Perhaps it was considered only just that a man who had helped lose one empire should have the task of consolidating another. Whatever the reason, Cornwallis had no desire to go. He was not by any means a fool, but he was a man who enjoyed English country pursuits and he was not known for his energy. But he did have a strong sense of duty towards his country. . . .

Cornwallis, like most other Englishmen who had never been to India, saw his duty as improving the conduct of the East India Company's servants and improving the administration. He succeeded in both. With the directors and Board of Control months away, he was all powerful. He was a simple imperialist who believed that Indians should be ruled by Europeans for their own benefit. Indians, who had previously been ruled by foreign Muslims for centuries, were not surprised. Cornwallis's instructions had been explicit: no territorial acquisition. He tried hard to avoid interference in Indian affairs. His reforms included the raising of pay of the Company's employees, which gave them more self-respect and encouraged them away from illegal private trading; he tried to instill them with a sense of duty like his own, something which [Robert] Clive and Warren Hastings, with their own questionable activities, had never really been able to do. The integrity of Cornwallis was unquestioned; he did not even draw all his salary. He improved the administration of justice in Bengal. Above all, he tried to get a fairer raising of revenue. . . .

Cornwallis had a poor opinion of Indians. "Every native of India, I verily believe, is corrupt," he said. In another of his reforms he dismissed all high Indian officials in the Company's service and replaced them with Europeans. This Europeanisation of the Company's service was the most important action of Cornwallis's regime, and it would be difficult to underrate it.

More and more, under Cornwallis, the Company's men were engaged in administration rather than in trade, inevitably, owing to income from tax having become far more important to the Company in India than income from trade; under him the two tasks were for the first time made quite separate, done by different men; for the administrators to engage in private trade, or financial dealings, under Cornwallis was a very serious offense; under his Governor-generalship many men were sent home. It was the beginning of the Civil Service in India. Employment was organized in three quite different classes: judicial, revenue, and commercial. Under Cornwallis, as well, the army grew more efficient. In this he was backed by Henry Dundas, who managed the Board of Control, a devious politician and a crony of Pitt. Recruiting in England, which had previously been done just before the departure of ships, was put on a more permanent basis.

After reading this selection, consider these questions:

1. Why did Cornwallis agree to go to India?
2. What explains Cornwallis's views of Indians?
3. How did Cornwallis deal with corruption among the employees of the East India Company?

CHAPTER 8
East Asian Traditions:
Is There a Price for Isolation?

In 1500 the two strongest traditions of east Asia were found in China and Japan. The men and women who lived in these cultures had developed their own sense of values and customs over hundreds of years.

Overshadowing east Asian peoples was the great respect given to the family and to Confucius, the great sage of ancient China. Children grew up with the idea that they were only temporary trustees of the family heritage. Adults honored the legacy of their ancestors from the remote past and looked forward to handing on the family reputation and property that had been entrusted to them. This common attitude among men and women, confirmed by Confucianism, resulted in the construction of an intricate code of etiquette that people were expected to follow. Individualism was not encouraged; a concern for fulfilling one's social role was.

Chinese society, unlike other civilizations, was built more on secular models than religious. The all-powerful emperor, with the title Son of Heaven, represented far distant deities who could either reward or punish according to the conduct of the court. While reverencing the divine spirits and offering the correct sacrifices were considered very important in the imperial routine, practical matters were dealt with on the advice of counselors and officials. Except for the court eunuchs, the civil service was staffed by men who obtained their position as a result of an examination system.

SELECTION 1:

Chinese Nationalism

The following selection from Susan Naquin and Evelyn S. Rawski discusses what it meant to be Chinese in the context of the eighteenth century.

To be Chinese was to be a member of a superior civilization: ethnographers studying overseas Chinese communities, as well as contemporary anthropologists studying outcast groups, have commented on the pervasiveness of this sense of identity, which crossed regional and socioeconomic lines.

But what was entailed in being Chinese? Some might associate this identity with the written language that had linked the educated elite of this culture for millennia. Even the illiterate peasant had a profound reverence for the written word—written in Chinese characters of course—if not a passing familiarity with it. The near-magical power of writing was certainly common to Daoist rituals, imperial edicts, legal contracts, and fine calligraphy, while written materials were a shared language for educated people from across the empire. Despite differences between dialects that were virtually separate languages, being Chinese seemed to involve some commitment to the unified and standardized written character.

The classical formulation for Chineseness identified clothing, diet, and ritual as key components. China's superior textile technology had long since become a hallmark of Chinese culture. The Chinese rejected the dairy products that the nomads ate and took pride in a culinary tradition that considered good eating essential to good health and placed eating at the core of community solidarity. Above all, to be Chinese was to value ritual and to follow tradition, especially in marriage and funerals.

Implicit in the centrality of ritual was a confidence in the linkage between external behavior and internalized values, an assumption by now so ingrained in Chinese culture that performance without belief could be seen to suffice. In a ritual, correct actions were thus more essential than the feelings of the participants. Individuals with widely different educations and background could invest the same ritual with different meanings. Ritual thus subsumed and harmonized differences even as it educated. Community rites cut across class and were not categorized as being associated exclusively either with the elite or with the masses, thus forming the basis for a truly popular (in the sense of pervasive) shared culture. Chinese followed Confucius not only in this faith in ritual but also in the core values expressed in such ceremonies: the asymmetrical and hierarchical relations between ruler and subject, father and child, husband and wife.

Proper behavior expressing orthodox values was associated in Confucian thought with a properly ordered and stable society presided over by a ruler who was in harmony with the cosmos. Harmony, order, and stability were goals not just for the state but for individuals as well. To the Chinese, civilization consisted of imposing order onto chaos, transforming societies in which individuals wore no clothing, "knew their mothers but not their fathers," and made no social distinctions.

The enemy of order was *luan*, internal confusion and chaos. Not something imposed from the outside, *luan* was the disorder that could arise within the state, the community, the household, or the individual when ethical norms and correct ritual were not followed. The desire to promote order and prevent *luan* permeated Chinese society

Susan Naquin and Evelyn S. Rawski, *Chinese Society in the Eighteenth Century* (New Haven, CT, and London: Yale University Press, 1987), pp. 91–93.

from top to bottom; most agreed that the nonviolent inculcation of values through a broadly educational effort, rather than reliance on coercion, was the best method of promoting order. Using the same paternalism with which children were socialized in each household, officials and literati attempted to indoctrinate the citizenry, beginning with an emphasis on proper action in a familial, social, and ritual context, because orthopraxy was seen as a means to promote orthodoxy among uneducated people. Crucial bulwarks against *luan* were the patrilineal family and the state. . . .

A belief system that de-emphasized personal salvation and stressed the collective patriline, that valued ritual and behavior based on venerable Confucian precepts concerning the sources of order in society and the cosmos, and that encouraged individuals to work hard and improve their lot in life—these are major elements found

not just in the eighteenth century but in traditional Chinese society generally. The eighteenth-century exposure of Han Chinese to non-Han minorities merely drew the latter into the powerful orbit of Chinese culture. Even the doubts about the foundations of classical education that were planted by evidential scholars in the minds of their contemporaries grew very slowly into disbelief and rejection.

After reading this selection, consider these questions:

1. What made up a consciousness of being Chinese?
2. Why was ritual so important in Chinese life?
3. What is *luan*? How did it matter in Chinese life?

SELECTION 2:

The Youth of the Wan Li Emperor

The obligation to be a Son of Heaven was a heavy burden for many of those who inherited it. One of these, in the days of a failing Ming dynasty, was the Wan Li Emperor. Encased forever within the confines of Beijing's Forbidden City, one of his first duties was to marry. The year was 1578. A modern writer describes the scene in the following selection.

The imperial wedding in early 1578 was not an exciting event. The emperor was only fourteen years old; his bride, daughter of a commoner hastily given an army commission, was barely thirteen. Needless to say, this was not a union of love. Wan Li merely abided by his mother's wish

to have many grandchildren as soon as possible. The installation of a principal wife to the ruler legitimated his nuptials with other consorts, of whom two were declared official only ten days after the wedding ceremony.

Most unfortunate was Empress Xiao Duan, as she is known to history. She was, from her wedding day, permanently encased in palatial pomp and comfort; yet, by the cruel exigency of tradition, her marriage was only a state necessity, re-

Ray Huang, *1587, a Year of No Significance: The Ming Dynasty in Decline* (New Haven, CT, and London: Yale University Press, 1981) pp. 26–29.

ducing her to an accessory to an institution, entitled to all kinds of meaningless honors but to little satisfaction as a wife. She bore the emperor a daughter and lived almost as long as he did. But at no time did she in any way affect the course of his life. As the principal daughter-in-law to Jen Sheng, the emperor's principal mother, she had both the privilege and the obligation of attending her in public, such as helping her from her sedan chair, a task Xiao Duan performed exactly as required, thus earning for herself a reputation for filial piety. Inside the palace, however, she was better remembered as a ruthless mistress who frequently ordered her chambermaids beaten, sometimes to death.

Yet, if Wan Li paid little attention to Xiao Duan, neither did he show much interest in the other two consorts. The important women in his life were yet to enter the picture, almost four years after his wedding to Xiao Duan, by the end of 1581 and later.

In the meantime the adolescent monarch was restless. The palace compound was magnificent but also oppressively monotonous. Even with those balustrades, incense burners, sculptured birds, and bronze lamps on stone bases, the Forbidden City comprised by and large the same architecture and routines over and over again. On fixed dates, the platoons and battalions of attendants changed from fur-lined robes with ear-covers, into silk, and then into light-weight gauze for the summer. Flowers were taken out from winter storage, leaves were raked, and ditches dredged—all according to a prearranged schedule. Yet palace life remained timeless and seasonless, lacking either the thrill of surprise or the excitement of anticipation. As emperor, Wan Li could not venture outside the palace compound. He could not even think of dropping in to visit his courtiers at home; no ritualistic proceedings to govern such behavior had been established in the dynasty's history.

But after his wedding Wan Li was at least free from Ci Sheng's [his mother's] daily supervision. Soon he discovered that life could be slightly more interesting. Sun Hai, a eunuch attendant, advised him to organize drinking parties with other attendants in the villas within the Imperial City. This was not exactly a city in the ordinary sense. The western portion of the enclosure was an immense park, with lakes, marble bridges, and white stone towers. The more than one thousand cranes hovering near the Lamaist temple in particular gave the area a feeling of warmth and informality, in contrast to the regimentation within the Forbidden City. Now the emperor often loitered both in and outside the gardens for fun, wearing tight-sleeved garments and carrying a sword, frequently under the influence of alcohol. One night in 1580, at seventeen, during one such merry hour Wan Li demanded that two palace women sing songs they were not familiar with. For their failure to obey the imperial order they were sentenced to death on the spot—a penalty carried out only symbolically, by cutting off tassels of their hair. . . .

The hundreds of palace women were the emperor's property; no relationship involving them with him was illicit, because any liaison could be legitimized by granting the lady in question the title of secondary wife. The Ruler of All Men was entitled to one empress, usually one principal consort, a number of associate consorts, and still more concubines. Ever since the Zheng De emperor had died without an heir, it had been generally recognized that the throne must widen the possibility of producing male offspring to assure regular succession.

Palace women were selected from the general population around Beijing. Sometimes as many as three hundred were admitted to the imperial household as a group. Between the ages of nine and fourteen, the young girls were nominated by the precinct and village elders according to quotas assigned to the communities, and subsequently went through many rounds of screening and selection before they entered the palace gate, which to most of them was a point of no return for the rest of their lives.

Those nymphs inside the Forbidden City became a frequent topic of erotic literature. They were likened to sculptured jade yet said to be freshly fragrant, appearing either as voluptuous as fully blossomed peach trees glowing in the morning sun, or as slender and delicate as jasmine vibrating in an evening breeze. In reality, palace women were never unpleasant to look at, yet hardly so glamorous and disturbingly beautiful as the romantic poets described them because eye-catching quality had never been the standard for selection.

The tears and loneliness of the girls who grew up within the palace compound must, however, have been real. Unless a palace woman caught the fancy of the emperor, the only male in the palace (as Ci Sheng herself had done, and thus was elevated to what she was today), her life was forlorn indeed. Having wasted her flourishing years as a chambermaid, she either had to find the sympathy of a compatible eunuch in her middle age or be sent to the northwest corner of the palace to perform miscellaneous labors. Upon her death her remains would be cremated and buried in an unmarked grave to assure that neither rumor nor legend could arise around one who theoretically had been accessible to emperor or emperors in her lifetime. With so slim a chance of eliciting imperial favor, the lot of palace women was so uninviting that when an impending selection was announced, many thoughtful parents quickly married off their young daughters to eliminate their eligibility.

After reading this selection, consider these questions:
1. What was the role of the emperor's wife in Ming China?
2. Why was life in the Forbidden City dull?
3. Would you consider being chosen to live in the Forbidden City a favor?

SELECTION 3:

Dinner in China

*D*espite its attempts to be isolated from the rest of the world, visitors insisted on coming to China. From the first Portuguese landing in 1514 the Chinese were never left alone. Christian missionaries sought to convert them while Western merchants tried to sell them products the Chinese did not want. Traders did want Chinese products and soon made fortunes bringing them to European markets. The Chinese emperors would allow trade only through a few ports, but this was enough to create a wedge in the Chinese wall of isolation.

Two descriptions of life there demonstrate European interest in Chinese culture. The first selection, written by a Jesuit missionary, Matteo Ricci, speaks of Chinese dining.

A few words about Chinese banquets, which are both frequent and very ceremonious. With some, in fact, they are of almost daily occurrence, because the Chinese accompany nearly every function, social or religious, with a dinner and consider a banquet as the highest expression of friendship. After the fashion of the Greeks they speak of drink meetings rather than of banquets and not without reason, too, because, although their cups do not hold more wine than a nutshell, the frequency with which they fill them

China in the Sixteenth Century: The Journals of Matthew Ricci, 1583–1610, ed. Louis J. Gallagher (New York: Random House, 1953), pp. 64–65.

makes up for their moderate content.

They do not use forks or spoons or knives for eating, but rather polished sticks, about a palm and a half long, with which they are very adept in lifting any kind of food to their mouths, without touching it with their fingers. The food is brought to the table already cut into small pieces, unless it be something that is soft, such as cooked eggs or fish and the like, which can be easily separated with the sticks.

Their drinks, which may be wine or water or the drink called Cia [tea], are always served warm, and this is so even in the hot summer. The idea behind this custom seems to be that it is more beneficial for the stomach and, generally speaking, the Chinese are longer-lived than Europeans and preserve their physical powers up to seventy or even eighty years of age. The custom might also account for the fact that they never suffer from gallstones, so common among the people of the West who are fond of cold drinks.

After reading this selection, consider these questions:
1. How does cooking link medieval and modern China?
2. What did Ricci note about Chinese tableware?
3. Do you see a connection between a long life and drinking tea?

SELECTION 4:

Chinese Customs

A later observation appeared in the first British envoy to China's writings, Lord George Macartney. A seasoned diplomat, he was London's first representative to the Qing Court of Beijing, sent there in 1793. At that time the Manchus governed the nation and the Chinese were their subjects. (Macartney calls the Manchus "Tartars.") His comments on Chinese life follow, with the prejudices of a diplomat whose basis for judgment was life in England.

Among the Chinese themselves, society chiefly consists of certain stated forms and expressions, a calm, equal apathetical deportment, studied, hypocritical attentions and hyperbolical professions.

Where women are excluded from appearing, all delicacy of taste and sentiment, the softness of address, the graces of elegant converse, the play of passions, the refinements of love and friendship must of course be banished. In their place gross familiarity, coarse pleasantry, and broad allusions are indulged in, but without that honesty and expansion of heart which we have sometimes observed to arise on such occasions among ourselves. Morality is a mere pretense in their practice, though a common topic of their discourse. Science is an intruder and gaming the resource. An attachment to this vice accompanies even the lowest Chinese wherever he goes. No change of country divests him of it. I have been assured that the Chinese settled in our new colony at the Prince of Wales's island, pay not less than ten thousand dollars per annum to the government for a license to keep gaming-houses and sell opium.

Every Chinese who aspires to preferment attaches himself to some Tartar of consequence,

An Embassy to China: Being the Journal Kept by Lord Macartney During His Embassy to the Emperor Ch'ien-lung, 1793–1794, ed. J.L. Cranmer-Byng (London: Longmans, Green, 1962), pp. 223–25.

and professes the utmost devotion to his service; but such is the strong and radical dislike in the client to the patron, that scarcely any benefits can remove it and plant gratitude in its place. As the nature of dependence is to grow false, it cannot be wondered at if these Chinese are not strict observers of truth. They have indeed so little idea of its moral obligation, that they promise you everything you desire, without the slightest intention of performance, and then violate their promises without scruple, having had no motive for making them that I could perceive, unless it were that they imagined what they said might be agreeable to you just at the moment. When detected or reproached they make light of the matter themselves, and appear neither surprised nor ashamed; but nevertheless it was evident that they particularly remarked our punctuality and our strict attention to truth in all our transactions with them, and respected us accordingly. . . .

A Chinese family is regulated with the same regard to subordination and economy that is observed in the government of a state; the paternal authority, though unlimited, is usually exercised with kindness and indulgence. In China children are indeed sometimes sold, and infants exposed by the parents, but only in cases of the most hopeless indigence and misery, when they must inevitably perish if kept at home; but where the thread of attachment is not thus snapped asunder by the anguish of the parent, it every day grows stronger and becomes indissoluble for life.

There is nothing more striking in the Chinese character through all ranks than this most respectable union. Affection and duty walk hand in hand and never desire a separation. The fondness of the father is constantly felt and always increasing; the dependence of the son is perfectly understood by him; he never wishes it to be lessened. . . .

The people, even of the first rank, though so fond of dress as to change it usually several times in a day, are yet in their persons and customs frowzy and uncleanly. Their outward garment of ceremony is richly embroidered with silks of different colors (those of the highest class of all with golden dragons), and their common habit is of plain silk, or fine broadcloth; but their drawers and their waistcoats (of which they usually wear several according to the season) are not very frequently shifted. They wear neither knit nor woven stockings, but wrap their legs round with a coarse cotton stuff, over which they have constantly drawn a pair of black satin boots without heels, but with soles nearly an inch in thickness. In summer everybody carries a fan in his hand, and is flirting it incessantly.

They wear but little linen or calico, and what they do wear is extremely coarse and ill washed, soap being never employed by them. They seldom have recourse to pocket handkerchiefs, but spit about the rooms without mercy, blow their noses in their fingers, and wipe them with their sleeves, or upon anything near them. This practice is universal, and what is still more abominable, I one day observed a Tartar of distinction call his servant to hunt in his neck for a louse that was troublesome to him.

After reading this selection, consider these questions:
1. What does Macartney think of the Chinese concern for ceremony?
2. How does the British diplomat view the relations between the Manchus and the Chinese?
3. What does Macartney find admirable in Chinese life?

SELECTION 5:

Riding Etiquette in Japan

Off the coast of China lay Japan, an archipelago of islands with a people quite different in ethnic background and language, but very similar to the Chinese in culture. From China the Japanese had borrowed much of their Buddhist faith, their writing system, and their ideas on human behavior that owed much to Confucius's teachings. Much as in China, certain norms were considered correct behavior, and no one, without disgrace, could dispense him- or herself from them.

In 1542 the Portuguese were also the first Europeans to reach Japan. At first the Japanese found them to be very interesting and wanted to learn as much as possible about Europe. In the journal in the following selection, the Portuguese João Rodrigues gives an account of the demands that Japanese courtesy made upon horsemen of different social ranks.

When a man on horseback sees a noble or honorable person coming on foot, he must dismount from the horse even if he does not know the person. This happens especially if the person is carrying aloft a lance, the usual ensign of nobles in Japan, because the lance is proper to such a person with two or three servants. But even if he does not carry a lance, the rider must still dismount at a greater or lesser distance according to the person's rank and the respect which the rider wishes to show him; the closer he dismounts, the less courtesy is shown. Usually he dismounts about fifteen paces away. The person on foot thanks him for the courtesy thus shown and begs him mount directly he has gone a little way past him.

If the person on foot is very noble, the rider continues walking for a while before remounting in order to show greater respect and the noble sends one of his servants to ask him to mount forthwith. The reason for this dismounting is because the man on horseback is in a higher and more exalted position than the man walking on foot, and to a certain extent looks down on him

and is, as it were, his superior, while the man on foot is in a low and inferior position.

When a man is riding a horse quickly and sees a person of rank traveling in front on foot and he must overtake him, he sends him a message asking permission to pass; when the man on foot turns round, the rider dismounts from his horse, offers his compliments as he passes and then remounts. If the other man is also going on horseback, all the rider does is ask permission, and as they pass each other they pay their compliments while still on horseback by bowing the body and head, and drawing up their hands in front of the pommel of the saddle. As they pass each other, he tries to pull over to the right, thus leaving the left-hand side for the other rider.

When a rider on horseback meets some closed litters in which some people are traveling, he always dismounts and withdraws to the right. When he meets another rider, who also wishes to pass, at the entrance to a bridge or some other narrow place, he withdraws to the right and once or twice tries to persuade the other to pass. If the other declines, the rider will show him the courtesy mentioned above and then pass. In the same way when a rider is fording a river and meets another man on horseback in the middle, he passes

This Island of Japon: João Rodrigues' Account of 16th Century Japan, ed. and trans. Michael Cooper (Tokyo and New York: Kodansha International, 1973), pp. 182–83.

and bows as has already been said. If a person of rank is crossing the river on foot and is met in the middle by a man on horseback, the rider will dismount after he has crossed the river and will there pay his respects.

After reading this selection, consider these questions:

1. Why do you suppose ritual played such an important role in Japan?
2. What does Japanese etiquette say about class distinctions in the country?
3. Do you see any advantages in following a norm of conduct similar to the one in Japan?

SELECTION 6:

The Search for Identity in Japan

As in China the Japanese emperors and the ruling nobility were anxious to keep the Europeans at arm's length. During the Tokugawa period the European merchants were allowed but one ship a year to dock at the port of Nagasaki. The once flourishing community of Japanese Christians, formed by the Jesuits in the sixteenth century, was persecuted to the extent that it almost collapsed. The Tokugawa shoguns (generals) did everything possible to remove any threat to their family's control of the nation and its economy.

In its relative isolation Japan went through significant change as it sought to define a national character. Led by the poet and scholar Norinaga Motoori, the Japanese were encouraged to develop their own culture and abandon their dependence on China, whether Buddhist or Confucian. A modern historian explains in the selection below.

The harsh measures taken by the Tokugawa rulers succeeded in their object. Japan experienced over two centuries of peace and security. Those centuries of order encouraged the development of outlooks and of institutions that transformed the quarrelsome samurai of 1600 into a more responsible and more civilian-style bureaucracy, one that administered what became a permanent military government. The arts of peace and education flourished, and popular literacy and culture showed the permeation throughout

Japanese society of values and learning that had previously been restricted to a small fraction of the elite.

One of the remarkable aspects of the Tokugawa years is that the Chinese literary heritage became more important than it had ever been. As a result, it was possible and in fact necessary for the Japanese to distinguish between "China" and Chinese culture. "China" as a country had fallen under Manchu rule, as centuries earlier it had fallen to the Mongols. This time, however, the awareness of that fact was far greater because changes within Japanese society had broadened the horizons of consciousness. Chinese books and Chinese refugees preserved the memory of the Manchu conquest long after censorship had

Marius B. Jansen, *Japan and Its World: Two Centuries of Change* (Princeton, NJ: Princeton University Press, 1995) pp. 19, 24–26, 28–29.

dulled it within China itself. . . .

Until the eighteenth century the only serious alternative to Confucian philosophy was Buddhist. Since both of these schools had come by way of China, the primacy of Chinese learning had not been challenged by that contention. But by the late eighteenth century there were also Japanese thinkers prepared to reject the entire Chinese model, Confucian as well as Buddhist. The most forthright of them were connected with the National Studies, or *kokugaku*, movement.

The eighteenth century witnessed tremendous development of literary and philosophical scholarship in Japan. Confucianists turned to the principal texts of their tradition with new rigor and determination in efforts to free those teachings from the accretions of subsequent interpretation. Specialists in Japanese poetry meanwhile developed their own enthusiasm for textual research. In the study of Japanese poetry they were dealing with the very center of Japanese aesthetics and values, and as they investigated the classics of Japanese antiquity they struggled to define what it was that lay at the center of the Japanese national character. In part this represented for them a psychological counter against the dominance of Confucianism and the influence of what seemed to them the formal, rule-centered scholarship of heavy-handed pedants. . . .

The Japanese spirit, the national scholars proclaimed, was pure, natural, and unbounded, and the norms of Confucian morality were antithetical to it. Emotion was pure and honest, and to curb it through rules or to sublimate it through religion was dishonest. Such foreign deception and falsehood, Motoori wrote, were contrary to human nature. A proper awareness of the pathos of things was most clearly present in Japan's tradition of emotive poetry. Thus their path led back to the classics of the Japanese literary tradition and to values that could be discerned at the dawn of Japanese history before imports from China obscured their purity. The ancient cult of Shintō was emphasized once again, with it the shrines at Ise, and with them the imperial cult, whose patron deity the Sun Goddess served as reminder of the superiority of Japanese spirit and polity over all possible competitors. In literary and philosophical writing the *kokugakusha* occasionally sounded Taoist, for that tradition had always contained the Chinese antithesis to Confucian order and decorum. . . .

The national scholars rejected the Chinese tradition of Confucian formalism, but they had little to substitute for it except an unstructured naturalism and an intuitive appreciation. Nor was their emphasis on national uniqueness and essence likely to stir them to seek other and more useful models. But by the time Motoori was writing his major works, an alternate approach to wisdom was far advanced. This was the study of the West, carried out with great difficulty with books brought by Dutch traders to Nagasaki.

After reading this selection, consider these questions:

1. Are there advantages for a people to turn inward in seeking to define their culture? Can you give any modern examples?
2. Why would Japanese scholars want to abandon Confucianism?
3. What do you see as providing the context for modern American culture?

CHAPTER 9
Africa: How Did European Contact Affect Its People?

In the early modern period visitors from Europe began to sail down both the western and eastern coasts of the Continent. In the west the goal of the Portuguese was to reach the African kingdoms that supplied gold to the caravans that crossed the Sahara Desert and then sold it to Europeans. Thanks to the voyages sponsored by Prince Henry the Navigator and expeditions overland from Egypt, the Europeans learned increasingly more about Africa. In the east an additional source of interest was the search for Prester John, a Christian prince who might well assist the Europeans in their never-ending wars with the Muslims.

Unfortunately, in West Africa the Portuguese merchants discovered, besides gold, a source of slaves. For many centuries in this region prisoners of war and criminals expected to be enslaved, so it was nothing new for men and women to be bought and sold, usually to be employed as domestic servants. However, once sugar plantation cultivation began in the Caribbean and Brazil and cotton and tobacco began growing in the British colonies, a great demand for human labor came to exist on the other side of the Atlantic. The American Indians proved unable to provide a sufficient number of workers and were forbidden by law to be enslaved, which left Africans to fill the need.

SELECTION 1:

A Description of Benin

The major West African kingdom was Benin. In the seventeenth century John Barbot visited this state and left this account of its government and society.

The king of Benin is absolute; his will being a law and a bridle to his subjects, which none of them dare oppose; and, as I have hinted before, the greatest men of the nation, as well as the inferior sort, esteem it an honor to be called the king's slave, which title no person dares assume without the king's particular grant; and that he never allows but to those, who, as soon as born, are by their parents presented to him: for which reason, some geographers have thought, that the king of Benin was religiously adored by all his subjects, as a deity. But that is a mistake, for the qualification of the king's slaves, is but a bare compliment to majesty; since none of the natives of Benin, can by the law of the land, be made slaves on any account. . . .

The present king is a young man of an affable behavior. His mother is still living, to whom he pays very great respect and reverence, and all the people after his example honor her. She lives apart from her son in her own palace out of the city Oedo, where she keeps her court, waited on and served by her proper officers, women and maids. The king her son uses to take her advice on many important affairs of state, by the ministry of his statesmen and counselors: for the king there is not to see his own mother, without danger of an insurrection of the people against him, according to their constitutions. The palace of that dowager is very large and spacious, built much after the manner, and of the same materials as the king's, and those of other great persons.

The king's household is composed of a great number of officers of sundry sorts, and slaves of both sexes, whose business is to furnish all the several apartments with all manner of necessaries for life and convenience, as well as the country affords. The men officers being to take care of all that concerns the king's tables and stables; and the women, for that which regards his wives and concubines: which all together makes the concourse of people so great at court, with the strangers resorting continually to it every day about business, that there is always a vast crowd running to and fro from one quarter to another. . . .

The king being very charitable, as well as his subjects, has peculiar officers about him, whose chief employment is, on certain days, to carry a great quantity of provisions, ready dressed, which the king sends into the town for the use of the poor. Those men make a sort of procession, marching two and two with those provisions in great order, preceded by the head officer, with a long white staff in his hand, like the prime court officers in England; and everybody is obliged to make way for him, though of never so great quality.

Besides this good quality of being charitable, the king might be reckoned just and equitable, as desiring continually his officers to administer justice exactly, and to discharge their duties conscientiously: besides that, he is a great lover of Europeans, whom he will have to be well treated and honored, more especially the Dutch nation, as I have before observed. But his extortions from such of his subjects as are wealthy, on one unjust pretense or other, which has so much impoverished many of them, will not allow him to be looked upon as very just.

John Barbot, "Benin," in *African History: Text and Readings*, ed. Robert O. Collins (New York: Random House, 1971), pp. 162–63.

He seldom passes one day, without holding a cabinet council with his chief ministers, for dispatching of the many affairs brought before him, with all possible expedition; besides, the appeals from inferior courts of judicature in all the parts of the kingdom, and audiences to strangers, or concerning the affairs of war, or other emergencies of state.

After reading this selection, consider these questions:

1. How was slavery regarded in the kingdom of Benin?
2. What was the special role of the queen-mother in Benin?
3. What provisions were made for the poor in the nation?

SELECTION 2:

The Growth of the West African Kingdoms

*R*oland *Oliver and J.D. Fage, well-known scholars of African affairs, note in the following selection how Benin and other West African states fared as French, Dutch, Danish, and English merchants sought to take over the slave trade monopoly that the Portuguese held. African kings were strong enough to keep the Europeans in forts on land that they leased to them along the coast. Europeans rarely ventured into the African interior.*

The general effect of the Atlantic slave trade was, indeed, to move the centers of wealth and power in West Africa away from the Sudan and towards the coast. The direct European share in this was negligible. The French, firmly established on the lower Senegal and at Gorée, and the British, Dutch, and Danes who occupied the Gold Coast forts, hardly possessed extensive political influence. Even the Gold Coast forts, impressive architectural monuments to the bitter European competition of the seventeenth century, were built on land leased from the local African states. In the last resort their lonely garrisons were unable to withstand determined opposition from the Africans of the towns which came to cluster round them. However, a community of interest existed, which came to ally the Europeans with their African neighbors when both were threatened by the growth of new states in the immediate hinterland, and from this, in the nineteenth century, the seeds of colonialism could grow.

The most impressive development of the seventeenth and eighteenth centuries was the growth of African states just inland from the coastlands. Benin's empire, which had already reached the sea when the Europeans came, proved unable to withstand the strains imposed on it by constant slave-raiding wars; the new centers of power were somewhat further inland. An early development was the short-lived empire of the Akan state of Akwamu, which between about 1680 and about 1730 expanded parallel with the eastern Gold Coast and the western Slave Coast in an attempt to engross the whole trade of their hinterlands with the south. Akwamu, however, failed to find a principle of administration capable of se-

Roland Oliver and J.D. Fage, *A Short History of Africa* (Harmondsworth: Penguin Books, 1962), pp. 124–25.

curing an enduring allegiance from its Ga and Ewe subjects, and its place as the major Gold Coast power was soon taken by Ashanti. In the early eighteenth century, Ashanti, learning from Akwamu experience, began to expand to the north, incorporating or making tributary states like Bono, Banda, Gonja, and Dagomba. Then, with the trade of the interior profitably secured, she turned south to seek direct contact with the European traders. Further east, Oyo had begun her southward expansion early in the seventeenth century. During the eighteenth century her paramountcy over her more southerly Yoruba kin was established, and much of the Nigerian slave trade became diverted from Benin to ports like Badagri and Lagos. Precariously situated between the Yoruba empire of Oyo and Ashanti rule, there emerged the new state of Dahomey, initially stimulated by the need to resist attacks from Oyo, to which in fact it long paid tribute. Nevertheless Dahomey too was attracted southward by the trade with the Europeans, to establish contact with the coast at Whydah.

By the end of the eighteenth century, then, over three centuries of European trade on the coasts of West Africa had led to little penetration of European influences. The Christian missionary effort in Guinea had been negligible; only the early Portuguese had been at all interested in the expansion of Christendom. Their early mission to Benin was soon withdrawn to Warri, where it lingered into the seventeenth century, but they were even less successful in creating a native Christian state here than in the Congo. Their other principal field of mission activity was in the coastlands opposite the Cape Verde Islands; here the best that could be achieved was the creation of a doubtfully-Christian class of half-caste traders.

With hardly another exception, the Europeans who had gone to West Africa were interested solely in exporting its produce, and in effect only in the slave trade. Permanent European settlement on the coast, as on the Gold Coast, and at the mouth of the Senegal, did tend to produce a thin layer of coastal Africans who were partly European in their outlook and even, sometimes, in their formal education. But the vast mass of West Africa and its peoples remained untouched by direct European influence.

After reading this selection, consider these questions:

1. How did the West African kings deal with Europeans?
2. Which African nation became the leading power in the early eighteenth century?
3. What was the major European impact on West Africa?

SELECTION 3:

Women of Dahomey

D*ahomey, one of the African kingdoms mentioned in the previous selection, also had its share of visitors who wanted to relate their impressions. One of these was Archibald Dalzel, whose report, excerpted below, was published in 1793. Dalzel was struck by the army of women recruited to serve the king.*

The King of Dahomey maintains a considerable standing army, commanded by an *Agaow*, or general, with several other subordinate military officers, who must hold themselves in readiness to take the field upon all occasions at the command of the sovereign. The payment of these troops chiefly depends on the success of the expeditions in which they are engaged. On extraordinary occasions, all the males able to bear arms, are obliged to repair to the general's standard; every *Caboceer* marching at the head of his own people. Sometimes the King takes the field, at the head of his troops; and, on very great emergencies, at the head of his women.

Whatever might have been the prowess of the *Amazons* among the ancients, this is a novelty in modern history, which ought not to be slightly passed over. Within the walls of the different royal palaces in Dahomey, are immured not less than *three thousand women*. Several hundreds of these are trained to the use of arms, under a female general and subordinate officers, appointed by the King, in the same manner as those under the Agaow. These warriors are regularly exercised, and go through their evolutions with as much expertness as the male soldiers. They have their large umbrellas, their flags, their drums, trumpets, flutes, and other musical instruments. In short, the singularity of this institution never fails to attract the particular attention of the Europeans, when, among other uncommon exhibitions, they are presented with the unusual spectacle of a *review* of female troops.

After reading this selection, consider these questions:

1. What do you recall about Dahomey from the previous selection?
2. Why would the king of Dahomey want to recruit a female army?
3. Do you think that men and women had an equal status in Dahomey?

Archibald Dalzel, *The History of Dahomy: an Inland Kingdom of Africa* (London, 1793; reprint, Frank Cass, 1967), pp. x–xi.

SELECTION 4:

A Slave Remembers

Only a few of the estimated 12 million Africans brought to the Americas ever succeeded in returning to their homelands and having a record made of their experience. One of these was Ayuba Suleiman Diallo of Bondu, whom the Europeans called Job ben Solomon. In 1734 he told his story to Thomas Bluett, who wrote it into a personal memoir. An extract appears in the following selection.

In February, 1730, Job's father hearing of an English ship at Gambia River, sent him, with two servants to attend him, to sell two Negroes, and to buy paper, and some other necessaries; but desired him not to venture over the river, because the country of the Mandingoes, who are enemies to the people of Futa, lies on the other side. Job not agreeing with Captain Pike (who commanded the ship, lying then at Gambia, in the service of Captain Henry Hunt, brother to Mr. William Hunt, merchant, in Little Tower Street, London)

Philip D. Curtin, ed., *Africa Remembered: Narratives by West Africans from the Era of the Slave Trade* (Madison, Milwaukee, and London: University of Wisconsin Press, 1967), pp. 39–41.

sent back the two servants to acquaint his father with it, and to let him know that he intended to go farther. Accordingly having agreed with another man, named Loumein Yoas, who understood the Mandingoe language, to go with him as his interpreter, he crossed the River Gambia, and disposed of his Negroes for some cows. As he was returning home, he stopped for some refreshment at the house of an old acquaintance; and the weather being hot, he hung up his arms in the house, while he refreshed himself. Those arms were very valuable; consisting of a gold-hilted sword, a gold knife, which they wear by their side, and a rich quiver of arrows, which King Sambo had made him a present of. It happened that a company of the Mandingoes, who live upon plunder, passing by at that time, and observing him unarmed, rushed in, to the number of seven or eight at once, at a back door, and pinioned Job, before he could get to his arms, together with his interpreter, who is a slave in Maryland still. They then shaved their heads and beards, which Job and his man resented as the highest indignity; though the Mandingoes meant no more by it, than to make them appear like slaves taken in war. On the 27th of February, 1730, they carried them to Captain Pike at Gambia, who purchased them; and on the first of March they were put on board. Soon after Job found means to acquaint Captain Pike that he was the same person that came to trade with him a few days before, and after what manner he had been taken. Upon this Captain Pike gave him leave to redeem himself and his man; and Job sent to an acquaintance of his father's, near Gambia, who promised to send to Job's father, to inform him of what had happened, that he might take some course to have him set at liberty. But it being a fortnight's journey between that friend's house

and his father's, and the ship sailing in about a week after, Job was brought with the rest of the slaves to Annapolis in Maryland, and delivered to Mr. Vachell Denton, factor to Mr. Hunt, before mentioned. Job heard since, by vessels that came from Gambia, that his father sent down several slaves, a little after Captain Pike sailed, in order to procure his redemption; and that Sambo, King of Futa, had made war upon the Mandingoes, and cut off great numbers of them, upon account of the injury they had done to his schoolfellow.

Mr. Vachell Denton sold Job to one Mr. Tolsey in Kent Island in Maryland, who put him to work in making tobacco; but he was soon convinced that Job had never been used to such labor. He every day showed more and more uneasiness under this exercise, and at last grew sick, being no way able to bear it; so that his master was obliged to find easier work for him, and therefore put him to tend the cattle. Job would often leave the cattle, and withdraw into the woods to pray; but a white boy frequently watched him, and whilst he was at his devotion would mock him, and throw dirt in his face. This very much disturbed Job, and added considerably to his other misfortunes; all which were increased by his ignorance of the English language, which prevented his complaining, or telling his case to any person about him.

After reading this selection, consider these questions:
  1. Why did Job make the journey to the mouth of the Gambia River?
  2. What did the Mandingoes want?
  3. What contributed to Job's distress in Maryland?

SELECTION 5:

The Portuguese in East Africa

The history of East Africa differed from that of West Africa. Here the Portuguese displaced the Arab merchants who plied the Indian Ocean and were able to hold on to their bases much longer than in West Africa. In this region the usual African products of the interior, gold, slaves, and ivory, were brought to them.

The beginning of the Portuguese contacts with East Africa is reported in the following selection.

The first step was taken by Vasco da Gama on his second voyage to India, in 1502. He called at Kilwa and forced the sultan to pay a yearly tribute to the king of Portugal. This was typical of Portugal's dealings with the coast. Tribute was demanded and unless it was paid the town was destroyed. If it was paid the local sultan was usually left in peace, provided he carried out the wishes of the Portuguese. After Kilwa, Zanzibar was the next place to suffer from the Portuguese. In 1503 a Portuguese commander called Ravasco showed the power of guns by using two boats with cannon to defeat canoes carrying 4,000 men. These canoes had been manned by the ruler of Zanzibar, in protest against Ravasco's unprovoked attack on a number of small local ships carrying goods that Ravasco wanted.

This was only the beginning. In 1505 a fleet of more than twenty ships set sail from Portugal for India. The newly-appointed viceroy of India, d'Almeida, was in command, and his first task was to gain control of three key places on the coast of East Africa: Sofala, Kilwa and Mombasa. Sofala was important to the Portuguese because it would give them control of the gold supply. It offered hardly any resistance, and a fort was built to protect the Portuguese colony that now replaced the old Arab settlement. But the

Portuguese inability to cooperate with either Arab or African was their undoing here, and in a few years Sofala could barely pay its way. Nor was its old overlord, Kilwa, in better shape; cut off from the gold-trade with Sofala, which had supplied much of its prosperity, it sank into a decline which only ended when the Zimba swarmed into the town and killed the inhabitants. A Dominican friar on the coast at the end of the sixteenth century wrote of the Zimba that they "worship no God, nor Idol, but their King, who (they say) is God of the Earth; and if it rains when he would not, they shoot their arrows at the sky for not obeying him. . . . They eat those which they kill in war."

Having laid waste Kilwa, d'Almeida's fleet then sailed away to deal with Mombasa, which of late had secured a larger share of trade than Kilwa; so that by 1505 Kilwa had only 4,000 inhabitants, compared to Mombasa's 10,000. Unlike Sofala and Kilwa, Mombasa did not yield without a fight, and throughout the 200 years during which the Portuguese ruled in East Africa, she was to be a thorn in their side, an island well-named the "Island of War." But the bowmen of Mombasa could not long resist guns and armor, and Mombasa too was conquered, and set on fire. Its resilience, though, was remarkable and may have been due not only to its favorable trading situation but also to its position as a mainland power as well as an island state. This position gave it the support of inland tribes in times of crisis.

Zoë Marsh and G.W. Kingsnorth, *An Introduction to the History of East Africa,* 4th ed. (Cambridge: Cambridge University Press, 1957), pp. 28–30.

Not one of these three places, Sofala, Kilwa, and Mombasa, however, was to be the headquarters of the Portuguese on the east coast. They found it more convenient to rule from Mozambique, which was "colonized" in 1507. The Portuguese representative on the north of the East African coast was the captain of Malindi. . . .

From the beginning the Portuguese found the East African part of their empire disappointing, because it never brought them the wealth they had expected. They had hoped to secure this by cutting off Arab trade with India, and by attacking the Arab coastal trade, both on sea and land. They intended to deal direct with the Africans themselves, and no share of their profits was to be taken by Arab or Indian middlemen. So the Portuguese were content to fill their warehouses with calico and beads from India and wait for the Africans to bring gold, ivory, and slaves from the interior. The Portuguese underestimated the importance of the local traders and they also lacked the men to staff these caravans.

It must also be remembered that they were not interested in setting up administrative machinery in their bases, and they never had enough Portuguese to staff them. Consequently the supply of ivory and slaves dried up and the Sofala gold-trade, which supported the prosperity of the East Coast, was diverted south with disastrous results. The old Arab settlements, which had been taken over by the Portuguese became poorer and weaker. This was most marked in the south, where Mozambique, Kilwa and Sofala had their Portuguese garrisons and forts. Things were a little easier in the north, where local sultans were still allowed to rule, provided they paid the annual tribute, but even here the conquerors were hated, and the Africans called the chief of the Portuguese *afriti*, or devil.

After reading this selection, consider these questions:

1. What hindered the Portuguese presence in the East African ports?
2. What city became the major Portuguese settlement in East Africa?
3. Why did the Portuguese East African colonies prove to be a disappointment?

SELECTION 6:

The East African Coast

The East African coast for centuries benefited from the Indian Ocean trade. Pushed in front of the monsoons, Persian and Arab traders brought the products of India to the African peoples and then sailed back to India with the goods of that continent. They gave to many of the inhabitants their religion, Islam, and their language, mixed with that of native tongues to form Swahili. Swahili became the written language of East Africa.

The Portuguese entered this world, uninvited, at the very end of the fifteenth century. Their superior ships and firepower meant the eclipse for Muslim traders of the Indian Ocean, as Europeans established themselves in the coastal cities of East Africa. About 1518 the Portuguese Duarte Barbosa passed along this coast on his way to India and left the following narrative of his voyage. It might be noted that the Arab sultans of Melinde regarded the merchants of Mombasa, now both port cities in *southern Kenya, their commercial rivals and were happy to welcome Portuguese aid in their struggle with that city.*

Further on, an advance along the coast towards India, there is an isle hard by the mainland, on which is a town called Mombaça [Mombasa]. It is a very fair place, with lofty stone and mortar houses, well aligned in streets [after the fashion of Quiloa]. The wood is well-fitted with excellent joiner's work. It has its own king, himself a Moor. [The men are in colour either tawny, black or white and also] their women go very bravely attired with many fine garments of silk and gold in abundance. This is a place of great traffic, and has a good harbour, in which are always moored craft of many kinds and also great ships, both of those which come from Çofala [now Beira in Mozambique] and those which go thither, and others which come from the great kingdom of Cambaya [in India] and from Melynde [an African port]; others which sail to the Isles of Zinzibar [now Zanzibar], and yet others of which I shall speak anon.

This Mombaça is a land very full of food. Here are found many very fine sheep with round tails, cows and other cattle in great plenty, and many fowls, all of which are exceeding fat. There is much millet and rice, sweet and bitter oranges, lemons, pomegranates, Indian figs, vegetables of divers kinds, and much sweet water. The men thereof are oft-times at war and but seldom at peace with those of the mainland, and they carry on trade with them, bringing thence great store of honey, wax and ivory.

The king of this city refused to obey the commands of the King our Lord, and through this arrogance he lost it, and our Portuguese took it from him by force. He fled away, and they slew many of his people and also took captive many, both men and women, in such sort that it was left ruined and plundered and burnt. Of gold and silver great booty was taken here, bangles, bracelets, ear-rings and gold beads, also great store of copper with other rich wares in great quantity, and the town was left in ruins.

Leaving Mombaça, and journeying along the coast towards India, there is a fair town on the mainland lying along a strand, which is named Melinde. It pertains to the Moors and has a Moorish king over it; the which place has many fair stone and mortar houses of many storeys, with great plenty of windows and flat roofs, after our fashion. The place is well laid out in streets. The folk are both black and white; they go naked, covering only their private parts with cotton and silk cloths. Others of them wear cloths folded like cloaks and waist-bands, and turbans of many rich stuffs on their heads.

They are great barterers, and deal in cloth, gold, ivory, and divers other wares with the Moors and Heathen of the great kingdom of Cambaya; and to their haven come every year many ships with cargoes of merchandize, from which they get great store of gold, ivory and wax. In this traffic the Cambay merchants make great profits, and thus, on one side and the other, they earn much money. There is great plenty of food in this city [rice, millet and some wheat which they bring from Cambaya], and divers sorts of fruit, inasmuch as there is here abundance of fruit-gardens and orchards. Here too are plenty of round-tailed sheep, cows and other cattle and great store of oranges, also of hens.

The king and people of this place ever were and are friends of the King of Portugal, and the Portuguese always find in them great comfort and friendship and perfect peace, and there the ships, when they chance to pass that way, obtain supplies in plenty.

After reading this selection, consider these questions:

1. What impresses Barbosa about the East African coast?
2. Why were the Portuguese welcomed in one city but rejected in another?
3. What caused the Indian Ocean trade to be so brisk?

The Book of Duarte Barbosa, trans. Mansel Longworth Dames (London: Hakluyt Society, 1918; Kraus reprint, 1967), pp. 19–23.

CHAPTER 10
The Americas: How Was Independence Achieved?

No political situation is ever stationary. Despite the efforts of Great Britain and Spain to keep their colonies attached to the mother countries, there was a growing maturity in the consciousness of people in the New World that encouraged them to move toward independence. Complaints arose for many reasons; political and economic causes were the major ones.

It was difficult for the men and women in Great Britain's thirteen colonies to accept the interference of London in their affairs. It is true that colonists enjoyed having the British army on this side of the Atlantic to protect them from their two foes, the American Indians and the French forces in Canada. Nevertheless, they resented having to pay taxes to support this army. A series of acts passed in Parliament to secure revenues from American pockets brought on the crisis.

In South America it was Napoleon's toppling of the Bourbon monarch in Madrid that caused politicians among the Creoles, people of European ancestry born in the Americas, to plan ways to be free from Spain. When Spanish armies again arrived in the New World they met resistance from local military units that were committed to keeping their freedom from European control.

SELECTION 1:

An Objection to Colonial Taxation

In the following selection you can read how the colonists had friends among some of the members of Parliament. William Pitt, first earl of Chatham, was one of these. Pitt had served Great Britain well as leader of Parliament for many years, and his foreign policy created much of the empire gained after the Seven Years' War in Europe. He was, however, much opposed to taxing the Americans, as seen in this speech delivered in Parliament.

It is my opinion, that this kingdom has no right to lay a tax upon the colonies. At the same time, I assert the authority of this kingdom over the colonies to be sovereign and supreme in every circumstance of government and legislation whatsoever. They are the subjects of this kingdom; equally entitled with yourselves to all the natural rights of mankind and the peculiar privileges of Englishmen; equally bound by its laws, and equally participating in the constitution of this free country. The Americans are the sons, not the bastards of England! Taxation is no part of the governing or legislative power.

Taxes are a voluntary gift and grant of the Commons alone. In legislation the three estates of the realm are alike concerned; but the concurrence of the peers and the Crown to a tax is only necessary to clothe it with the form of a law. The gift and grant is of the Commons alone. In ancient days, the Crown, the barons, and the clergy possessed the lands. In those days, the barons and the clergy gave and granted to the Crown. They gave and granted what was their own! At present, since the discovery of America, and other circumstances permitting, the Commons are the proprietors of the land. The Church (God bless it!) has but a pittance. The property of the lords, compared with that of the Commons, is as a drop of water in the ocean; and this House represents those Commons, the proprietors of the lands; and those proprietors virtually represent the rest of the inhabitants. When, therefore, in this House, we give and grant, we give and grant what is our own. But in an American tax, what do we do? "We, your Majesty's Commons for Great Britain, give and grant to your Majesty"—what? Our own property? No! "We give and grant to your Majesty" the property of your Majesty's Commons of America! It is an absurdity in terms.

The distinction between legislation and taxation is essentially necessary to liberty. The Crown and the peers are equally legislative powers with the Commons. If taxation be a part of simple legislation, the Crown and the Peers have rights in taxation as well as yourselves; rights which they will claim, which they will exercise, whenever the principle can be supported by power.

There is an idea in some that the colonies are virtually represented in the House. I would fain know by whom an American is represented here. Is he represented by any knight of the shire, in any county in this kingdom? Would to God that respectable representation was augmented to a greater number! Or will you tell him that he is represented by any representative of a borough?

Lord Chatham, speech in Parliament, in *The Library of Original Sources*, ed. Oliver J. Thatcher (Milwaukee: University Research Extension, 1901), pp. 69–70.

A borough which, perhaps, its own representatives never saw! This is what is called the rotten part of the Constitution. It can not continue a century. If it does not drop, it must be amputated. The idea of a virtual representation of America in this House is the most contemptible idea that ever entered into the head of a man. It does not deserve a serious refutation.

After reading this selection, consider these questions:
1. How did Pitt divide the issue of sovereignty from taxation?
2. What does Pitt mean when he says we "give and grant what is our own"?
3. What was meant by American virtual representation in Parliament?

SELECTION 2:

Common Sense

In 1775 Thomas Paine shipped out of England for the colonies. In his pocket he carried letters of introduction from Benjamin Franklin. His employment record was not a happy one in Great Britain, where he had moved from one job to another. During these years of uncertainty Paine developed a passionate interest in independence for the colonies, and in January 1776 published his ideas in a pamphlet he entitled Common Sense.

Paine's work was an instant success. Over half a million copies were printed and bought up by the colonists, now eager to read of their oppression in words that kindled their imagination. As the following selection demonstrates, Paine's words are still stirring.

I have heard it asserted by some, that, as America has flourished under her former connection with Great Britain, the same connection is necessary towards her future happiness, and will always have the same effect. Nothing can be more fallacious than this kind of argument. We may as well assert, that, because a child has thrived upon milk, that it is never to have meat; or that the first twenty years of our lives are to become a precedent for the next twenty. But even this is admitting more than is true; for I answer roundly, that America would have flourished as much, and probably much more, had no European power had anything to do with her. The commerce by which she has enriched herself, are the necessaries of life, and will always have a market while eating is the custom of Europe.

But she has protected us, say some. That she has engrossed us, is true, and defended the continent at our expense, as well as her own, is admitted; and she would have defended Turkey from the same motive, viz., the sake of trade and dominion.

Alas! we have been long led away by ancient prejudices, and made large sacrifices to superstition. We have boasted of the protection of Great Britain, without considering that her motive was interest, not attachment; that she did not protect us from our enemies on our account, but from her enemies on her own account; from those who had no quarrel with us on any other account, and who will always be our enemies on the same account. Let Britain waive her pretensions to the continent, or the continent throw off the dependence; and we shall be at peace with France and Spain, were

Thomas Paine, *Common Sense,* in *The Library of Original Sources,* pp. 211–13.

they at war with Britain. The miseries of Hanover, last war, ought to warn us against connections.

It has lately been asserted in Parliament, that the colonies have no relation to each other but through the parent country; i.e., that Pennsylvania and the Jerseys, and so on for the rest, are sister colonies by the way of England. This is certainly a very round-about way of proving relationship, but it is the nearest and only true way of proving enemyship, if I may so call it. France and Spain never were, nor perhaps ever will be our enemies, as Americans, but as our being the subjects of Great Britain.

But Britain is the parent country, say some. Then the more shame on her conduct. Even brutes do not devour their young, nor savages make war upon their families; wherefore the assertion, if true, turns to her reproach; but it happens not to be true, or only partly so; and the phrase—parent, or mother country—has been jesuitically adopted by the king and his parasites, with a low papistical design of gaining an unfair bias on the credulous weakness of our minds. Europe, and not England, is the parent country of America. This new world has been the asylum for the persecuted lovers of civil and religious liberty, from every part of Europe. Hither have they fled, not from the tender embraces of the mother, but from the cruelty of the monster; and it is so far true of England, that the same tyranny which drove the first emigrants from home, pursues their descendants still. . . .

But, admitting that we are all of English descent, what does it amount to? Nothing. Britain, being now an open enemy, extinguishes every other name and title: and to say that reconciliation is our duty, is truly farcical. The first King of England of the present line (William the Conqueror), was a Frenchman, and half the peers of England are descendants from the same country; wherefore, by the same method of reasoning, England ought to be governed by France.

Much has been said of the united strength of Britain and the colonies; that, in conjunction, they might bid defiance to the world. But this is mere presumption. The fate of war is uncertain; neither do the expressions mean anything; for this continent would never suffer itself to be drained of inhabitants to support the British arms in either Asia, Africa, or Europe.

I challenge the warmest advocate for reconciliation, to show a single advantage that this continent can reap by being connected with Great Britain; I repeat the challenge—not a single advantage is derived. Our corn will fetch its price in any market in Europe; and our imported goods must be paid for, buy them where you will.

After reading this selection, consider these questions:

1. What does Paine think of the past relations between Great Britain and the colonies?
2. Why does Paine hold that Great Britain retains an interest in the colonies?
3. Can you answer Paine's challenge and name some advantages that the colonists gained from their relationship with Great Britain?

SELECTION 3:

The Middle Class in America

After the American Revolution the United States began to forge a nation based upon a written constitution that structured the government according to the best thinking of the Enlightenment. In its ten amendments the document guaranteed its citizens remarkable rights. For the first time in modern history, democracy was put to the test.

In the following selection, taken from Gordon Wood's Radicalism of the American Revolution, *the author attempts to prove that in the process of becoming a single nation, the United States truly became a society in which most people thought and acted on the supposition that they belonged in the middle class, neither the rich nor the poor. Wood sees this as a great strength in a democracy and attributes much of the subsequent history of the nation owing to this fact.*

By the second decade of the nineteenth century Americans were already referring to themselves as a society dominated by the "middling" sort. To be sure, these terms were being used in England at the same time, but their significance in America was different. In England the term "middle class" had a more literal meaning than it did in America: it described that stratum of people who lay between the aristocracy and the working class. But in America, in the North at least, already it seemed as if the so-called middle class was all there was. Middling sorts in America appropriated the principal virtues of the two extremes and drained the vitality from both the aristocracy and the working class. By absorbing the gentility of the aristocracy and the work of the working class, the middling sorts gained a powerful moral hegemony over the whole society. The aristocracy lost its monopoly of civility and politeness and the working class lost its exclusive claim to labor. Leisure became idleness, work became respectable, and nearly every adult white male became a gentleman. It happened nowhere else in the Western world quite like this.

"Patrician and plebeian orders are unknown . . . ," wrote Charles Ingersoll [a famous American commentator on the early days of the nation] in 1810, in one of the first avowed defenses of America's national character against foreign criticism. "Luxury has not yet corrupted the rich, nor is there any of that want, which classifies the poor. There is no populace. All our people. What in other countries is called the populace, a compost heap, whence germinate mobs, beggars, and tyrants, is not to be found in the towns; and there is no peasantry in the country. Were it not for the slaves of the south," wrote Ingersoll, "there would be one rank."

The exception is jarring, to say the least; by modern standards Ingersoll's judgment that America had become classless is absurd. We today see the distinctions of early-nineteenth-century society vividly, not only those between free and enslaved, white and black, male and female, but those between rich and poor, educated and barely literate. Yet if we are to understand the wonder, the astonishment, and judgments of observers like Ingersoll, we must see, as they did, this society of the early Republic in the context of what American society had once been and what societies elsewhere in the Western world still resembled. In that context America had experienced an unprecedented democratic revolution and had created a huge sprawling society that was more egalitarian, more middling, and more dominated by the interests of ordinary people than any that had ever existed before.

After reading this selection, consider these questions:

1. What was unique about early American society?
2. In polls taken today in the United States, an overwhelming number of people think of themselves as middle class. How do you explain this sentiment?
3. Why was it easier to create a more egalitarian society in the United States in comparison to other world societies?

Gordon S. Wood, *The Radicalism of the American Revolution* (New York: Knopf, 1992), pp. 347–48.

SELECTION 4:

The American Democracy

Alexis de Tocqueville was born a French nobleman but early in life ex-hibited an interest in the experiment in democracy occurring across the Atlantic. In 1830 he arrived in the United States and remained for the next eighteen months, observing the American democracy during the presiden-cy of Andrew Jackson.

Tocqueville did more than observe. He was anxious to make an analy-sis of what he saw. He was impressed by the amount of individual freedom that the Constitution offered citizens, but he had concerns over the power that a majority might use against minorities.

It is interesting to compare what he says as a confirmation of the Wood thesis that you have just read. These two pieces illustrate how historians use primary sources. Tocqueville's following eyewitness account provides a basis for Wood's modern history.

Many important observations suggest them-selves upon the social condition of the Anglo-Americans, but there is one which takes prece-dence of all the rest. The social condition of the Americans is eminently democratic; this was its character at the foundation of the Colonies, and is still more strongly marked at the present day. I have stated . . . that great equality existed among the emigrants who settled on the shores of New England. The germ of aristocracy was never planted in that part of the Union. The only influ-ence which obtained there was that of intellect; the people were used to reverence certain names as the emblems of knowledge and virtue. Some of their fellow citizens acquired a power over the rest which might truly have been called aristo-cratic, if it had been capable of transmission from father to son. . . .

In America the aristocratic element has always been feeble from its birth; and if at the present day it is not actually destroyed, it is at any rate so completely disabled that we can scarcely assign to it any degree of influence in the course of af-fairs. The democratic principle, on the contrary, has gained so much strength by time, by events, and by legislation, as to have become not only predominant but all-powerful. There is no family or corporate authority, and it is rare to find even the influence of individual character enjoy any durability. . . .

America, then, exhibits in her social state a most extraordinary phenomenon. Men are there seen on a greater equality in point of fortune and intellect, or, in other words, more equal in their strength, than in any other country of the world, or in any age of which history has preserved the remembrance.

After reading this selection, consider these questions:

1. What does Tocqueville observe of the class structure in the United States?
2. Why has the democratic spirit been so strong in American history?
3. In a democracy, what safeguards the rights of minorities?

Alexis de Tocqueville, *Democracy in America*, trans. Henry Reeve, 2 vols., rev. ed. (Colonial Press, 1900), vol. 1, pp. 46, 52–53.

SELECTION 5:

The Revolutions in South America

The revolutions in South America early in the nineteenth century took place as a result of events occurring in Europe. Napoleon's overthrow of the Bourbon monarch in Spain created a very difficult situation for the representatives of the Spanish crown in Latin America. Were they to give their loyalty to Napoleon's candidate now sitting in Madrid, keep their allegiance to their deposed monarch, or await events with a provisional government? The issue was complicated because of a great social gap between the peninsulares, *officials born in Spain sent out to the colonies as high officials, and the Creoles, people born in South America who had no influence in charting government policy. The* peninsulares *monopolized all the major positions in both the government and state to the chagrin of the Creoles, even though it was the latter who paid the taxes, managed the ranches, and owned the mines that gave Spanish America its wealth. The following selection by a modern historian analyzes the situation.*

In 1808, a wave of Spanish patriotism and loyalty to the Crown had swept the colonies, and in meetings all over Spanish America people had sworn allegiance to the imprisoned Ferdinand VII and to those who governed in his name. Since then, the throne had been vacant for two years, and people had begun to think that it might long remain so. The colonial authorities who claimed to represent the caretaker government in Seville tried to conceal the news of that government's collapse, but without success. As news of the disaster spread, it brought in its wake an escalation of revolutionary activity.

The groups who now constituted themselves as local leaders also presented themselves as loyal subjects of the beleaguered Spanish Crown. For a number of reasons, such leaders were slow to push openly for independence. Great Britain

was unlikely to look with favor on such a move because of its Spanish alliance, and, for their part, the leaders of the new round of ad hoc [temporary] governing bodies viewed themselves not as rebels but as the rightful heirs of an authority that had entered an apparently permanent eclipse. There was no reason for them to emphasize a break with that authority when they intended to use it for their own purposes. Both colonial officials and insurgent leaders now struggled to present themselves as the legitimate heirs of the old order. . . .

After 1810, these prudent revolutionaries could no longer turn back, even had they so desired. The executions of the year before indicated the consequences of defeat. Wrapping themselves in the mantle of legitimate rule strengthened them against internal challengers, but the decisive battle had still to be won. Royal administrators, clergy, and military officers immediately opposed a Creole movement clearly inimical to their own interests, which depended on the continued vitality of Spanish imperial power. The

Tulio Halperín Donghi, *The Contemporary History of Latin America*, ed. and trans. John Charles Chasteen (Durham, NC and London: Duke University Press, 1993), pp. 50–51, 65–66.

result was a civil war led by these two opposing factions of the ruling class. Each side quickly sought allies in the larger population. The elite search for allies began, once again, in an entirely traditional manner when the new authorities simply ordered their subordinates to join the revolution. In New Granada [modern Colombia] and in Chile they encountered little opposition, but the situation was different in Peru, which remained securely under the control of a particularly able viceroy, and in Venezuela and the Río de la Plata, where fighting quickly erupted. . . .

In 1817, Simon Bolívar was the only leader capable of uniting the many regional chiefs created by the Venezuelan revolution. He had broken with the timid aristocratic revolutionaries of Caracas (partly by threatening to free the slaves who formed the base of their plantation economy) and demonstrated his ability to gain a following among the country people of the Andean region. He now set about broadening his support among the veteran rebels of the coastal region east of Caracas and, most decisively, among the horsemen of the Orinoco plains, who had defeated him in 1814. Entering Venezuela once again with a small force of three hundred men in 1817, the year of San Martín's invasion of Chile, Bolívar finally found the key to victory in an alliance with a new guerrilla chief of the Orinoco plains, José Antonio Páez. The horsemen of Páez were reinforced by the arrival of several thousand volunteers, including a (mostly Irish) Britannic Legion.

The alliance with Páez gave the revolution a base in the Venezuelan interior, but it caused dissension with the llaneros' [Colombian cattle ranchers] former adversaries, the veteran patriot fighters of the eastern coast, who were now of secondary importance in Bolívar's strategy. Finding Caracas too well defended, he took his army of three thousand across the Orinoco plains to attack the highlands of New Granada from behind, scaling the eastern slopes of the Andes, catching the royalist defenders of Bogotá by surprise, and shattering them at the decisive battle of Boyacá in 1819. This victory began the formation of the Republic of Colombia (usually called Gran Colombia by historians because it incorporated Venezuela and Ecuador, former dependencies of the viceroyalty of New Granada), which received a provisional institutional structure at the Congress of Angostura at the end of the year. Each of the partially liberated states of the federation would have a vice president in charge of the administrative tasks, while Bolívar, as president and "Liberator," continued the war against the enemy forces still in control of the Venezuelan coast. Meanwhile, news of the liberal revolution in Spain had weakened the cohesion of the royalist cause. In 1821, the Spanish forces abandoned Caracas, and word arrived that Bolívar's lieutenant Antonio José de Sucre had captured Quito. The defeat of the remaining royalist holdouts at Pasto, between New Granada and Quito, completed the liberation of Gran Colombia and freed Bolívar to lead the army south against the royalist bastion in the Andes of Peru.

During the Peruvian campaign, Gran Colombia came close to falling apart. The Congress of Cúcuta in 1821 discarded the federal organization of Angostura and imposed a centralized administration to be directed from Bogotá by Vice President Francisco de Paula Santander. The reformist initiatives of Santander encountered predictable resistance from such vested interests of the colonial order as the church and the slave-owning aristocracy. Merchants and artisans balked at his policy of free trade, which they correctly expected to favor British traders and manufacturers. The leaders of the revolution were hesitant to move too strongly against the conservative interests for fear of opening the door to the kind of social revolution that had occurred in the slave revolt of Haiti, an image never far from the minds of the Creole leadership in the region of the Caribbean.

The northern revolution thus returned to the tradition of moderate reform but was handicapped by the destruction of the previous decade of fighting and the burden of the Peruvian campaign. Nor did Santander have the support that the imperial structure had provided to earlier reformers. In the absence of such support, he could hardly overcome the opposition of the most powerful elements among the governed, who quickly began to send protests to Bolívar and to agitate for more local autonomy. Santander's authority in Venezuela was sharply curtailed by the influence of Páez. In Bogotá, the divisions recalled the first revolutionary cycle, when the United Provinces of New Granada had feuded with the Republic of Cundinamarca [a self-proclaimed government in central Colombia]. Santander had fought with the United Provinces against Cundinamarca at that time, a circumstance that did not endear him to the populace of Bogotá. Dissidents throughout tottering Gran Colombia pinned their hopes on the return of the Liberator. Without breaking with Santander, whose liberal convictions he did not share, Bolívar tacitly encouraged their appeals.

After reading this selection, consider these questions:

1. What happened in Spanish America when news arrived that King Ferdinand VII of Spain had been overthrown in 1808?
2. At the beginning of the nineteenth century, what were the Creoles' grievances against the *peninsulares*? Do you think they were justified?
3 Who were Simón Bolívar's supporters?

SELECTION 6:

Bolívar's Resignation

Simón Bolívar, who figures so prominently in the previous selection, holds the imagination of South American patriots much as George Washington in the United States. He was born in Venezuela of prominent Creole parents and completed his education in Spain. On his return to Venezuela Bolívar joined the movement for independence. He tried and failed several times in his attempts to drive out the Spaniards before success came his way.

In February 1819, Bolívar was able to resign his military command to the National Congress of Venezuela, but as pointed out above, the federal structure he envisioned did not last. The following speech delivered at Angostura gives an insight into his contribution to the independence movement in Spanish America.

Gentlemen:

Happy is the citizen who under the protection of the army of his command has convoked national sovereignty to exercise its absolute will! I, therefore, count myself among those most favored by Divine Providence since I have had the honor to gather the representatives of the people of Venezuela in this august Congress, the source of legitimate authority, depository of sovereign will and the arbiter of the destiny of the nation.

In transferring to the representatives of the people the supreme power with which I have been entrusted, I fulfill the wishes of my own heart, those of my fellow citizens and those of our future generations which expect everything from your wisdom, uprightness, and prudence. In discharging this sweet duty, I free myself from the overburdening of immense authority and the unlimited responsibility weighing upon my weak

Simón Bolívar, "Address at Angostura," in *The Dynamics of Nationalism*, ed. Louis L. Snyder (Princeton, NJ: D. Van Nostrand, 1964), pp. 285–86.

shoulders! Only a compelling necessity coupled with the commanding will of the people could have made me assume the tremendous and dangerous charge of *Dictator, Supreme Chief of the Republic.* But I can breathe easier now in handing back to you that authority, which I have succeeded in maintaining with so much risk, difficulty and hardships amid the most awful tribulations that could ever afflict any social political body.

The epoch in the life of the republic over which I have presided has not been a mere political storm; it has been neither a bloody war, nor yet one of popular anarchy. It has been indeed, the development of all disorganizing elements; it has been the flooding of an infernal torrent which has overwhelmed the land of Venezuela. A man, aye, such a man as I am, what check could he offer to the march of such devastation? In the midst of this sea of woes I have simply been a mere plaything of the revolutionary storm, which tossed me about like a frail straw. I could do neither good nor harm. Irresistible forces have directed the trend of our events. To attribute this to me would not be fair, it would be assuming an importance which I do not merit. Do you desire to know who are the authors of past events and the present order of things? Consult then the annals of Spain, of America, of Venezuela; examine the laws of the Indies, the rule of the old executives; the influence of religion and of foreign domination; observe the first acts of the republican government, the ferocity of our enemies and our national temperament.

Do not ask me what are the effects of such mishaps, ever to be lamented. I can scarcely be accounted for but as a mere instrument of the great forces which have been at work in Venezuela. However, my life, my conduct, all my acts, both public and private, are subject to censure by the people.

Representatives! You are to judge them. I submit the history of my tenure of office to your impartial decision; I shall not add one thing more to excuse it; I have already said all that could be my apology. If I deserve your approval, I have attained the sublime title of a good citizen, to me preferable to that of *Liberator*, given me by Venezuela, that of *Pacificator*, which Cundinamarca accorded me, and all the titles that the whole world could bestow upon me.

Legislators! I deposit in your hands the supreme command of Venezuela. Yours is now the august duty of devoting yourselves to achieving the happiness of the republic; you hold in your hands the scales of our destinies, the measure of our glory; your hands will seal the decrees insuring our liberty. At this moment the Supreme Chief of the Republic is nothing but a plain citizen, and such he wishes to remain until death. I will serve, however, in the career of a soldier while there are enemies in Venezuela.

The country has a multitude of most worthy sons capable of guiding her; talents, virtues, experience, and all that is required to direct free men, are the patrimony of many of those who are representing the people here; and outside of this sovereign body, there are citizens, who at all times have shown their courage in facing danger, prudence in avoiding it, and the art, in short, to govern themselves and of governing others. These illustrious men undoubtedly merit the vote of Congress, and they will be entrusted with the Government that I have just resigned so cordially and sincerely and forever.

After reading this selection, consider these questions:

1. Why does Bolívar claim he is happy to resign his position as head of the republic?

2. Does Bolívar think he controlled events during the war of independence?

3. What does Bolívar envision for the future of Venezuela?

UNIT 2

The Nineteenth Century

CONTENTS

MAP   124

CHAPTER 11:
The French Revolution and Napoleon: How Did They Change the
History of Europe?   126

CHAPTER 12:
European Industrialization and Urbanization: What Were the
Consequences?   137

CHAPTER 13:
Europe: How Did Nationalism Shape the Nineteenth Century?   147

CHAPTER 14:
Asia and Africa: What Were the Challenges of the Colonial Period?   156

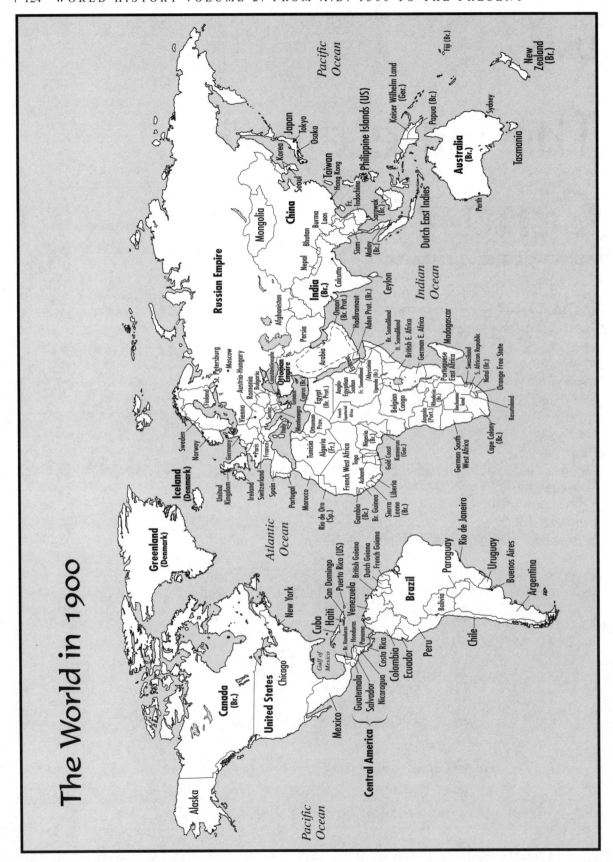

The World in 1900

Unit 2
The Nineteenth Century

A true turning point in European history appeared as a result of the French Revolution and the Napoleonic era. The idea of a monarch with no checks on his or her authority and of an upper class with its special privileges was vigorously challenged. When the smoke had cleared, Europe had become a society where a middle class represented the nation. This class expected to have a say in politics and was intent upon pursuing wealth through commerce and manufacturing, but in most European countries professing to be democratic only males owning property had the vote.

Another aspect of the period was the great expansion of population. Cities grew to hold more and more people as farmers abandoned their villages and moved into towns. The industrialization of the Continent offered employment to the new arrivals.

The growth of nationalism is a key to understanding the foreign relations of nineteenth-century Europe. Each state, with almost the full support of its population, sought to ensure its security by building large military establishments. After 1870 this safety net was supposedly strengthened by a series of international alliances.

Nationalism was also a central cause of spreading colonialism after 1870. Africans and Asians were now even more closely linked to markets in Europe and the Americas and found themselves at a great disadvantage when trying to keep the Europeans and Americans at bay.

The competition between the European states for the largest armies, the strongest economies, and the most territories was obviously a dangerous undertaking. However, it was only discovered just how risky it was as Europe moved toward the events of 1914 and the opening of World War I.

CHAPTER 11
The French Revolution and Napoleon: How Did They Change the History of Europe?

After the American Revolution, the second of the popular insurrections against the established government took place in France. This revolution marked a major change in the way many west Europeans thought about government. Essentially the French Revolution swept away the political and social structure of the Middle Ages. It replaced this structure with a new order that promised greater social justice and political equality. The slogan of the revolutionaries, borrowed from Rousseau, "Liberty, Equality, and Fraternity," summed up their highly idealistic goal. It is the French Revolution of 1789 that begins the modern history of Europe.

France at the close of the eighteenth century was a rich nation, holding the largest population of any country of Europe, but many people remained poor. These included the day laborers in the towns and the rural peasants who did not own their land. Oppressive taxation, rents, fees, and other financial exactions met them at every turn, prohibiting opportunities to get ahead.

SELECTION 1:

The Useless Nature of Nobility

The peasants were part of the Third Estate, the classification that encompassed everyone who was not a churchman or born into the nobility. These two classes composed the Second and First Estates and enjoyed all the privileges and none of the responsibilities of French citizenship. However, it was not only peasants who fell into the Third Estate, for it also included wealthy merchants and professionals, who deeply resented their position. It was in the Third Estate, those who read the authors of the Enlightenment, that revolutionary fervor was strongest.

A French priest, Abbé Emmanuel Joseph Sieyès, struck a responsive chord in the members of the Third Estate with his pamphlet What Is the Third Estate? *It served as a major piece of ammunition against the privileged classes. The following selection gives an excerpt from Sieyès's explosive little book.*

It suffices to have made the point that the so-called usefulness of a privileged order to the public service is a fallacy; that, without help from this order, all the arduous tasks in the service are performed by the Third Estate; that without this order the higher posts could be infinitely better filled; that they ought to be the natural prize and reward of recognized ability and service; and that if the privileged have succeeded in usurping all well-paid and honorific posts, this is both a hateful iniquity towards the generality of citizens and an act of treason to the commonwealth.

Who is bold enough to maintain that the Third Estate does not contain within itself everything needful to constitute a complete nation? It is like a strong and robust man with one arm still in chains. If the privileged order were removed, the nation would not be something less but something more. What then is the Third Estate? All; but an "all" that is fettered and oppressed. What would it be without the privileged order? It would be all; but free and flourishing. Nothing will go

well without the Third Estate; everything would go considerably better without the two others.

It is not enough to have shown that the privileged, far from being useful to the nation, can only weaken and injure it; we must prove further that the nobility is not part of our society at all: it may be a *burden* for the nation, but it cannot be part of it.

First, it is impossible to find what place to assign to the caste of nobles among all the elements of a nation. I know that there are many people, all too many, who, from infirmity, incapacity, incurable idleness or a collapse of morality, perform no functions at all in society. Exceptions and abuses always exist alongside the rule, and particularly in a large commonwealth. But all will agree that the fewer these abuses, the better organized a state is supposed to be. The most ill-organized state of all would be the one where not just isolated individuals but a complete class of citizens would glory in inactivity amidst the general movement and contrive to consume the best part of the product without having in any way helped to produce it. Such a class, surely, is foreign to the nation because of its *idleness*.

The nobility, however, is also a foreigner in our

Emmanuel Joseph Sieyès, *What Is the Third Estate?* trans. M. Blondel (New York and London: Frederick A. Praeger, 1964), pp. 56–58.

midst because of its *civil and political* prerogatives.

What is a nation? A body of associates living under *common* laws and represented by the same *legislative assembly*, etc.

Is it not obvious that the nobility possesses privileges and exemptions which it brazenly calls its rights and which stand distinct from the rights of the great body of citizens? Because of these special rights, the nobility does not belong to the common order, nor is it subjected to the common laws. Thus its private rights make it a people apart in the great nation. It is truly *imperium in imperio* [a state within a state].

As for its *political* rights, it also exercises these separately from the nation. It has its own representatives who are charged with no mandate from the People. Its deputies sit separately, and even if they sat in the same chamber as the deputies of ordinary citizens they would still con-stitute a different and separate representation. They are foreign to the nation first because of their origin, since they do not owe their powers to the People; and secondly because of their aim, since this consists in defending, not the general interest, but the private one.

The Third Estate then contains everything that pertains to the nation while nobody outside the Third Estate can be considered as part of the nation. What is the Third Estate? *Everything.*

After reading this selection, consider these questions:

1. What complaint does Sieyès make against the First and Second Estates?
2. What does the author think to be the role of the Third Estate?
3. What do you suppose Sieyès wanted to happen in France?

SELECTION 2:

Women in the French Revolution

It was not long before revolutionary fervor spilled over into the masses. Their concerns were much more basic than political change, for many went to bed hungry every night. The women of Paris were especially concerned that the price of bread, the staple in their family's diet, was so high that they could no longer afford it. If there was to be a revolution they knew what they expected from it. Taking the matter into their own hands a group of angry women charged the Paris city hall, the Hôtel de Ville, bent upon showing French politicians exactly how they felt. Next it was off to Versailles and King Louis XVI. The following selection, by a modern historian, describes what happened.

At dawn, on Monday, 5 October [1789], a group of between eight hundred and two thou-sand women converged—not par hazard [without a plan]—on the Hôtel de Ville, forced the doors, and rushed inside. They then proceeded to throw out the men who had helped them to force the door and denied any of them entry. Then they

Olwen H. Hufton, *Women and the Limits of Citizenship in the French Revolution* (Toronto: University of Toronto Press, 1992), pp. 7–11.

ransacked the place for arms and found a number of pikes though no ammunition. They seized as many papers and files as they could lay their hands on and prepared to make a huge bonfire of them in the hall, claiming that they contained nothing which would help them to get a better supply of bread. They were, according to one rendering, dissuaded from this by Maillard, a member of the National Guard, brother to a petty official at the Hôtel de Ville and, most pertinently, one of the *vainqueurs de la Bastille* [conquerors of the Bastille] and hence someone they trusted. Then either they persuaded him to lead them in their march to Versailles or, some versions say, he offered to go with them to keep an eye on them (but this was not his testimony). Whatever the agreement between Maillard and the women it also involved taking two cannons with them though they had no ammunition. Then the women set off for another rendezvous. Some went to the Invalides to see if any ammunition could be found, and the rest went home to round up as many women as they could. Children went around the parish of Saint Eustache with a bugle and a bell. In this way the number of women was doubled or perhaps even trebled. The least reliable part of the evidence pertains to numbers. There was a general rendezvous at the Place Louis XV and the women who gathered carried brooms and kitchen tools. Very few had pikes. It was almost afternoon before they set off with eight drummers at their head and with Maillard out front. They were followed several hours later by the National Guard headed by Lafayette, who, according to some accounts, did not want to go either because he feared what might happen in his absence in the capital or because he thought that the Guard might make the women's protest more dangerous. In some interpretations, he cedes to pressure from the Guard to express to the monarchy their outrage at the conduct of the Flanders regiment. Later still, after work, groups of men set off.

The women chanted and sang in festive mood about what they were going to do at Versailles. En route and in a persistent drizzle they picked up more women. There may have been some coercion involved but there was no lack of opportunity for the coerced to fall away. The crowd was far from unified. Some groups became angry, when at Sèvres, Maillard encountered opposition from shopkeepers over the supply of refreshments but without serious incident, and although this event has been used to imply that the women in question were *bacchantes* [drunk and out of control], the amount of wine involved was very small, so small, in fact, that the quantity serves as evidence for those who wish to reduce the size of the crowd of women who went on that day.

They arrived in Versailles around five o'clock, and after some discussion about their first move they took themselves to the National Assembly where some filled the tribunes; some remained outside and some looked for a place to camp. The weather was bad and the women were already soaked. Some of them removed their outer clothing and spread it out to dry in the assembly hall.

The Assembly had been warned to expect their arrival. It was in course of debating the issue of compensation for feudal rights, and the women became impatient. This was not business they deemed relevant. They were granted permission to deliver a petition and Maillard was their spokesman. The petition was a complaint in highly personalized terms about speculation in the grain trade. They said that they wanted an audience with the king. The occasion was initially quite orderly though it became rowdier as the women got used to their surroundings and they directed particularly offensive remarks towards the clergy who tried to bring them to order. *A bas les calotins* [Down with the priests]. Both the bishop of Langres and the Abbé Grégoire suffered particularly smarting insults. The delegation of about twelve, including a seventeen-year-old girl named Louise Chabry, was accompanied to the palace to see the king around seven o'clock. She is said to have mouthed the words 'du pain' [bread] and to have fallen in a breathless faint at the feet of the king (a nice damsel in distress touch but, one feels, one more suitable for Louis XV) and the king promised to see to it that the city was adequately provisioned.

The delegation returned and reported to the women and the majority were totally dissatisfied. What guarantees had the monarch offered? Had the delegation got anything in writing? The fainting seventeen-year-old was accused of accepting bribes and some accounts, though the least reliable, say that an attempt was made to hang her. [French historian Jules] Michelet strenuously denies this. However, the women were certainly angry. If they went back to Paris with no more than promises, how was their situation improved? The king was still locked in the court with his whore of a wife.

The few who thought they had done well enough went back home. Maillard took the opportunity to leave as well. The women were now split into groups. Many went back to the Assembly, which came to resemble an unruly camp. Women occupied the president's chair and imitated the proceedings in the midst of the drying clothes.

The politicians, or at least some of them, decided they must carry on and continued in desultory fashion. Some of the women slept on the Assembly benches. Others invaded the Hôtel de la Surintendance and ministerial offices which gave them shelter from what was now driving rain. Inside the château, the king and his advisers were absorbed in discussion. The women's presence was disconcerting and there was news that a larger crowd was on the way. The flight of the royal family was discussed, but the king was not convinced of the need. By ten in the evening, news came to the Assembly that the king had accepted the constitution with its limitations on royal sovereignty. The women in the hall were not sure how this benefited them.

By ten o'clock the National Guard arrived and Lafayette told the king that order and his personal safety could only be guaranteed if he and his family came to the capital. The king would not agree. In the small hours the men arrived and in the semi-darkness the mood became uglier. Some of the crowd broke into the palace and tried to force entry to the queen's bedchamber. In the confrontation, two of the royal bodyguards were slain (not by women). At this stage of the mêlée the role of the women had conspicuously diminished though it is at this juncture that we hear from the more royalist accounts of men dressed up as women. The National Guard intervened and when order had been restored the king appeared publicly on the balcony before perhaps as many as then ten thousand people. He promised bread and, overwhelmed by the shouting, finally agreed to go back to the capital.

It was a triumphal procession. [French author Louis-Sébastien] Mercier says it was twenty thousand strong by the time it got to the Tuilleries [the royal palace], though again estimates of the numbers are not to be trusted.

After reading this selection, consider these questions:
1. What were the Parisian women's grievances that touched off their march on Versailles?
2. How did the National Guard and the National Assembly react to the women's march?
3. Why did the king agree to accompany the women back to Paris?

SELECTION 3:

Violence Claims the Revolution

The Revolution passed through a number of stages at approximately two-year intervals. These were the National Assembly, the Legislative Assembly, and the Convention. It was while the Convention was in power that in 1793 government by terror became the rule as the most radical revolu-

tionaries formed the Committee of Public Safety, as a modern historian describes in the following selection.

"It is impossible," declared Saint-Just in the name of the Committee of Public Safety, "for revolutionary laws to be executed if the government itself is not constituted in a revolutionary way." He therefore proposed that the Committee itself should take on the central direction of the entire state apparatus, subject only to the oversight of the Convention. Such "Revolutionary Government" would be temporary; but the government of France was declared revolutionary until the peace.

Thus began the most famous stage of the French Revolution, when in the course of nine months around 16,000 people perished under the blade of the guillotine. The cold, mechanical efficiency of the method had all Europe watching with fascinated horror. The Terror began—and ended far into 1794—with famous victims. Marie-Antoinette went to the scaffold, her defiant appearance in the tumbril memorably sketched by David, on 17 October. Two weeks later (31 October) 21 Girondins [representatives from Gironde], including [Jacques-Pierre] Brissot and [Pierre-Victurnien] Vergniaud, followed her, after a show trial cut short when the eloquence and debating skills of the accused threatened to prolong it indefinitely. They went to their deaths defiantly singing the "Marseillaise."

Those who had signed the secret protest against their purging in June were imprisoned as Girondins after its existence was revealed in the preparations for the trial; but Robespierre always blocked moves to have them too put on trial. Of those who had escaped in June, four went to the guillotine in Bordeaux, while [Jerôme] Pétion and Buzot shot themselves. Their bodies were later found, half-eaten by wolves. [Jean-Marie] Roland too committed suicide when he heard of his wife's execution in November. November also saw the execution of Égalité, no Girondin, but a prince of royal blood with an *émigré* son; and suspect figures from the past like [Antoine-

Pierre] Barnave, arrested a year previously when his 1791 intrigues with the queen were revealed; and [Jean-Sylvain] Bailly, still hated by the sansculottes for his part in the massacre of the Champ de Mars. For him a special guillotine was erected at the scene of the crime. The others all met their deaths where the guillotine now permanently stood, close to where Louis XVI's head had fallen in the place de la Révolution.

Even so, only 177 people were executed in Paris between October and the end of 1793. The pathetic spectacle of the once mighty and famous now brought low distracted attention from the thousands of less well-known provincials who made up the bulk of the Terror's victims. Just as the show trials in Paris were beginning, Lyons finally surrendered to the besieging armies after two months of bombardment and resistance during which its defense was increasingly reliant on royalist volunteers commanded by a returned *émigré*. Hoping to be relieved by a Piedmontese invasion from the east, the starving city had held out over the summer. . . .

On receipt of the news of its fall, on 12 October, the Committee moved a decree that Lyons should be destroyed. Its very name was to disappear, except on a monument among the ruins which would proclaim "Lyons made war on Liberty. Lyons is no more." "The collection of houses left standing"—for the destruction of the city was glossed later in the decree as the destruction of the houses of the rich—was to be renamed Freed-Town (*Ville Affranchie*). . . . Thousands of suspects were imprisoned as parties of sansculottes swept the city with "domiciliary visits," but by the end of November scarcely more than 200 "Federalists" had been condemned by the special courts. . . . By April 1,880 Lyonnais had been condemned. Arriving in the city with a detachment of the Paris Revolutionary Army on 22 January, a German adventurer who had joined them gazed in horror at:

whole ranges of houses, always the most handsome, burnt. The churches, convents, and all the dwellings of the former patri-

William Doyle, *The Oxford History of the French Revolution* (Oxford: Clarendon Press, 1989), pp. 252–54.

cians were in ruins. When I came to the guillotine, the blood of those who had been executed a few hours beforehand was still running in the street . . . I said to a group of sansculottes . . . that it would be decent to clean away all this human blood.—Why should it be cleared? one of them said to me. It's the blood of aristocrats and rebels. The dogs should lick it up.

After reading this selection, consider these questions:
1. What explains the Convention's turn to violence?
2. What do you suppose was behind the executions?
3. What lessons about human nature can be gained from studying the terror?

SELECTION 4:

A Critique of the Revolution

*E*dmund Burke, one of the most articulate politicians of Great Britain, viewed events in France as frightening. How could a people kill its king and attempt to tear down the traditions and customs of centuries? Burke put his ideas into a work titled Reflections on the French Revolution, *from which the following selection is excerpted.*

France has bought poverty by crime! France has not sacrificed her virtue to her interest, but she has abandoned her interest, that she might prostitute her virtue. All other nations have begun the fabric of a new government, or the reformation of an old, by establishing originally, or by enforcing with greater exactness, some rites or other of religion. All other people have laid the foundations of civil freedom in severer manners, and a system of a more austere and masculine morality.

France, when she let loose the reins of regal authority, doubled the license of a ferocious dissoluteness in manners, and of an insolent irreligion in opinions and practices; and has extended through all ranks of life, as if she were communicating some privilege, or laying open some secluded benefit, all the unhappy corruptions that usually were the disease of wealth and power. This

is one of the new principles of equality in France.

France, by the perfidy of her leaders, has utterly disgraced the tone of lenient council in the cabinets of princes, and disarmed it of its most potent topics. She has sanctified the dark, suspicious maxims of tyrannous distrust; and taught kings to tremble at (what will hereafter be called) the delusive plausibilities of moral politicians. Sovereigns will consider those, who advise them to place an unlimited confidence in their people, as subverters of their thrones; as traitors who aim at their destruction, by leading their easy goodnature, under specious pretenses, to admit combinations of bold and faithless men into a participation of their power. This alone (if there were nothing else) is an irreparable calamity to you and to mankind. Remember that your parliament of Paris told your king, that, in calling the states together, he had nothing to fear but the prodigal excess of their zeal in providing for the support of the throne. It is right that these men should hide their heads. It is right that they should bear their part in the ruin which their counsel has

Edmund Burke, *Reflections on the French Revolution*, vol. 24 of the Harvard Classics, ed. Charles W. Eliot (New York: P.F. Collier & Son, 1909), pp. 186–87.

brought on their sovereign and their country. Such sanguine declarations tend to lull authority asleep; to encourage it rashly to engage in perilous adventures of untried policy; to neglect those provisions, preparations, and precautions, which distinguish benevolence from imbecility; and without which no man can answer for the salutary effect of any abstract plan of government or of freedom. For want of these, they have seen the medicine of the state corrupted into its poison. They have seen the French rebel against a mild and lawful monarch, with more fury, outrage, and insult, than ever any people has been known to rise against the most illegal usurper, or the most sanguinary tyrant. Their resistance was made to concession; their revolt was from protection; their blow was aimed at a hand holding out graces, favors, and immunities.

This was unnatural. The rest is in order. They have found their punishment in their success. Laws overturned; tribunals subverted; industry without vigor; commerce expiring; the revenue unpaid, yet the people impoverished; a church pillaged, and a state not relieved; civil and military anarchy made the constitution of the kingdom; everything human and divine sacrificed to the idol of public credit, and national bankruptcy the consequence; and, to crown all, the paper securities of new, precarious, tottering power, the discredited paper securities of impoverished fraud and beggared rapine, held out as a currency for the support of an empire, in lieu of the two great recognized species that represent the lasting, conventional credit of mankind, which disappeared and hid themselves in the earth from whence they came, when the principle of property, whose creatures and representatives they are, was systematically subverted.

After reading this selection, consider these questions:

1. Why does Burke condemn the French revolutionaries for degrading religion? Do you agree with his position? Why or why not?

2. What potential for tyranny does Burke see in Revolutionary France? Do you agree with his position? Why or why not?

3. What evidence does Burke see that the French revolutionaries are undermining property rights?

SELECTION 5:

Napoleon's Invasion of Russia

The churning of the Revolution was at last spent by 1799 and had produced, of all unlikely results, a military dictatorship led by a general who was not even a Frenchman, Napoleon Bonaparte. Napoleon was born in Corsica and later attended the Military School of Paris. As a lieutenant in the army he found himself in the right place at the right time, espoused the Revolution, and rose to become a general.

In time a new French constitution allowed him to become first consul, and a second change in government named him emperor. An accomplished military strategist, Napoleon went from victory to victory, but in 1812 he made a fateful decision to invade Russia. This famous campaign receives notice in the following selection from a modern biography, Napoleon: The Myth of the Saviour.

The French troops crossed the Niemen at Kovno on 24 June. Napoleon swooped on Vilna to separate the Russian forces; he hoped to annihilate them one after the other and then dictate the terms of peace. But he found nothing. The Russian soldiers were withdrawing from the invader, leaving a desert behind them. Napoleon thought he would catch them at Smolensk on 17 August, but they avoided him again.

In two months no serious battle had been fought, meanwhile the strength of the Grande Armée was continually being sapped. A hundred and fifty thousand soldiers were already out of action. Sickness, desertion and lack of supplies caused the loss of some five to six thousand men a day. According to the evidence of the future Bishop of Butkevic who was in Lithuania at the time, the French seemed badly prepared. The dragoons who had become lancers had had to exchange their guns for lances which they did not know how to use; "horses reared, cavalrymen grew impatient"; equally "the lack of experience in shoeing the artillery horses in order to cross the frozen steppes in the north, necessitated the abandoning of many cannon." To satisfy French opinion, Napoleon had counted on Prussian and Polish resources only. The hostility of the Prussians, reservations in Poland, bad roads and insufficient harvests all played their part. Furthermore Napoleon failed to catch the enemy while his army disintegrated little by little, his men worn out by forced marches in too lengthy stretches.

The ideas advocated by Count Lieven and [Carl von] Clausewitz triumphed. After all, Clausewitz, who was now in the service of the Tsar, had asserted in the Russian military headquarters that Napoleon would perish, conquered by the gigantic dimensions of the Empire, if only Russia knew how to play her hand—this meant sparing her strength until the last moment and making peace under no circumstances. He recommended "the evacuation of the whole countryside up to Smolensk and that they only start to fight properly in this region."

This was to be the version circulated by the Russians after the campaign. In fact, Clausewitz, in his account of the campaign, has clearly shown that the scorched-earth tactics were only applied accidentally by headquarters. If the generals withdrew, it was, above all, through fear of confronting Napoleon and of being beaten by him, and not through calculation.

But would the holy city of Moscow allow itself to be taken without a battle? The old general, [Mikhail] Kutusov, was ordered to block the invader's path. He installed himself on the Moskva, to the south of Borodino. After a relentless and appallingly bloody battle, Napoleon broke through on 7 September. Tolstoy* was later to sing of the "Russian victory at Borodino." It is fairer to speak of the "French success on the Moskva" since, on the 14th, the Grande Armée entered Moscow. But the losses were considerable and, furthermore, an immense fire destroyed three-quarters of the city making it uninhabitable. Finally, [Russian emperor] Alexander firmly refused to negotiate.

Once again, Napoleon discovered national war, one which combines patriotism with religious fanaticism, and puts a whole people against the invader. War seen as a game of chess between decent people gave way to a conflict in which no holds were barred, where the rules were no longer respected.

Napoleon was cut off from his Empire by distance—a courier took fifteen days to liaise between Moscow and Paris. So, tired of waiting on Alexander's goodwill, and despite supplies which would have lasted through the winter, Napoleon gave the order to retreat in mid-October. On the 19th, the army evacuated the city. Nothing would have been lost, despite the heavy casualties already suffered, if Napoleon had not returned by the same route as he had come. Unfortunately for him, Kutusov forced him, by the Battle of Maloyaroslavets on 24 October, to take the Smolensk route across countryside which had been devastated first by the Russians and then by the French army marching on Moscow. What is more, the

Jean Tulard, *Napoleon: The Myth of the Saviour*, trans. Teresa Waugh (London: Weidenfeld & Nicolson, 1984), pp. 302–304.

*The great Russian novelist Leo Tolstoy, who in the 1860s wrote his masterpiece *War and Peace* about the French invasion.

soldiers were as heavily laden with booty as they were with supplies. Cold was added to hunger. After Smolensk the temperature fell to –20°C and even to –30°C. Interminable nights without fire or light. Daybreak revealed a long line of men wrapped in rags from head to foot (their shoes had long ago worn out), dragging themselves through the snow and leaving corpses, wagons and cannon in their wake. Anything was better than to fall into the hands of the Cossacks who harried the column. In his memoirs, a Russian officer, Boris Uxkull, tells how moujiks [partisans] bought French prisoners in order to throw them into cauldrons of boiling water or to impale them. They cost two roubles a man. Russian historiographers have dwelt insistently on the part played by partisans which seems to them to have been more decisive than the climate.

Even if the extent of the disaster has been exaggerated in the imaginations of many, the scenes of horror recounted by the survivors were not invented. The crossing of the Beresina by two bridges made of planks, which were set up in the icy water by Eblé's pontoneers, took a dramatic turn. [Russian soldier Comtesse de] Ségur described it:

The leaders, pushed by those who followed, pushed back by the guards or the pontoneers, or impeded by the river, were crushed, trampled under foot or hurled into the drifting ice of the Beresina. There arose from the immense and horrible throng, sometimes a deafening hum, sometimes a great clamor mixed with wailing and dreadful curses.

On 16 December, only eighteen thousand men apparently recrossed the Niemen; during the days that followed others arrived in small groups. The total losses in deaths, prisoners and deserters are estimated at one hundred and eighty thousand soldiers. It was three of the greatest disasters in history and its very magnitude has enhanced the Napoleonic legend.

After reading this selection, consider these questions:

1. What strategy did the Russians use against Napoleon?
2. Why did Napoleon believe the war would end after the capture of Moscow?
3. Why was the retreat of the French army such a disaster?

SELECTION 6:

Looking Back

*A*fter Waterloo, Napoleon in exile had a chance to look back on his life in conversations with one of his friends, Benjamin Constant de Rebecque, excerpted in the following selection.

"I wanted to rule the world, and in order to do this I needed unlimited power. . . . I wanted to rule the world—who wouldn't have in my place?

The world begged me to govern it; sovereigns and nations vied with one another in throwing themselves under my scepter."

[And in a later conversation:]

"When I took power, people would have liked me to be another Washington. Words come cheap, and no doubt those who made such glib

Napoleon Bonaparte, "Conversations with Benjamin Constant," in *The Mind of Napoleon*, ed. and trans. J. Christopher Herold (New York: Columbia University Press, 1955), p. 276.

statements were doing so in ignorance of the time and place, of men and things. If I had been in America, I would gladly have been a Washington, and without deserving much credit for it; indeed, I don't see how it could have been reasonably possible to act otherwise. But if Washington had been a Frenchman, at a time when France was crumbling inside and invaded from outside, I would have dared him to be himself; or, if he had persisted in being himself, he would merely have been a fool and would have prolonged his country's misfortunes.

As for me, I could only be a crowned Washington. And I could become that only at a congress of kings, surrounded by sovereigns whom I had either persuaded or mastered. Then, and then only, could I have profitably displayed Washington's moderation, disinterestedness, and wisdom. In all reason, I could not attain this goal except by means of world dictatorship. I tried it. Can it be held against me?"

After reading this selection, consider these questions:

1. How does Napoleon explain his desire to "rule the world"?
2. Do you think that Napoleon's comparison between himself and Washington is a fair one?
3. Do you see Napoleon's view of himself a justification for his ambition?

CHAPTER 12
European Industrialization and Urbanization: What Were the Consequences?

The nineteenth century was a pivotal point in European history for two related reasons. One was the introduction of industrialization to the Continent. This meant that the millennia-old ways of working were replaced by the energy of machines. Human and animal power no longer were the basic elements of work.

Industrialization drew a massive emigration of people from rural areas into cities. Here people lived close to work in the factories that sprang up first in Great Britain after 1780 and, two generations later, on the Continent. What disturbed many people was the obvious fact that the wealth generated because of industrialization was very badly distributed. While workers hardly received wages that allowed them to survive, the owners and managers enjoyed a standard of living that was the most comfortable ever before seen in European history.

SELECTION 1:

Population Out of Control

The gap between the new, wealthy European capitalists and the poverty of the factory workers was difficult to explain. Some blamed industry itself; others faulted the selfishness of the bourgeoisie, the class of owners and businessmen. Thomas Malthus, a clergyman at Albury, Surrey, while studying the problem, authored An Essay on the Principle of Population. *In his book, published in 1798, he contended that the problem lay in the fact that the growth in population kept people poor. Put bluntly, poor people have too many children; hence they never escape from poverty. He expressed part of his argument in this way, in the following selection.*

It is observed . . . that there is no bound to the prolific nature of plants or animals but what is made by their crowding and interfering with each other's means of subsistence. Were the face of the earth, he says, vacant of other plants, it might be gradually sowed and overspread with one kind only; as, for instance, with fennel: and were it empty of other inhabitants, it might in a few ages be replenished from one nation only; as, for instance, with Englishmen.

This is incontrovertibly true. Through the animal and vegetable kingdoms nature has scattered the seeds of life abroad with the most profuse and liberal hand; but has been comparatively sparing in the room and the nourishment necessary to rear them. The germs of existence contained in this spot of earth, with ample food, and ample room to expand in, would fill millions of worlds in the course of a few thousand years. Necessity, that imperious all-pervading law of nature, restrains them within the prescribed bounds. The race of plants and the race of animals shrink under this great restrictive law; and the race of man cannot by any efforts of reason escape from it.

In plants and animals the view of the subject is simple. They are all impelled by a powerful instinct to the increase of their species; and this in-

stinct is interrupted by no reasoning or doubts about providing for their offspring. Wherever, therefore, there is liberty, the power of increase is exerted; and the superabundant effects are repressed afterwards by want of room and nourishment, which is common to plants and animals; and among animals, by their becoming the prey of each other.

The effects of this check on man are more complicated. Impelled to the increase of his species by an equally powerful instinct, reason interrupts his career, and asks him whether he may not bring beings into the world for whom he cannot provide the means of support. If he attend to this natural suggestion, the restriction too frequently produces vice. If he hear it not, the human race will be constantly endeavoring to increase beyond the means of subsistence. But as by that law of our nature which makes food necessary to the life of man, population can never actually increase beyond the lowest nourishment capable of supporting it; a strong check on population, from the difficulty of acquiring food, must be constantly in operation. This difficulty must fall somewhere, and must necessarily be severely felt in some or other of the various forms of misery, or the fear of misery, by a large portion of mankind.

That population has this constant tendency to increase beyond the means of subsistence, and that it is kept to its necessary level by these causes, will sufficiently appear from a review of the

Thomas R. Malthus, *An Essay on the Principle of Population*, ed. Patricia James, 2 vols. (Cambridge: Cambridge University Press, 1989), vol. 1, pp. 10–11.

different states of society in which man has existed. But before we proceed to this review the subject will, perhaps, be seen in a clearer light if we endeavor to ascertain what would be the natural increase of population if left to exert itself with perfect freedom; and what might be expected to be the rate of increase in the productions of the earth under the most favorable circumstances of human industry. A comparison of these two rates of increase will enable us to judge of the force of that tendency in population to increase beyond the means of subsistence, which has been stated to exist.

It will be allowed, that no country has hitherto been known where the manners were so pure and simple, and the means of subsistence so abundant, that no check whatever has existed to early marriages from the difficulty of providing for a family, and that no waste of the human species has been occasioned by vicious customs, by towns, by unhealthy occupations, or too severe labor. Consequently in no state that we have yet known has the power of population been left to exert itself with perfect freedom.

Whether the law of marriage be instituted or not, the dictate of nature and virtue seems to be an early attachment to one woman; and where there were no impediments of any kind in the way of a union to which such an attachment would lead, and no causes of depopulation afterwards, the increase of the human species would be evidently much greater than any increase which has been hitherto known.

After reading this selection, consider these questions:

1. What does Malthus consider the difference between human reproduction and that of other animals?
2. Why is he pessimistic about the future of humanity?
3. Has Malthus been proven right or wrong since he published his book?

SELECTION 2:

Precious Metals as Wealth

Equally put to question was the very concept of what constituted wealth. For several centuries the mercantile system answered that query, positing that a nation's wealth was synonymous with the amount of precious metals that it held. Therefore, Europe's kingdoms did whatever they could to enhance their supply of bullion, convinced that this made them richer. But a corollary of mercantilism held that the amount of wealth in the world was an absolute. If one country obtained more, then another country had to lose. This was one of the major reasons for the fierce European competition for colonies in Asia and Africa, for it was expected that they should provide raw materials and markets for products produced in the homeland.

This accepted wisdom was challenged by a Scotsman, Adam Smith. In 1751 he became professor of logic and later of moral philosophy at the University of Glasgow. For ten years of retirement he worked on Wealth of Nations, for which he is so well remembered. Published in 1776 it argued, among other things, that a country is rich because it has natural resources and a labor force that can make use of them.

That wealth consists in money, or in gold and silver, is a popular notion which naturally arises from the double function of money, as the instrument of commerce, and as the measure of value. In consequence of its being the instrument of commerce, when we have money we can more readily obtain whatever else we have occasion for, than by means of any other commodity. The great affair, we always find, is to get money. When that is obtained, there is no difficulty in making any subsequent purchase. In consequence of its being the measure of value, we estimate that of all other commodities by the quantity of money which they will exchange for. We say of a rich man that he is worth a great deal, and of a poor man that he is worth very little money. A frugal man, or a man eager to be rich, is said to love money; and a careless, a generous or a profuse man, is said to be indifferent about it. To grow rich is to get money; and wealth and money, in short, are in common language considered as in every respect synonymous.

A rich country, in the same manner as a rich man, is supposed to be a country abounding in money; and to heap up gold and silver in any country is supposed to be the readiest way to enrich it. For some time after the discovery of America, the first inquiry of the Spaniards, when they arrived upon any unknown coast, used to be, if there was any gold or silver to be found in the neighborhood? By the information which they received, they judged whether it was worth while to make a settlement there, or if the country was worth the conquering.

Plano Carpino, a monk sent ambassador from the king of France to one of the sons of the famous Ghengis Khan, says that the Tartars used frequently to ask him if there were plenty of sheep and oxen in the kingdom of France. Their inquiry had the same object with that of the Spaniards. They wanted to know if the country was rich enough to be worth the conquering. Among the Tartars, as among all other nations of shepherds, who are generally ignorant of the use of money, cattle are the instruments of commerce and the measures of value. Wealth, therefore, according to them, consisted in cattle, as according to the Spaniards it consisted in gold and silver. Of the two, the Tartar notion perhaps was the nearest to the truth. . . .

Others admit that if a nation could be separated from all the world, it would be of no consequence how much or how little money circulated in it. The consumable goods which were circulated by means of money, would only be exchanged for a greater or a smaller number of pieces; but the real wealth or poverty of a country, they allow, would depend altogether upon the abundance or scarcity of those consumable goods. But it is otherwise, they think, with countries which have connections with foreign nations, and which are obliged to carry on foreign wars, and to maintain fleets and armies in distant countries. This, they say, cannot be done but by sending abroad money to pay them with; and a nation cannot send much money abroad, unless it has a good deal at home. Every such nation, therefore, must endeavor in time of peace to accumulate gold and silver, that, when occasion requires, it may have wherewithal to carry on foreign wars.

In consequence of these popular notions, all the different nations of Europe have studied, though to little purpose, every possible means of accumulating gold and silver in their respective countries. Spain and Portugal, the proprietors of the principal mines which supply Europe with those metals, have either prohibited their exportation under the severest penalties, or subjected it to a considerable duty. The like prohibition seems anciently to have made a part of the policy of most other European nations. It is even to be found, where we should least of all expect to find it, in some old Scotch Acts of Parliament, which forbid under heavy penalties the carrying gold or silver forth of the kingdom. The like policy anciently took place both in France and England.

After reading this selection, consider these questions:

1. Why is it customary for people to equate wealth with money?

Adam Smith, *Wealth of Nations*, in *The Library of Original Sources*, ed. Oliver J. Thatcher (Milwaukee: University Research Extension, 1901), pp. 399–401.

2. What is false in the understanding of wealth in this way?

3. What did countries in the past do to keep their share of precious metals from leaving?

SELECTION 3:

The Working Class in Nineteenth-Century England

Studies of working people in the British Isles involve painstaking research through government reports and factory and commercial account books. Working from this data, historians are able to generalize about the economic history of the times. E.P. Thompson has done just that in the following selection. Part of what he has discovered shows a very complex picture, as each industry had its own problems and opportunities. Because jobs were scarce, workers had to compete for employment in many occupations, causing skilled laborers to lose status and wages. To hold on to their positions, they had to compete with unskilled workers, many of them women and children, as well as machines.

The first half of the 19th century must be seen as a period of chronic under-employment, in which the skilled trades are like islands threatened on every side by technological innovation and by the inrush of unskilled or juvenile labour. Skilled wages themselves often conceal a number of enforced outpayments: rent of machinery, payment for the use of motive power, fines for faulty work or indiscipline, or compulsory deductions of other kinds. Sub-contracting was predominant in the mining, iron and pottery industries, and fairly widespread in building, whereby the "butty" or "ganger" [names given to the bosses from among the workers] would himself employ less skilled labourers; while children—pieceners in the mills or hurryers in the pits—were customarily employed by the spinner or the collier. . . .

Woodworkers and shoemakers could obtain

their own materials cheaply and owned their own tools, so that the unemployed artisan set up as an independent "garret-master" or "chamber-master," working his whole family—and perhaps other juveniles—round a seven-day week and hawking the products on his own account. Carpenters requiring a more costly outlay were reduced to "strapping-shops" where a sickening pace of gimcrack work was kept up under the foreman's patrol and where each man who fell behind was sacked. Tailoring workers, who could rarely purchase their own cloth, became wholly dependent upon the middlemen who farmed out work at sweated prices. Dressmaking—a notoriously "sweated" trade—was largely done by needlewomen (often country or small-town immigrants) in shops contracted by large establishments.

The building worker, who could neither buy his bricks nor hawk a part of a cathedral round the streets, was at the mercy of the sub-contractor; even the skilled "society" men expected to be laid

E.P. Thompson, *Making of the English Working Class* (New York: Pantheon Books, 1963), pp. 243, 258–59.

off in the winter months; and both classes of worker frequently attempted to escape from their predicament by direct speculative building—"the land," as [British economic historian Sir John Clapham] Clapham says "rented in hope, materials secured on credit, a mortgage raised on the half-built house before it is sold or leased, and a high risk of bankruptcy." On the other hand, the coach-builder, the shipwright, or engineer, who did not own all his tools nor purchase his own materials, was nevertheless better situated, by reason of the character of his work and the scarcity of his skill, to maintain or extend trade union defences.

A similar collapse in the status of the artisan took place in older provincial centres. There are many complexities and qualifications. On one hand, the boot and shoe industry of Stafford and of Northamptonshire had long lost its artisan character and was conducted on an outwork basis when the London shoemakers were still trying to hold back the dishonourable trade. On the other hand, the extreme specialisation of the Sheffield cutlery industry—together with the exceptionally strong political and trade union traditions of the workers who had been the most steadfast Jacobins [strong supporters of workers' rights]—had led to the maintenance of the skilled worker's status in a twilight world of semi-independence, where he worked for a merchant (and, sometimes, for more than one), hired his motive-power at a "public wheel," and adhered to strict pricelists. Despite the Sheffield Cutlers Bill (1814) which repealed the restrictions which had limited the trade to freemen and which left a situation in which "any person may work at the corporated trades without being a freeman, and may take any number of apprentices for any term," the unions were strong enough—sometimes with the aid of "rattening" and other forms of intimidation—to hold back the unskilled tide, although there was a continual threat from "little mesters," sometimes "illegal" men or self-employed journeymen, who sought to undercut the legal trade.

After reading this selection, consider these questions:

1. What seems to be the key that enabled some workers to hold on to their jobs as skilled laborers while others could not?
2. Does this selection prove that Malthus was right (selection 1)?
3. Does Thompson's view support the necessity for unions in industrialized countries?

SELECTION 4:
Bourgeoisie and Proletariat

The upper and middle classes' enthusiasm for industrialization and urbanization was not always shared by those who had to work in factories for long hours with little pay. Life for them and their families was very difficult and their hope for improvement bleak.

Thinkers of the age wrestled with the problem of the laborer's plight and came up with a number of solutions. Many involved government intervention to protect the health of workers, especially women and children. Others saw the formation of labor unions to balance the power of the industrialist as an answer. The most radical solutions urged a workers' revolution, by which the working class, the proletariat, would overthrow all of the institutions set up by the bourgeoisie, the propertied class.

A call for class revolution was issued by two Germans, Karl Marx and Friedrich Engels, in memorable dramatic prose in The Communist Manifesto. *Its opening paragraphs, excerpted in the following selection, seek to explain the issue.*

A specter is haunting Europe—the specter of Communism. All the powers of old Europe have entered into a holy alliance to exorcise this specter: Pope and Czar, Metternich and Guizot, French radicals and German police spies.

Where is the party in opposition that has not been decried as communistic by its opponents in power? Where the opposition that has not hurled back the branding reproach of Communism against the more advanced opposition parties, as well as against its reactionary adversaries?

Two things result from this fact:

I. Communism is already acknowledged by all European powers to be itself a power.

II. It is high time that communists should openly, in the face of the whole world, publish their views, their aims, their tendencies, and meet this nursery tale of the specter of communism with a Manifesto of the party itself.

To this end, communists of various nationalities have assembled in London and sketched the following Manifesto, to be published in the English, French, German, Italian, Flemish, and Danish languages.

The history of all hitherto existing society is the history of class struggles.

Freeman and slave, patrician and plebeian, lord and serf, guild-master and journeyman, in a word, oppressor and oppressed, stood in constant opposition to one another, carried on an uninterrupted, now hidden, now open fight, a fight that each time ended, either in a revolutionary reconstitution of society at large or in the common ruin of the contending classes.

In the earlier epochs of history, we find almost everywhere a complicated arrangement of society into various orders, a manifold gradation of social rank. In ancient Rome we have patricians, knights, plebeians, slaves; in the Middle Ages, feudal lords, vassals, guild-masters, journeymen, apprentices, serfs; in almost all of these classes, again, subordinate gradations.

The modern bourgeois society that has sprouted from the ruins of feudal society has not done away with class antagonisms. It has but established new classes, new conditions of oppression, new forms of struggle in place of the old ones.

Our epoch, the epoch of the bourgeoisie, possesses, however, this distinctive feature: it has simplified the class antagonisms. Society as a whole is more and more splitting up into two great hostile camps, into two great classes directly facing each other: bourgeoisie and proletariat.

From the serfs of the Middle Ages sprang the chartered burghers of the earliest towns. From these burgesses the first elements of the bourgeoisie were developed.

The discovery of America, the rounding of the Cape opened up fresh ground for the rising bourgeoisie. The East Indian and Chinese markets, the colonization of America, trade with the colonies, the increase in the means of exchange and in commodities generally, gave to commerce, to navigation, to industry, an impulse never before known, and thereby, to the revolutionary element in the tottering feudal society, a rapid development.

The feudal system of industry, under which industrial production was monopolized by closed guilds, now no longer sufficed for the growing wants of the new markets. The manufacturing system took its place. The guild-masters were pushed on one side by the manufacturing middle class; division of labor between the different corporate guilds vanished in the face of division of labor in each single workshop.

Meantime the markets kept ever growing, the demand ever rising. Even manufacture no longer sufficed. Thereupon, steam and machinery revolutionized industrial production. The place of manufacture was taken by the giant, modern industry, the place of the industrial middle class, by

Karl Marx and Friedrich Engels, *The Communist Manifesto,* in *Karl Marx: Essential Writings*, ed. Frederic L. Bender (New York: Harper and Row, 1972), pp. 240–43.

industrial millionaires, the leaders of whole industrial armies, the modern bourgeois.

Modern industry has established the world market, for which the discovery of America paved the way. This market has given an immense development to commerce, to navigation, to communication by land. This development has, in its turn, reacted on the extension of industry; and in proportion as industry, commerce, navigation, railways extended, in the same proportion the bourgeoisie developed, increased its capital, and pushed into the background every class handed down from the Middle Ages.

We see, therefore, how the modern bourgeoisie is itself the product of a long course of development, of a series of revolutions in the modes of production and of exchange.

Each step in the development of the bourgeoisie was accompanied by a corresponding political advance of that class.

After reading this selection, consider these questions:

1. How does the manifesto understand past history?
2. What does this interpretation of history neglect?
3. What does the future hold for the bourgeoisie according to Marx and Engels?

Selection 5:

Railroads and Steamships

Eighteenth-century Great Britain was the first country to industrialize, aided by the invention of the steam engine. It proved to be one of the most useful inventions, leading to the general use of mechanical power. Soon factories sprouted over the British countryside, built near the coal mines whose product fueled the machinery in the factories. In a matter of time the steam engine was put on wheels. In 1829, the first railroad, the Liverpool and Manchester Railway, began carrying people between these two cities. A second major step forward was made when the steamship became common on the seas, expanding international trade by huge amounts. A modern historian describes this in the selection below.

The railway was an innovation with a long period of slow development followed by one of sudden, tremendous growth. The potentialities of railways were obscured both by their technical unfamiliarity and by the economic difficulty of experimenting with them on an appreciable scale, owing to the very heavy initial outlay which was involved. It was therefore only to be expected that the introduction of public railways operated by steam locomotives should have been over short distances in districts where economic advance was most marked, and where, consequently, the need for better transport was most urgently felt and the cost of providing it could best be met. The earliest developments were in Great Britain and the eastern United States, but the success of local lines encouraged larger schemes there and, as soon as railways had demonstrated how much difference they could make to economic life, railway building was taken up rapidly

William Ashworth, *A Short History of the International Economy Since 1850* (London: Longman, 1952), pp. 62, 65, 68, 69, 70.

in most European countries. In the half-century before the First World War new railway construction reached its maximum, and railways spread far into the interior of some parts of every continent as a means of extending commerce. . . .

For more than half a century the railway was practically unchallenged as a means of inland transport, but from about 1920 its position was seriously affected by competition and, although the demand for transport as a whole continued to increase, the railways in many countries experienced little or no increase in their total traffic. The inland carriage of passengers and freight over long distances, both nationally and internationally, was still mainly effected by railways, though some inland waterways underwent a revival as motor-driven vessels brought new cost reductions. But a great deal of local traffic was carried by automobile. . . .

To the increased movement of goods internationally after the middle of the nineteenth century the outstanding contributions came from technical improvement in shipping and from the achievements of civil engineers in expanding port facilities. In the second half of the nineteenth century the chief improvements in shipping were the replacement of wood by iron and later by steel in construction, and the substitution of steam for sail. The steamship was in process of development throughout the nineteenth century, but came only slowly into general use, mainly because of the extravagant fuel consumption of early marine engines, which raised costs very

much on long voyages, so that the steamship was for many years used for little but river, coastal, and ferry traffic, and for such ocean traffic as could afford high charges.

Nothing of any importance except the North Atlantic passenger services came within this last category. But there was a great change from the eighteen-sixties, when the compound engine, which sharply reduced fuel consumption and costs, came into use. The potentialities of the steamship for general use were clearly demonstrated in 1865, when the Holt Line introduced a service between Liverpool and Mauritius, a distance of 8,500 miles, without any intermediate port of call. The opening of the Suez Canal in 1869 gave further encouragement to the adoption of the steamship, for it could not be used by sailing-ships, yet it offered great savings for traffic between Europe or America and the Far East. From this time steamship services began to be concerned mainly with cargo traffic.

After reading this selection, consider these questions:
1. What delayed the full use of railroads for transporting people and goods?
2. What happened to challenge the railroads' lock on inland transportation in the twentieth century?
3. What inventions contributed to the use of the steamship in the nineteenth century?

SELECTION 6:

The Progress of Industrialization

In the following selection, W.O. Henderson has summarized European and American industrialization and economic development. He notes the new interest in government circles to expand the opportunities for economic development. Politicians came to realize that a strong economy promoted internal stability and national prestige. Ordinary people because of *their savings helped power the expansion, providing the capital needed for a nation to build railroads, factories, and utilities to serve them.*

In the period 1840–70 the encouragement of industry and agriculture by the state and the founding of credit banks and joint-stock companies were probably the most significant incentives to economic progress on the European mainland. The slump of 1847 and the Revolutions of 1848 were followed by a period of economic expansion interrupted only by the depression of 1857 and the dislocation of the cotton industry during the blockade of the Southern states at the time of the Civil War in the United States. The authoritarian regimes holding power in countries such as Austria, France and Prussia in the period of reaction that followed the Revolutions relied upon the support of the middle classes and passed laws favorable to the expansion of industrial and commercial activities. In Prussia, for example, the reform of the mining laws lifted numerous restrictions which had long inhibited private mining enterprise. Throughout Europe the urban middle classes, still largely unable to participate directly in the political life of their countries, devoted their energies to economic undertakings.

In the 1850s and 1860s various factors greatly extended the market for European manufactured goods. The continued growth of population, the extension of railway networks in Europe and the United States, the introduction of iron steamships, the opening of the Suez Canal, and a re-newed bid for colonial possessions, all greatly benefited international trade. . . .

Bankers and financiers now played a vital role in fostering new enterprises. In the 1850s a new kind of finance house came into prominence, the Crédit Mobilier in France, the Darmstadt Bank in Germany, and the Kreditanstalt in Austria being among the most important examples. They attracted the savings of small investors and used them to buy shares in new industrial enterprises. In 1856 the French consul in Leipzig reported that in Germany "every town and state, however small it may be, wants its bank and its Crédit Mobilier."

These credit banks, which soon spread to Italy, Spain, Holland and other countries, were more closely involved with industry than the older British banks. Being the first nation to industrialize, Britain . . . "was able to build her plant from the ground up . . . beginning with rudimentary machines that were not too expensive for private purses and ploughing profits into growth and technological advance." In Britain joint-stock companies and credit institutions were less important than they proved to be elsewhere.

After reading this selection, consider these questions:

1. How are political decisions and an expanding economy connected?
2. Why are banks needed for economic growth?
3. What were reasons for economic expansion in the 1850s and 1860s?

W.O. Henderson, *The Industrialization of Europe: 1780–1914* (Harcourt, Brace & World, 1969), pp. 28–29, 31.

CHAPTER 13
Europe: How Did Nationalism Shape the Nineteenth Century?

Few people would debate that in nineteenth-century Europe it was nationalism that dominated the political scene. Nationalism, devotion to the nation, replaced whatever was left of religious allegiance as the identifying characteristic of European peoples. Men and women began to think in terms of "I am a Frenchman," "I am a German," or "I am an Irishman."

Nationalism is basically a state of mind, so those elements that make it up are difficult to sort out. Certainly a common language helps to define nationality—although people in New Zealand and Canada both speak English, yet there is no common bond of nationality between them. A shared history helps to define nationality, but exceptions again appear. So also do culture and religion help, but not definitively, forge a nation's self. An extremely important constituent of every nationality has certainly been a desire to have a land that can be called its own. Yet even this criterion is not always present. For example, European Gypsies have apparently never felt a need for their own country or government.

It has been ethnic majorities that declare what nationalism is about. This means that minorities in a nation often were considered "outsiders" and suffered from overt or covert discrimination. This was surely true for the Bretons of France, the Poles of Germany, and the Basques of Spain. Drawing ethnic boundaries in the nineteenth century put minorities at risk.

The rise of nationalism in Italy and Germany demanded self-determination in the former, a unified country in the latter. In the Habsburg, Ottoman, and Russian Empires it sought the establishment of independent states, freed from the central control of Vienna, Istanbul, and St. Petersburg, respectively. It is little wonder that in these capitals, nationalism received no encouragement, for to do so would mean the end of the eastern European empires. When World War I occurred that is exactly what happened.

SELECTION 1:

Building a Nation

In the following selection, author Anthony D. Smith looks at the ingredients that go into constructing nationalism. He defines those qualities that Europeans in the nineteenth century and Africans and Asians today must construct to build a sense of community. He uses the French term ethnie *to describe what patriots call the national consciousness. Can you think of reasons why* ethnie *is strong in some countries and weaker in others? Can you think of other factors that contribute to national consciousness?*

Once nationalists had set out on the road to nation-formation, the problem of cultural and social integration became paramount, along with that of ethno-political congruence. To achieve integration and legitimate a set of borders and a "homeland," myths of descent were needed, not only for external consumption, but for internal mobilization and co-ordination. These myths might, or might not, make sense to outsiders, depending on their prior attitudes; far more important was their role in fostering internal solidarity and the sense of territorial "rootedness." National unity requires both a sense of cohesion of "fraternity" and a compact, secure, recognized territory or "homeland"; all nationalisms, therefore, strive for such fraternity and homelands. But, since neither are born overnight or *ex nihilo* [out of nothing], both presuppose a long history of collective experience. So "history" becomes the focal point of nationalism and nation-formation. The "rediscovery" or "invention" of history is no longer a scholarly pastime; it is a matter of national honour and collective endeavour. Through the tracing of our history, "we" discover (or "rediscover") who we are, whence we came, when we emerged, who our ancestors were, when we were great and glorious, who our heroes are, why we declined. . . . But the rediscovery of the "na-

tional self" is not an academic matter; it is a pressing practical issue, vexed and contentious, which spells life or death for the nationalist project of creating the nation.

Because of this urgent and deep-seated need, modern nationalisms have had to resort increasingly to unifying ethnic myths, even when there are competing *ethnie* [national memories] from which the new national culture must be forged. It is true that ruling elites, fearful of importing a "Balkans" situation into Africa, have tried to suppress what they term "tribalism," and have equated *ethnie* with what European colonialists called "tribes." But their pronouncements have rarely been matched by their actions. In practice, they have had to allocate resources on ethnic grounds, assign administrative posts according to ethnic population proportions, and even render to each ethnic culture its due in the areas where the majority are from particular *ethnie*. Of course, this has not been a voluntary or even-handed policy. Dominant *ethnie* have usually reaped advantages greater than those of the minority *ethnie*, and in some cases, like Kenya, have occupied most of the strategic political positions.

At the same time, such a one-sided recourse to the traditions and personnel of the dominant ethnic community, itself a tilt towards an "ethnie model" of the nation, carries grave dangers. The alternative strategy is to construct a new "political culture" out of the various ethnic traditions within the territorial state, by combining myths

Anthony D. Smith, *The Ethnic Origin of Nations* (Oxford: Basil Blackwell, 1986), pp. 148–49.

and symbols, seeking common denominators in the past (colonialism, racial discrimination) and even inventing a distant common origin or "age of heroism" such as other nationalisms have admired. In effect, this means that the new territorial nation-to-be must acquire ethnic dimensions and characteristics, if it lacks them; in Rousseau's words, it must be given a "national character."

The upshot of our brief account of the formation of nations in the modern world is that all nations bear the impress of both territorial and ethnic principles and components, and represent an uneasy confluence of a more recent "civic" and a more ancient "genealogical" model of social and cultural organization. No "nation-to-be" can survive without a homeland or a myth of common origins and descent. Conversely no "*ethnie*-aspiring-to-become-a-nation" can achieve its goals without realizing a common division of labour and territorial mobility, or the legal equality of common rights and duties for each member, that is, citizenship.

After reading this selection, consider these questions:
1. What is needed for a people to become a nation?
2. Is it possible for a people to exist without a homeland? Can you cite some examples?
3. What are some symbols of American nationalism?

SELECTION 2:

Evils of the Revolutionary Spirit

The statesmen who ruled Europe after the Napoleonic era all opposed nationalism. They recognized that if nationalism succeeded it would mean the end of monarchies in multiethnic states where a dominant group held power to the exclusion of others. This was especially true in eastern Europe.

The strongest and most able of those resisting the growth of nationalism was Prince Klemens Metternich, the Austrian minister of foreign affairs from 1809 to 1848. His imprint was on every major political decision made in central Europe during this period. He devoted his policies to suppress any liberal or revolutionary movements that called for limits on the power of rulers or the breakup of multinational empires. In his memoirs, excerpted below, he discusses the "evils" of revolution and change that he feared would upset the thrones of Europe's kings.

The evil exists and it is enormous. We do not think we can better define it and its cause at all times and in all places than we have already done by the word "presumption," that inseparable companion of the half-educated, that spring of an unmeasured ambition, and yet easy to satisfy in times of trouble and confusion.

It is principally the middle classes of society which this moral gangrene has affected, and it is only among them that the real heads of the party are found.

For the great mass of the people it has no attraction and can have none. The labors to which this class—the real people—are obliged to de-

Memoirs of Prince Metternich, 1815–1829, ed. Richard Metternich, 5 vols. (New York: Howard Fertig, 1970), vol. 3, pp. 465–67.

vote themselves, are too continuous and too positive to allow them to throw themselves into vague abstractions and ambitions. The people know what is the happiest thing for them: namely, to be able to count on the morrow, for it is the morrow which will repay them for the cares and sorrows of today. The laws which afford a just protection to individuals, to families, and to property, are quite simple in their essence. The people dread any movement which injures industry and brings new burdens in its train.

Men in the higher classes of society who join the revolution are either falsely ambitious men or, in the widest acceptation of the word, lost spirits. Their career, moreover, is generally short! They are the first victims of political reforms, and the part played by the small number among them who survive is mostly that of courtiers despised by upstarts, their inferiors, promoted to the first dignities of the state; and of this France, Germany, Italy, and Spain furnish a number of living examples.

We do not believe that fresh disorders with a directly revolutionary end—not even revolutions in the palace and the highest places in the government—are to be feared at present in France, because of the decided aversion of the people to anything which might disturb the peace they are now enjoying after so many troubles and disasters.

In Germany, as in Spain and Italy, the people ask only for peace and quiet.

In all four countries the agitated classes are principally composed of wealthy men—real cosmopolitans, securing their personal advantage at the expense of any order of things whatever—paid state officials, men of letters, lawyers, and the individuals charged with the public education.

To these classes may be added that of the falsely ambitious, whose number is never considerable among the lower orders, but is larger in the higher ranks of society.

There is besides scarcely any epoch which does not offer a rallying cry to some particular faction. This cry, since 1815, has been *Constitution*. But do not let us deceive ourselves: this word, susceptible of great latitude of interpretation, would be but imperfectly understood if we supposed that the factions attached quite the same meaning to it under the different *régimes*. Such is certainly not the case. In pure monarchies it is qualified by the name of national representation. In countries which have lately been brought under the representative *régime* it is called development, and promises charters and fundamental laws. In the only state which possesses an ancient national representation [Great Britain] it takes reform as its object. Everywhere it means change and trouble.

After reading this selection, consider these questions:

1. Why does Metternich blame the middle class for stirring up nationalist sentiment?
2. Why does he claim that the masses of people have no interest in nationalism? Do you think he was correct in this assumption?
3. Why does Metternich have no use for constitutions?

SELECTION 3:

A Revolution on Trial

In 1848 Metternich's system of repressing nationalism and liberalism fell apart as revolution swept across Europe. In the cities, workers, students, and professionals demanded change, taking to the streets in mass demon-

strations. The police and army were called out, but their members were often sympathetic to those whom they were called upon to resist. Lives were lost in clashes between the opposing sides. Metternich had to flee Vienna leaving behind his house in flames.

In February 1848 the French set the spark as demonstrators in Paris sought to be free of the staid and corrupt government of their king, Louis-Philippe, and to set up a republic. Among them were Socialists who looked to Louis Blanc for inspiration. In the provisional government the Socialists had their way in setting up national workshops for the unemployed. National elections then followed, returning a National Assembly much more conservative than the Parisian partisans who wanted social change. Traditionalists in the National Assembly made the national workshops a special target. In June the National Assembly called on the army to take over Paris, and its soldiers effectively crushed the workers' social revolution, leaving four hundred dead and three thousand arrested. The leaders among Blanc's supporters and their followers were put under arrest and brought to trial. The testimony that follows is that of a railway worker conscripted to fight for the revolution.

Accused Hearing the recall I went out with my musket. They gave me some drinks and led me to the barricade blocking the way. There they [the Parisian leaders] said to me, "Look, are you going to shoot?" "Hell," I said, "what at?" "Are you going to shoot?" they repeated, "If not, you'll have to hand over your musket." And they took it away. The next day they made me take one from a wounded man. . . . I only fired twice.

Q: Why did you agree to fire?

R: I was carried away, like lots of others. The ones who wouldn't go along with them got called idlers and were maltreated.

Q: But did you not know that when you fired on Paris you were firing on your brothers?

R: Yes. But they told us it wasn't the same thing. A man like me up from the country, who had never heard these things talked about, had never seen anything, and who couldn't read or write—a man like me is easily led astray.

*An insurgent leader at the Barrières de Charenton . . . gave as the reason for the revolt the desire for a democratic and social republic. I asked him to explain what he meant by social; he replied . . . the right of workers to form associa-*tions and to take part, according to their ability, in public and private enterprises.

[In another trial the accused was an engineering worker.]

Accused Citizens, the Republic has always been my only idea, my only dream. Twice I have been thrown into jail for working for the setting up of the democratic republic. . . .

Q: What do you mean by a social Republic?

R: I mean a republic with social reforms. Universal suffrage has been decreed, but that doesn't do the people any good. It is an instrument that the people do not use, that they do not know how to use. I want free and compulsory education for all and the organisation of work through association; finally I want to ensure that the worker receives the product of his labour, a proportion of which is at present taken away from him by the man who provides the capital. Then there would be no poverty, and so there would be no Revolution to fear. If the authorities had done that instead of fruitlessly spending vast sums on the National Workshops there would not have been an uprising in June. The workers enrolled in the National Workshops would rather have done proper work than received money for doing nothing.

Roger Price, ed., *Documents on the French Revolution of 1848* (New York: St. Martin's Press, 1996), pp. 94–95.

After reading this selection, consider these questions:

1. Do you believe the testimony of the railway worker that he and many like him may have been coerced into the struggle?
2. Why do you think that in the country-side there was not the same enthusi-asm for the revolution?
3. Do you think that the national work-shops were possibly a solution to unemployment? Can you think of modern examples?

SELECTION 4:

The Prussian Revolution

By March 1848 the revolutionary fever had spread to the German states, especially Prussia, where there was a significant group of liberals who wanted German unification and constitutional government. King Frederick William IV hesitated to use troops against demonstrators in Berlin and agreed to call a constitutional assembly. Over time the conservatives surrounding Frederick William convinced him that he should act vigorously to restore his rule, with the result that the Prussian Constitution was issued by the king, not the National Assembly.

In the following selection, a modern historian reflects on why the liberals in Prussia failed, much like those in France.

In provincial and state parliaments, city councils, clubs and associations, and in the private correspondence of liberal notables, we can detect a new sense of crisis and opportunity. In this already volatile setting, the revolutionary violence which began in Italy and France during the first weeks of 1848 had an immediate catalytic effect. At the end of February, the news of the French monarchy's fall set off widespread political agitation and popular disorder east of the Rhine. For better or worse, people throughout central Europe were about to begin their first large-scale effort at effecting fundamental political change from below.

The energy and initial success of the revolution came from the fact that many different groups in German society were brought together by their dissatisfaction with the status quo. Like almost every modern revolution, 1848 was a "revolution of conflicting expectation," carried out by men who did not share a common vision of how discontents might be dissolved.

From the beginning, there were important differences between those who saw the revolution as primarily a political phenomenon aimed at constitutional reform and those who saw it as a way to relieve economic and social problems. The relative importance of and relationship between these groups, which Bruno Bauer called the "national" and "social" elements of the revolution, varied from place to place. In a few regions there was not a great deal of social unrest, and liberals remained the only visible spokesmen for change. But sometimes popular unrest swept aside or simply ignored the liberals: this happened in the south and west where peasants attacked manor houses to express their hatred of seigniorial

James J. Sheehan, *German Liberalism in the Nineteenth Century* (Chicago and London: University of Chicago Press, 1978), pp. 52–53, 55.

obligations and in cities where artisans destroyed machines which they felt threatened their livelihood; elsewhere men seized the opportunity created by the revolution to assault an unpopular official or protest against an unpopular policy. . . .

More important than the election law [for the National Assembly] and its application were those habits of mind and action which shaped Germans' relationship to their political system. It is hardly surprising that a political culture which had developed over decades was not suddenly transformed by an election campaign lasting a few weeks. In some areas (and these are the ones we tend to know the most about), the local leadership was able to generate considerable interest in the campaign. But elsewhere apathy and habits of deference persisted and popular involvement

in the political process remained rather low. Overall, it seems probable that less than half of the adult males in the population took advantage of their right to vote.

The election campaign in various parts of Germany suggests that a great many liberal leaders, no less than the masses of the electorate, remained closely tied to the habits of the prerevolutionary era.

After reading this selection, consider these questions:

1. What did German liberals expect from a revolution?
2. Why are revolutions always difficult?
3. Was the conservatism of the Germans similar to that of the French (selection 3)?

SELECTION 5:

The Argument for an Independent Italy

The growth of nationalist spirits and liberalism could not be curbed, neither by Metternich's arguments nor by the failure of the revolutions of 1848. Liberals continued to demand greater personal freedom and national unification, and among the middle class their arguments were persuasive.

Italy, like Germany, represented a geographic region still politically divided, but with much agitation for change. As an example of nationalist fervor, the writings of Giuseppe Mazzini could not be equaled. His target was the Austrian army that occupied the north of Italy and controlled, through threats, the rest of the peninsula. In 1845 Mazzini wrote the following letter to an Englishman describing the situation of Italy, but it was only in 1870 that Mazzini's goal of a united nation was finally achieved.

Italy is a vast prison, guarded by a certain number of jailers and gendarmes, supported in case of need

Giuseppe Mazzini, "Letter to Sir James Graham," in *Selected Writings*, ed. N. Gangulee (Westport, CT: Greenwood Press, 1974), pp. 70–71.

by the bayonets of men whom we don't understand and who don't understand us. If we speak, they thrust a gag in our mouths; if we make a show of action, they platoon us. A petition, signed *collectively*, constitutes a crime against the state.

Nothing is left us but the endeavor to agree in

secret to wrench the bars from the doors and windows of our prison—to knock down gates and jailers, that we may breathe the fresh life-giving air of liberty, the air of God. Then, a career by pacific means of progress will be open to us; then will begin our guilt and condemnation if we cannot bring ourselves to be content with it.

I am no partisan of that Jesuitical maxim, *the end justifies the means*; but I must confess, it seems to me equally absurd, equally unjust, to exalt into an axiom the opinion that on all occasions and at all times censures the application of physical force. It appears to me more rational to say—whenever a way remains open to you in a just cause for the employment of moral force, never have a recourse to violence; but when every moral force is seared up—when tyranny stretches so far as formally to deny you the right of expressing in any manner so ever what you conceive to be the truth,—when ideas are put down by bayonets,—then, reckon with yourself: if, though convinced justice is on your side, you are still in a weak minority, fold your arms and bear witness to your faith in prison or on the scaffold—you have no right to imbrue your country in a hopeless civil war: but if you form the majority, if your feeling prove to be the feeling of millions, rouse yourselves, and beat down the oppression by force. Cowardly to bow the head before brutal violence upholding injustice, when the arms that God has given you suffice for its overthrow, is to degrade yourself to the passive condition of the animal—to betray the sacred cause of truth and of God—to enthrone tyranny for ever, under the pretext of abhorring physical force.

You cannot in conscience apply the principles of your normal state to our peculiar condition. You cannot censure or repudiate our means of action, the only ones left us, without declaring by implication that despotism is a good thing, that the liberty of which England boasts is an evil.

I put to every true Englishman this simple question—imagine eighty thousand French soldiers stationed in Ireland or Scotland; imagine that, whenever the people in that portion of the English territory remaining free called for improvement, advancement, or change in their internal laws, the eighty thousand foreigners should intrude the points of their bayonets, and say, "In the name of brute force, stir not"; what would you do?

What would you do, we have made up our minds to do; we are trying to understand each other, so as to be able to do it. That sums up the Italian question: in that consists what today you brand with the name of *conspiracy*—what you would hail to-morrow, should we triumph, with the title of *glorious victory*.

After reading this selection, consider these questions:

1. How does Mazzini describe the Austrian occupation of Italy?
2. How does he justify the use of armed insurrection against his country's oppressors?
3. Does success or failure determine whether the "conspiracy" or "victory" shall be attached to a revolution?

SELECTION 6:

The Final Chapter for Garibaldi

The great hero of Italian patriots was Giuseppe Garibaldi, one of the most flamboyant revolutionaries of the nineteenth century. Garibaldi was constantly at war against the foreigners who governed Italy, and since his early insurrections ended in failure, much of his life was spent in exile. It was finally time for a victory in 1860. He landed first in Sicily and then took Naples away from its king, but the superior forces of Sardinia-Piedmont forced him to compromise. Instead of a republic, the kingdom of Sardinia-Piedmont merged with the conquests of Garibaldi in southern Italy.

But Rome and the territory around it still remained outside Italy. Until 1870 a French army guaranteed papal rule there. Then, with the outbreak of a war between France and Prussia, Garibaldi believed that the moment he had been waiting for had arrived. Despite the opposition of the Italian king and cabinet he called on volunteers to take Rome, disgusted with the hesitancy of the government in Florence, then serving as the Italian capital. It was several months later that, with all French troops withdrawn, the Piedmontese army entered Rome. (In 1929 the pope was given rule over tiny Vatican City.) The following is a modern historian's account.

Leaving the military men and the politicians arguing behind him, Garibaldi marched. Nearly all his old officers and his friends tried to dissuade him; but, encouraged to believe that all he had to do was to "fire a few musket shots even in the air" and the Italian army would be with him, he launched his attack, pushing past the papal forces at Monterotondo. His march, though, had been made too late. Louis Napoleon, given due warning of his intentions, had sent a strong French force back to Civitavecchia. Mazzini warned Garibaldi of his danger, and advised him to retire towards Naples and await a more favourable opportunity. But Garibaldi "obstinately marching to defeat was in no temper to listen to anybody, Mazzini least of all." And on 3 November he came upon the French army, armed with the new Chassepot-rifle and supported by papal troops, at Mentana.

"Garibaldi commanded his men in person," the American consul in Rome reported, "and endeavoured many times to check the retreat of his forces. They could not, however, stand against the greater coolness and steadiness of the advance of the regular troops. . . . It is generally reported in the Italian papers that the pontifical force was defeated and only saved by the presence of the French. This is utterly untrue."

There could be no doubt, though, that Garibaldi's ultimate defeat was overwhelming. His army suffered heavy casualties, lost 1,600 men as prisoners, and was driven back in confusion across the frontier.

Garibaldi was himself arrested for the last time, protesting in vain as the police pulled him out of the special train he had ordered to take him back to the coast, that the King and the politicians had encouraged him to attack Rome and then abandoned him. He was taken first to Varignano and then escorted back to Caprera [his home]. . . . Garibaldi looked an old man now. He was pale and thin, his face lined with pain and disappointment, and his hair and beard were almost white. He felt bitter and betrayed, resentful towards the politicians and the Court, the French, the Church, the Italian army and Mazzini, whom he blamed unjustly for the desertion from his force before the battle of Mentana, denying now that the man had ever been his master.

"In great need of money," as he put it, he settled down to write a novel, holding the pen with difficulty in his stiff fingers and on some days unable to grasp it at all.

It was a distressingly bad book.

After reading this selection, consider these questions:

1. Why was Italy still not a single nation up to 1870?
2. Why do you think Garibaldi paid little attention to others' advice?
3. When Rome did fall to Italian forces, it was a Piedmontese army that annexed it to Italy. Why do you suppose it had greater success than Garibaldi?

Christopher Hibbert, *Garibaldi and His Enemies* (Boston and Toronto: Little, Brown, 1965), pp. 355–57.

CHAPTER 14
Asia and Africa: What Were the Challenges of the Colonial Period?

In the late nineteenth and early twentieth centuries, Europeans controlled most of the surface of the earth. In 1800 they occupied 35 percent of the world's land, but by 1914 that figure had risen to 84 percent. This mastery was due to the military and technological inventions made in Europe and North America.

The colonial pattern allowed the Europeans, represented by a small number of merchants, military, and civil administrators, to live in comfort, as far as possible replicating the life they knew in Europe. Although in the early years of colonization Europeans had frequent contacts with native peoples, as the years passed and colonial numbers increased, they tended to live in self-contained cocoons, knowing only a relationship of servant to master. Racist views were accepted as matter of fact.

For colonized men and women, imperialism meant rapid change from a traditional way of life to one that brought them into the European cultural world, especially its capitalist economy. Traditional elites tended to hold on to their positions on the local level, but by its very definition imperialism meant that native peoples could not be considered equals. Nevertheless, an indigenous middle class did develop since managers were essential and the seeds of nationalism began to sprout in their consciousness. Eventually this nationalism and the trauma of World War II was to dissolve the colonial period of world history.

SELECTION 1:

The Impact of Colonialism

The following selection provides a general overview of colonialism by the historian E.J. Hobsbawm.

This still leaves us with the questions about the impact of western (and from the 1890s Japanese) expansion on the rest of the world, and about the significance of the "imperial" aspects of imperialism for the metropolitan countries.

The first of these questions can be answered more quickly than the second. The economic impact of imperialism was significant, but, of course, the most significant thing about it was that it was profoundly unequal, for the relationship between metropoles and dependencies was highly asymmetrical. The impact of the first on the second was dramatic and decisive, even without actual occupation, whereas the impact of the second on the first might be negligible, and was hardly ever a matter of life or death.

Cuba stood or fell by the price of sugar and the willingness of the USA to import it, but even quite small "developed" countries—say Sweden—would not have been seriously inconvenienced if all Caribbean sugar had suddenly disappeared from the market, because they did not depend exclusively on that area for sugar. Virtually all the imports and exports of any region in sub-Saharan Africa came from or went to a handful of western metropoles, but metropolitan trade with Africa, Asia and Oceania, while increasing modestly between 1870 and 1914, remained quite marginal. About 80 percent of European trade throughout the nineteenth century, both exports and imports, was with other developed countries, and the same is true of European foreign investments. Insofar as these were directed

overseas, they went mostly to a handful of rapidly developing economies mainly populated by settlers of European descent—Canada, Australia, South Africa, Argentina, etc.—as well as, of course, to the USA. In this sense the age of imperialism looks very different when seen from Nicaragua or Malaya than it does from the point of view of Germany or France.

Among the metropolitan countries imperialism was obviously of greatest importance to Britain, since the economic supremacy of that country had always hinged on her special relationship with the overseas markets and sources of primary products. In fact it is arguable that at no time since the industrial revolution had the manufactures of the United Kingdom been particularly competitive on the markets of industrializing economies, except perhaps during the golden decades of 1850–70. To preserve as much as possible of its privileged access to the non-European world was therefore a matter of life and death for the British economy. In the late nineteenth century it was remarkably successful in doing so, incidentally expanding the area officially or actually under the British monarchy to a quarter of the surface of the globe (which British atlases proudly colored red).

If we include the so-called "informal empire" of independent states which were in effect satellite economies of Britain, perhaps one-third of the globe was British in an economic, and indeed cultural, sense. For Britain exported even the peculiar shape of her post-boxes to Portugal, and so quintessentially British an institution as Harrods department store to Buenos Aires. But by 1914 much of this zone of indirect influence, especially in Latin America, was already being infiltrated

E.J. Hobsbawm, *The Age of Empire, 1875–1914* (New York: Pantheon Books, 1987), pp. 73–74, 76–77.

by other powers.

However, not a great deal of this successful defensive operation had much to do with the "new" imperialist expansion, except that biggest of bonanzas, the diamonds and gold of South Africa. This generated a crop of (largely German) instant millionaires—the Wernhers, Beits, Ecksteins, *et al.*—most of whom were equally instantly incorporated into British high society, never more receptive to first-generation money if it was splashed around in sufficiently large quantities. It also led to the greatest of colonial conflicts, the South African War of 1899–1902, which eliminated the resistance of two small local republics of white peasant settlers. . . .

Yet the Age of Empire was not only an economic and political but a cultural phenomenon. The conquest of the globe by its "developed" minority transformed images, ideas and aspirations, both by force and institutions, by example and by social transformation. In the dependent countries this hardly affected anyone except the indigenous elites, though of course it must be remembered that in some regions, such as sub-Saharan Africa, it was imperialism itself, or the associated phenomenon of Christian missions, which created the possibility of new social elites based on education in the western manner. The division between "francophone" and "anglophone" African states today exactly mirrors the distribution of the French and British colonial empires.

Except in Africa and Oceania, where Christian missions sometimes secured mass conversions to the western religion, the great mass of the colonial populations hardly changed their ways of life if they could help it. And, to the chagrin of the more unbending missionaries, what indigenous peoples adopted was not so much the faith imported from the West as those elements in it which made sense to them in terms of their own system of beliefs and institutions, or demands. Just like the sports brought to Pacific islanders by enthusiastic British colonial administrators (so often selected from among the more muscular products of the middle class), colonial religion often looked as unexpected to the western observer as Samoan cricket. This was so even where the faithful nominally followed the orthodoxies of their denomination. But they were also apt to develop their own versions of the faith, notably in South Africa—the one region in Africa where really massive conversions took place—where an "Ethiopian movement" seceded from the missions as early as 1892 in order to establish a form of Christianity less identified with the whites.

What imperialism brought to the elites or potential elites of the dependent world was therefore essentially "westernization." It had, of course, begun to do so long before then. For all governments and elites of countries faced with dependency or conquest it had been clear for several decades that they had to westernize or go under.

After reading this selection, consider these questions:

1. What made the relationship between the metropolitan country and its colonies an unequal one?
2. How did colonial people react to European control?
3. Was westernization a positive force in the colonies?

SELECTION 2:

The Opium Trade

Throughout the early nineteenth century Great Britain was the major industrial power of Europe. Its merchants covered the globe. Although India proved to be its most lucrative colony, opportunities to trade with China also beckoned the merchants who made up the British East India Company. The company, a private concern, found a novel way to conduct its trade with China. Instead of paying its bills in scarce gold coins, it would send opium into the country to settle its debts. By 1833 the value of this exchange netted the company £15 million.

Because of the obvious effects this was having on the population, in 1839 an energetic Chinese official, Lin Ze Xu, seized and burned the warehouses of the British merchants in south China, beginning what is known as the Opium War. Lin Ze Xu wrote to Queen Victoria the following memorandum to explain his action.

Looking over the public documents accompanying the tribute sent (by your predecessors) on various occasions, we find the following:—"All the people of my (i.e., the king of England's) country, arriving at the Central Land [or Inner Land, the Chinese name for their country] for purposes of trade, have to feel grateful to the great emperor for the most perfect justice, for the kindest treatment," and other words to that effect.

Delighted did we feel that the kings of your honorable nation so clearly understood the great principles of propriety, and were so deeply grateful for the heavenly goodness (of our emperor):—therefore, it was that we of the heavenly dynasty nourished and cherished your people from afar, and bestowed upon them redoubled proofs of our urbanity and kindness. It is merely from these circumstances, that your country—deriving immense advantage from its commercial intercourse with us, which has endured now two hundred years—has become the rich and flourishing kingdom that it is said to be!

But, during the commercial intercourse which has existed so long, among the numerous foreign merchants resorting hither, are wheat and tares, good and bad; and of these latter are some, who, by means of introducing opium by stealth, have seduced our Chinese people, and caused every province of the land to overflow with that poison. These then know merely to advantage themselves, they care not about injuring others! This is

a principle which heaven's Providence repugnates; and which mankind conjointly look upon with abhorrence! Moreover, the great emperor hearing of it, actually quivered with indignation, and especially dispatched me, the commissioner, to Canton, that in conjunction with the viceroy and lieutenant-governor of the province, means might be taken for its suppression!

Every native of the Inner Land who sells opium, as also all who smoke it, are alike adjudged to death. Were we then to go back and take up the crimes of the foreigners, who, by selling it for many years have induced dreadful calamity and robbed us of enormous wealth, and punish them with equal severity, our laws could not but award to them absolute annihilation! But, considering that these said foreigners did yet repent of their crime, and with a sincere heart beg for mercy; that they took 20,283 chests of opium piled up in their store-ships, and through [Sir George] Elliot, the superintendent of the trade of your said country, petitioned that they might be delivered up to us, when the same were all utterly destroyed, of which we, the imperial commissioner and colleagues, made a duly prepared memorial to his majesty.

Considering these circumstances, we have happily received a fresh proof of the extraordinary goodness of the great emperor, inasmuch as he who voluntarily comes forward, may yet be deemed a fit subject for mercy, and his crimes be graciously remitted him. But as for him who again knowingly violates the laws, difficult indeed will it be thus to go on repeatedly pardoning! He or they shall alike be doomed to the penalties of the new statute. We presume that

---

"Letter of Commissioner Lin to Queen Victoria," in *Modern Asia and Africa*, ed. William H. McNeill and Mitsuko Iriye (New York: Oxford University Press, 1971), pp. 112–13.

you, the sovereign of your honorable nation, on pouring out your heart before the altar of eternal justice, cannot but command all foreigners with the deepest respect to reverence our laws! If we only lay clearly before your eyes, what is profitable and what is destructive, you will then know that the statutes of the heavenly dynasty cannot but be obeyed with fear and trembling!

After reading this selection, consider these questions:

1. What does Lin Ze Xu resent about the British merchants in China?
2. What penalties fell upon a native Chinese convicted of using opium?
3. How did Lin Ze Xu handle the immediate problem of opium in China?

SELECTION 3:

The Attack on Delhi

Within India the British East India Company recruited native Indian Hindus and Muslims to serve in its private armies. Generally these forces were better paid and commanded than the Mughal armies of the maharajas. However, in 1857 a mutiny broke out in the ranks of the company's forces. Known as the Sepoy Rebellion, it was started by rumors that the use of newly issued bullets contained the fat of pigs—repugnant to Muslims—and of cows—a sacrilege to Hindus. Action commenced at Meerut and then passed to Delhi, where a British officer, N.A. Chick, recalls the events.

Meanwhile the regiments were ordered out, the guns loaded and every possible preparation made. The Brigadier harangued the troops in a manly style, told them that now was the opportunity to show their fidelity to the Company to whom they had shown fidelity, and by whom they had never been deceived. His brief, pithy address was received with cheers. The 54th especially seemed eager to exterminate the mutineers, and loudly demanded to be led against them. The Brigadier responding to their seeming enthusiasm, put himself at their head and led them out of the Cashmere Gate to meet the rebels, whose near approach had been announced.

As they marched out in gallant order, to all appearance proud and confident, a tumultuous array appeared advancing from the Hindun. In front

and in full uniform with medals on their breasts gained in fighting for British supremacy, confidence in their manner and fury in their gestures, galloped on about 250 of the 3rd cavalry troopers: behind them at no great distance, and almost running in their efforts to reach the golden minarets of Delhi, appeared a vast mass of infantry, their red coats soiled with dust, and their bayonets glittering in the sun. No hesitation was visible in all that advancing mass; they came on as if confident of the result. Now the cavalry approach nearer and nearer! At this headlong pace they will soon be on the bayonets of the 54th.

These latter are ordered to fire; the fate of India hangs on their reply. They do fire, but alas! into the air; not one saddle is emptied by that vain discharge. And now the cavalry are amongst them; they fraternize with them; they leave the officers to their fate; and these are remorselessly cut down wherever they can be found!

N.A. Chick, comp., and David Hutchinson, ed., *Annals of the Indian Rebellion, 1857–58* (London: Charles Knight, 1974), pp. 41–42.

After reading this selection, consider these questions:

1. What was the initial response of the British officers to the approach of the mutineers?

2. Why do you suppose the sepoys deceived their officers?

3. Why do soldiers sometimes desert?

SELECTION 4:

Great Britain and India

*A*fter the Sepoy Rebellion's eventual suppression in 1858 the London government elected to take over the direct control of India. The country now became part of the growing British Empire, convinced that it was all to the good of the Indians and the British. A modern historian explains in the following selection.

Most Englishmen in India seemed to feel the general principles guiding British administration, while subject to refinement and minor improvements, were satisfactory on the whole. As long as the natives did not rebel, and as long as India continued to be profitable for British public and private interests, the great majority of Englishmen were content with the autocratic character of the Raj [the name given the British rule]. For the indefinite future, there was no need to share political power with Indians. To do so would lessen India's economic and strategic value.

The value of the Indian connection was obvious and growing in the last two decades of the century. As one official wrote in 1892, "if British rule should end, the value of the interests affected would be so great that practically no adequate compensation would be possible." Englishmen had invested heavily in Indian agricultural and extractive industries, including tea, coffee, jute, indigo, and coal; they had bought shares in the Indian railways, some of which had had a guaranteed rate of profit and had been located to serve British manufacturing and military needs; they

were able to sell British textiles in a sizable market in competition with the young, unprotected Indian textile industry; and they owned the largest banks, insurance companies, export houses, and shipping lines. Almost one-fifth of the total British overseas investment was in India and about one-fifth of British exports went to India. In return, the Government of India sent about one-fifth of its annual revenues to Britain as payment for loans, investments, administrative services, and military supplies and personnel.

India was also vital to British economic and strategic interests in the rest of Asia and in east Africa. British Indian banks serviced British trade in the Indian Ocean and further east, and Indian labor was exported to build railways, mine minerals, and work on British plantations. In strategic terms, India was Britain's most valued possession, representing her "oriental barracks," a reservoir of military manpower, a subsidy for the cost of the British military establishment, and a potential second front against Russia. The Indian Army was used for imperial and expansionist purposes which the British public tolerated because India paid a major share of the cost. In the forty years after the Mutiny, the Indian Army went to China (1859), Ethiopia (1867), Singapore (1867), Hong Kong (1868), Afghanistan

John R. McLane, *Indian Nationalism and the Early Congress* (Princeton, NJ: Princeton University Press, 1977), pp. 22–23.

(1878), Egypt (1882), Burma (1885), Nyasa (1893), the Sudan (1896), and Uganda (1896).

Although the Indian taxpayers' share of the costs was gradually decreased in response to nationalist complaints, India was still required to contribute to Britain's non-Indian interests. As late as 1908, the Liberal secretary of state for India, Lord John Morley, agreed to the War Office's request to increase India's annual contribution to English army reserves from £420,000 to £720,000. When Lord [Horatio] Kitchener objected, the War Office replied:

> The principles of fair dealing enunciated by Lord Kitchener might be applicable enough to two independent states in alliance with each other. They are inapplicable to a dependency inhabited by alien races, our hold over which is not based on the general goodwill of those disunited races.

India, in other words, was held as she had been taken—by the sword.

The sword, it was hoped, would remain sheathed except to awe the native population, and the ordinary work of administration was performed by the civilians of the Indian Civil Service. The largely British I.C.S. was a powerful opponent of nationalist aspiration in its own right. The more than 900 members were a well-paid elite who looked forward to a varied and exotic career and the option of retiring with a generous pension after 25 years. All but a few Indians were kept out by giving the I.C.S. entrance examinations in England in subjects which ordinarily required years of schooling in England.

After reading this selection, consider these questions:
1. What made the British complacent about their position in India?
2. How did trade with India benefit the British?
3. How was the Indian army used to support British expansion?

Selection 5:

Africa in the Colonial Age

The continent of Africa began to attract European colonial powers late in the nineteenth century. Europeans surveyed African lands as sources for minerals, tropical plants such as rubber, and food crops. In addition there was an antislavery lobby that urged intervention to stop the slave trade that was still a fact of East Africa. In West Africa political and economic interests, spurred on by nationalists, resulted in a British and French occupation of the region. In this incisive analysis of the colonial system in West Africa, historian Michael Crowder makes the following points.

Superior weapons, a skilful manipulation of hostilities between African states or the internal divisions within them, enabled the Europeans to conquer West Africa with small forces and with comparative ease. For the most part Africans were cut off from sources of supply of modern European weapons and even had they been available lacked instructors to teach them how to use them. Too often they met the invaders with the same military tactics they used against each other. Cav-

Michael Crowder, *West Africa Under Colonial Rule* (Evanston, IL: Northwestern University Press, 1968), pp. 159, 165–66.

alry charges, hails of arrows or spears, and hand-to-hand fighting were no use against repeater rifles and Maxim guns. The great mud walls that would withstand a six-month siege by an African army crumbled before the European artillery.

Too little use was made by Africans of their superior knowledge of the terrain on which they were fighting. Only few leaders like Bai Bureh and Samory [native African rulers] knew that the only way to deal with superior forces was to use guerrilla tactics. The hardest to conquer were often not the great states with regular armies, but people like those of the southern Ivory Coast and the eastern states of Nigeria where invasion was resisted village by village.

But given the lack of unity in West Africa at the time, and the technological inferiority of the African armies, the Africans defended their independence with much greater vigor than has often been allowed. True some welcomed the European, but the general picture was of a people who fiercely resisted the invader with the few means at their disposal. . . .

Little time was left to colonial conquistadors of West Africa to consider the advantages and disadvantages of the systems of administration they decided to impose on the peoples whose lands they had occupied. In the first place they were largely ignorant of the nature of the societies they were about to govern; in the second place they were usually preoccupied with the next stage of the conquest. Even where they did have time to ponder the merits of a particular system of administration, there was little chance that they would remain in a specific area long enough to see it put into practice.

The administrations imposed by the occupying powers were necessarily *ad hoc* [temporary administrations] and greatly influenced by the personality of the man imposing them and the circumstances under which a particular area was occupied—by conquest or treaty. More important still was the character of the society to be governed: different techniques had to be employed to govern the large centralized state, the small independent village and the desert nomad tribe. So by 1906, with the Soko Caliphate [of Nigeria] finally subjugated, and most of the rest of West Africa

under European rule, there was to be found a bewildering variety of administrations.

Such heterogeneity naturally offended the Cartesian French [Descartes, a French philosopher, was known for his search for order], and even upset the tidy mind of the Empirical Briton. There was, furthermore, growing concern among the European colonial powers over the whole question of colonial responsibility: how could African peoples be governed so that both they and the colonial power would benefit from it? It must not be forgotten that during this period a searchlight was turned on the African colonies because of the scandals in King Leopold's Congo [Leopold, king of Belgium, had invested much of his wealth in the Congo] and there was increasing concern with the "Native Question." Thus E. D. Morel, one of Leopold's most ardent critics, also visited Nigeria in 1912 to see how that colony was administered, and he was received by the colonial authorities as though he were a general conducting an annual inspection.

During the early years of colonial rule there was considerable debate as to what type of colonial rule was desirable for Tropical Africa. This debate became most involved in France and has been summarized in a number of useful studies. The British debate was more restricted in character, and somewhat one-sided, since nearly all agreed that indirect rule, or the government of Africans through their own institutions, was desirable. . . .

From these debates, and from the practical experiences of the administrators on the spot, there emerged three dominant trends in colonial policy in West Africa which were to be characteristic of the period of colonial rule from 1918 to 1939. The first major trend in colonial policy as practiced in West Africa was that of *assimilation* or that body of colonial theory which advocated identity between the colony and the mother country, though the nature of this identity varied from one exposition to another. The second was that of *indirect rule*, or that body of theory which held that there could be no identity between such divergent cultures as those of Europe and Africa and that as a consequence the metropolitan power should rule its African subjects through their own institutions, since these were clearly the ones best suited to them. The third body of theory was one that resulted from dilemma. It could not accept assimilation as a realistic policy for the administration of peoples as culturally different as the African from the European; nor did it consider traditional institutions a suitable basis for the administration of colonies which were to be exploited to the mutual benefit of the indigenous inhabitant and the metropolitan power.

After reading this selection, consider these questions:

1. What gave European armies in West Africa the advantage?
2. Why was the administration of African colonies so haphazard?
3. What possibilities appeared for governing African colonies?

SELECTION 6:

Japan's Economy Under the Tokugawa Shoguns

Japan's first experience with Europeans began in 1542 when Portuguese sailors landed in the country. The Japanese at first welcomed the material goods and even the Christian faith of the foreigners. Then in 1603, when Ieyasu Tokugawa became the shogun, the welcome was withdrawn. He ordered the Christians to return to Buddhism and limited European merchants in the country. Later his grandson and successor in the shogunate threw out all the Portuguese, allowing only a single Dutch ship to anchor in the harbor of Nagasaki.

The attempt to isolate Japan served the Tokugawa shoguns well. They were able to hold unchallenged power. Such stability caused an increase in population and economic development on a considerable scale. The following selection is an assessment of the economy of the Tokugawa period.

One cannot estimate the country's production accurately, of course, though on Malthusian principles population is an indicator of sorts: it grew from about 18 million in 1600 to something like 30 million by 1850. . . .

It is clear from these very broad-brush statements that well before there was any stimulus from Western capitalism Japan had reached a stage of development from which modern economic growth was within its reach. The national economy had a high degree of integration. In the more advanced regions villagers were already making use of cash for purchases, rather than subsisting on what they grew and made themselves. Some of them were becoming landlords and entrepreneurs, marketing crops and fertilizer, manufacturing sake [rice wine] or textiles. In the towns there were merchants capable of handling large wholesale deals, organizing regular shipping routes, raising loans and transferring credits of significant size. . . .

About the short-term consequences of Tokugawa economic change there is less uncertainty.

W.G. Beasley, *The Rise of Modern Japan* (New York: St. Martin's Press, 1990), pp. 10–12.

The most conspicuous was its effect on government finance. Both Bakufu [the central government] and domains [lands where the emperor was the landlord] raised much the greatest part of their revenues in rice. Leaving aside the stipends they paid to samurai [the military class], their expenditures were largely in the money economy of the towns, where prices not only drifted steadily upward over the years, but also fluctuated widely at quite short intervals. Matching expenditure to revenue in these circumstances was beyond the capacity of most feudal officials, who turned to merchants for advice and to borrowing as a means of making good the occasional deficiencies. Before the end of the seventeenth century most administrations were heavily in debt. . . .

Of more significance for the future was the creation of monopolies, especially by domains, in which government not only provided a framework of authority, but also took a major share of the gains. Their basis was a partnership between the lord's treasury and the privileged merchants of the castle-town for the purpose of buying some specialized product of the region—not infrequently at fixed prices, paid in domain paper money—then "exporting" it to Osaka or other commercial markets. There were cases, like Kagoshima's [a region on the island of Kyushu] sugar crop, where the profits were enhanced by draconian rules against selling outside the monopoly and by seizing part of the crop by way of tax.

One result of this development, which reached its peak in the early decades of the nineteenth century, was to bequeath to post-Tokugawa Japan a modicum of commercial knowledge among samurai officials, together with a habit of intervention in the economy.

After reading this selection, consider these questions:

1. What explains the prosperity of Japan during the Tokugawa shogunate?
2. What advantages came from Japan's economic isolation?
3. Why do you think that in the United States, we have laws against monopolies, yet the Japanese welcomed them?

UNIT 3

A Century of Change

CONTENTS

MAP   167

CHAPTER 15:
World War I: What Explains Its Tragedy?   169

CHAPTER 16:
The Russian Revolution: How Did Communism Affect Russia?   179

CHAPTER 17:
World War II: What Were Its Origins and Its Impact on World Events?   189

CHAPTER 18:
The Cold War: What Explains the Conflict Between the Communist
Nations and the West After World War II?   199

CHAPTER 19:
Nationalism in Action: How Did It Cause the End of Empire and the
Creation of New Countries?   209

CHAPTER 20:
The Collapse of Communism in the Soviet Union and Eastern
Europe and Its Survival in China: What Other Forces Now Shape
the Modern World?   221

The World in About 1990

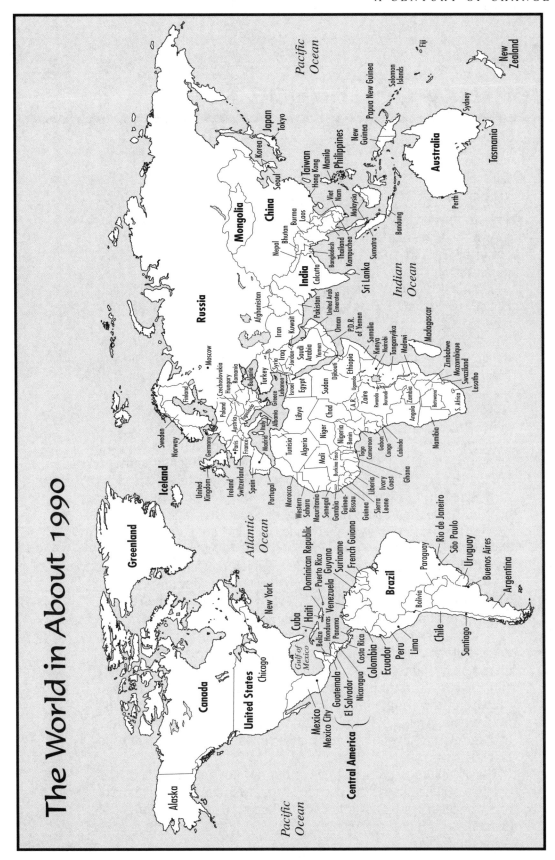

UNIT 3
A Century of Change

The third unit of this book of readings looks at the period from 1914 to the present. It aptly speaks of this part of the twentieth century as a time marked by rapid developments in world history. Never before did improvements come so fast in technology, transportation, and communication.

The First World War demonstrated to all the world that nationalism needed to have checks put upon it. The European diplomats who failed to stop the conflict never expected that a four-year bloodletting would occur. Neither were they prepared to learn that the great Russian Empire would fall into the hands of revolutionary Marxists. Humans always seem to forget that ideas, or the lack of them, often have unforeseen consequences.

It has often been stated that the seeds of World War II were sown at the Peace Conference of Paris that followed the First World War. Then the general dismay of the German people, coupled with the effects of the Great Depression, allowed Adolf Hitler to come to power. His goal of bringing all Europe under Nazi rule came close to realization, but it collapsed thanks to the Soviet army and the entry of the United States on the side of Great Britain and its allies.

After the shooting war had ended, a new cold war began as Joseph Stalin and Mao Zedong threatened the Western view of how the world should run. On both sides suspicions were raised about the threat of nuclear disaster, a prospect much diminished after Mikhail Gorbachev's reforms in the Soviet Union resulted in the collapse of communism in Eastern Europe.

New nations by the dozens appeared on the world map with the demise of the colonial system. Some came into being when the soldiers sent to fight in Europe returned home. Others had special circumstances surrounding their origins. Israel was established because of the emigration of Jews, survivors of the Holocaust and from hostile Arab neighbors. South Africa, though not a new nation, had an internal revolution, and a new constitution gave equality to black Africans.

Unfortunately a promised new order did not emerge. There was enough violence in the last decade of the twentieth century to make one wonder if lessons of tolerance and peace can ever be taught or learned.

CHAPTER 15
World War I: What Explains Its Tragedy?

Although no one wanted or expected it, in 1914 the major powers of Europe went to war. Unfortunately an alliance system forged by the German chancellor Otto von Bismarck in an effort to ensure stability had the opposite effect. Germany and its allies faced off against France and those nations bound by treaty with it. The result was a general war that devastated Europe for the next four years.

The most unstable and dangerous area of Europe was in the Balkans. As the Ottoman Empire began to crumble, both Russia and Austria-Hungary sought to fill the vacuum by sponsoring the creation of small Balkan national states or by annexing new territory outright. It was Russia that gave its support to Bulgarian and Serbian independence and Austria-Hungary that took over the region of Bosnia-Herzegovina.

When the heir to the Habsburg throne, Archduke Franz Ferdinand, and his wife, Sophie, visited the Bosnian capital of Sarajevo on June 28, 1914, Serbian nationalists were outraged. This was the national holiday of Serbia, a nation intent on annexing the Bosnians into its own small landlocked state. A Serbian nationalist, Gavrilo Princip, and fellow conspirators lay in wait for the archduke's car to pass. When the chauffeur of the imperial couple made a wrong turn and had to back up, Princip shot and killed them both.

The Austro-Hungarian government believed that Serbian officials had sponsored the attack and demanded that their agents conduct an inquiry in Belgrade, the Serbian capital. This the Serbian government refused and Europe stood on the brink of war. Russia promised to support Serbia, and Germany stood behind Austria-Hungary.

SELECTION 1:

The Last Chance for Peace

In the following selection, the modern historian Barbara Tuchman relates the events of the last days of peace. Germany had sent an ultimatum to St. Petersburg warning the Russians that they must cancel an order for mobilization.

At noon on Saturday, August 1, the German ultimatum to Russia expired without a Russian reply. Within an hour a telegram went out to the German ambassador in St. Petersburg instructing him to declare war by five o'clock that afternoon. At five o'clock the Kaiser [William II] decreed general mobilization, some preliminaries having already got off to a head start under the declaration of *Kriegesgefahr* (Danger of War) the day before. At five-thirty Chancellor Bethmann-Hollweg, absorbed in a document he was holding in his hand and accompanied by little Jagow, the Foreign Minister, hurried down the steps of the Foreign Office, hailed an ordinary taxi, and sped off to the palace. Shortly afterward General von Moltke, the gloomy Chief of General Staff, was pulled up short as he was driving back to his office with the mobilization order signed by the Kaiser in his pocket.

A messenger in another car overtook him with an urgent summons from the palace. He returned to hear a last-minute, desperate proposal from the Kaiser that reduced Moltke to tears and could have changed the history of the twentieth century.

Now that the moment had come, the Kaiser suffered at the necessary risk to East Prussia, in spite of the six weeks' leeway his Staff promised before the Russians could fully mobilize. "I hate the Slavs," he confessed to an Austrian officer. "I know it is a sin to do so. We ought not to hate anyone. But I can't help hating them.". . .

In Berlin on August 1, the crowds milling in the street and massed in thousands in front of the palace were tense and heavy with anxiety. Socialism, which most of Berlin's workers professed, did not run so deep as their instinctive fear and hatred of the Slavic hordes. Although they had been told by the Kaiser, in his speech from the balcony announcing *Kriegesgefahr* the evening before, that the "sword has been forced into our hand," they still waited in the ultimate dim hope of a Russian reply. The hour of the ultimatum passed. A journalist in the crowd felt the air "electric with rumor. People told each other Russia had asked for an extension of time. The Bourse writhed in panic. The afternoon passed in almost insufferable anxiety."

Bethmann-Hollweg issued a statement ending, "If the iron dice roll, may God help us." At five o'clock a policeman appeared at the palace gate and announced mobilization to the crowd, which obediently struck up the national hymn, "Now thank we all our God." Cars raced down Unter den Linden with officers standing up in them, waving handkerchiefs and shouting, "Mobilization!" Instantly converted from Marx to Mars, people cheered wildly and rushed off to vent their feelings on suspected Russian spies, several of whom were pummeled or trampled to death in the course of the next few days.

Once the mobilization button was pushed, the whole vast machinery for calling up, equipping, and transporting two million men began turning automatically. Reservists went to their designated depots, were issued uniforms, equipment, and arms, formed into companies and companies into

Barbara W. Tuchman, *The Guns of August* (New York: Macmillan, 1962), pp. 73–75.

battalions, were joined by cavalry, cyclists, artillery, medical units, cook wagons, blacksmith wagons, even postal wagons, moved according to prepared railway timetables to concentration points near the frontier where they would be formed into divisions, divisions into corps, and corps into armies ready to advance and fight. One army corps alone—out of the total of 40 in the German forces—required 170 railway cars for officers, 965 for infantry, 2,960 for cavalry, 1,915 for artillery and supply wagons, 6,010 in all, grouped in 140 trains and an equal number again for their supplies. From the moment the order was given, everything was to move at fixed times according to a schedule precise down to the number of train axles that would pass over a given bridge within a given time.

Confident in his magnificent system, Deputy Chief of Staff General Waldersee had not even returned to Berlin at the beginning of the crisis but had written to Jagow: "I shall remain here ready to jump; we are all prepared at the General Staff; in the meantime there is nothing for us to do." It was a proud tradition inherited from the elder, or "great," Moltke who on mobilization day in 1870 was found lying on a sofa reading

Lady Audley's Secret.

His enviable calm was not present today in the palace. Face to face no longer with the specter but the reality of a two-front war, the Kaiser was as close to the "sick Tom-cat" mood as he thought the Russians were. More cosmopolitan and more timid than the archetype Prussian, he had never actually wanted a general war. He wanted greater power, greater prestige, above all more authority in the world's affairs for Germany but he preferred to obtain them by frightening rather than by fighting other nations. He wanted the gladiator's rewards without the battle, and whenever the prospect of battle came too close, as at Algeciras and Agadir [crises in Morocco], he shrank.

After reading this selection, consider these questions:
1. Why was the kaiser reluctant to call for mobilization?
2. What made the army general staff so confident?
3. How do you explain the German dislike of the Slavs?

SELECTION 2:

Germany's War Aims

Much has been written about the mood of the people as the war approached. Somehow there was little awareness of what a general conflict might bring. For the moment there was simply excitement over the adventure that appeared to engulf all shades of opinion, even that of the Communists and Socialists who had pledged not to support "capitalist" wars. An historian explains the sentiments of the government in the selection below.

In the fantastic national upsurge of August, 1914,

considerations of war aims at first hardly entered into the consciousness of the mass of the German people. When, on August 4, the Reichstag met in solemn session in the White Hall of the royal palace in Berlin, and the Emperor, in his speech

Fritz Fischer, *Germany's Aims in the First World War* (London: Chatto & Windus, 1967), pp. 95–97.

from the throne, uttered his famous words: "It is no lust of conquest that inspires us," he was beyond doubt voicing the feelings of the overwhelming majority of the German people. The popular enthusiasm which erupted in patriotic songs in streets and squares was rooted in a sincere feeling of having been made victims of a long-planned "encirclement" and deliberate assault by jealous enemies—as the Chancellor said often enough on later occasions. Both public opinion and the government's official utterances strongly stressed the defensive character of the war; and up to the end of the war, and after it, all official commentaries explaining Germany's attitude during the war took this line. The German official version of the First World War as a purely defensive struggle has proved so enduring that it has largely determined the picture of German war aims, not only from 1914 to 1918, but down to our own days.

By adopting the slogan of a war of defense, the government seemed to have renounced in advance all conquests. But it was only a few weeks before the slogan changed from "war of self-defense" to the necessity—in view of the possibility of a second war—of acquiring "safeguards" and "guarantees" for the future of the German Empire before arms could safely be laid down. This led to a determination to achieve decisive victory and to dictate the peace terms to the enemy. On that same August 4 on which the Reichstag listened to the Emperor's speech from the throne, the *Militärwochenblatt* [the military newspaper] struck the key-note for the future in the following passage: "Russia has forced war on us unscrupulously for the sake of—Serbia! The hour of reckoning, which could not long have been postponed, has struck. . . . If God in His grace should grant us the victory, then . . . *vae victis* [woe to the conquered]!"

A week later, when the First Foot Guards left for the front, the Emperor swore not again to sheathe the sword until he could dictate the peace. In exactly the same way, the King of Bavaria, Ludwig III, promised to carry on the war "until the enemy accepts the conditions which we dictate to him."

The German government could not openly proclaim its desire to make profit out of the war, or at least to keep a free hand for the eventuality of ultimate victory; it had to present itself both to world public opinion and to its own people in an attitude consonant with its solemn announcement that its war was one of self-defense. This was particularly necessary in dealing with the Social Democrats who had been the strongest party in the Reichstag since 1912, and with the Socialist Trade Unions, which constituted the biggest political mass organization in imperial Germany. Without the Social Democrats and the workers controlled by it the war could not be carried on. This was why the mobilization of anti-Tsarist emotion among the Social Democrats was essential for the establishment of the national united front of August 4, 1914. In fact, even before war broke out, Bethmann-Hollweg was able to report with satisfaction to the Prussian Ministry of State, on July 30, that feeling was "generally good" and that

he believed himself entitled to conclude from his conversations with the deputy Südekum that there was no reason to fear any particular trouble from the Social Democrats or their party leaders. There would be no question of a general strike or of partial strikes or of sabotage.

The Conservatives, at least, who had at that time to be counted as a government party, were from the first firmly resolved not to exclude conquests by war. The Social Democrats, who, by virtue of their special position in imperial Germany, were the one party capable of speaking up in the Reichstag, proposed on August 4 to include in their statement, to be read out by Hugo Haase (President of the party and of its parliamentary representatives), a passage to the effect that the Social Democrats would oppose any attempt to make a war of conquest out of the conflict. Laborious negotiations followed, and Count Westarp, the spokesman for the Conservatives, forced the Social Democrats to revise their attitude by threatening that if they made such a declaration, he would answer Haase's speech with another which, in the nature of things, could only be directed against the "impossible and internationally detrimental passage" about the war of conquest. The Social Democrat deputies retreated and contented themselves with a vague remark that peace must be restored after the security of Germany's frontiers against foreign enemies had been established.

After reading this selection, consider these questions:

1. Do you think the German claim that the war was defensive a valid one?
2. Why was there more talk of territorial expansion once the conflict started?
3. How did the different political parties react to the war?

SELECTION 3:

Intellectual Responsibility

The enthusiasm for the war has been studied at length by numerous historians. Some have argued that the intellectual atmosphere contributed to the outbreak of the war and therefore deserves condemnation. In the following selection, Roland N. Stromberg takes exception to that view.

The intellectual atmosphere had very little to do with the beginning of the war. In a lecture rightly calling attention to the need for more study of this atmosphere, James Joll has argued that historians need to "re-create the climate of opinion in which political leaders operated." But it is doubtful that the political leaders concerned in the vital decisions of July and early August paid much attention to this factor. The game was not one of thinking about whether to go to war or not and then asking whether public opinion wanted this or would put up with it; it was rather one of responding to urgent situations abroad, beginning with the Austrian response to the assassination on June 28 and continuing with decisions in St. Petersburg, Berlin, and Paris about whether to support an ally, fearful of the consequences if they did not.

Statesmen were immersed in their own world. We may suppose that had there been a powerful adverse reaction, they might have been forced to find another route. For them, obviously, war was by no means unthinkable. But in fact there *was*

something of an adverse response early in the crisis, meetings and demonstrations against the war were held in France and Germany July 27–29, and the Socialist International called a meeting of its executive council. British opinion seemed overwhelmingly antiwar down to August 4, and many a person shared Carl Zuckmayer's amazement that he had viewed war with "disgust and loathing" only three days before he was inflamed with passion for battle and rushed to enlist.

The screaming crowds which poured into the streets, some shouting "À Berlin!", or surrounding Buckingham Palace for days, while other crowds cheered the Kaiser through the streets of Berlin—"as though a human river had burst it banks and flooded the world"—followed rather than preceded the declarations of war. They were unleashed, having been latently, more than consciously, present. . . .

Much evidence belies the trite explanation of the war as a breaking forth of evil, whether Christian Original Sin or, more fashionably, Freudian inner aggressions. Too many went forth joyfully to war, cheered on by happy crowds, in a spirit of adventure but also serious search for fulfillment in a worthy purpose, and for true companionship. Doubtless they found hell, but they did not go

Roland N. Stromberg, *Redemption by War: The Intellectuals and 1914* (Lawrence: Regents Press of Kansas, 1982), pp. 182–83, 190–91.

seeking it; rather than an itch to kill, hurt, or torture their fellow men, as Freud claimed, they felt something much more akin to love. Odd as this may seem, the testimony of articulate warriors bears it out. [French writer Romain] Rolland reflected that "a war in which two men such as Dehmel and Péguy can kill each other with the same fervor, for the liberty of the world, is it not monstrous and ridiculous." Doubtless it was, but it happened that way—Dehmel and Péguy were spiritual companions who would have loved each other personally, but they marched happily off to fight in rival armies, and in Péguy's case, of course, to die. [Both were poets.]

The war had psychic explanations, but these are not of the order of hidden springs of malevolence; they involve, rather, a powerful thirst for identity, community, purpose—positive and, in themselves, worthy goals, perverted and misdirected but not poisoned at the springs.

We would do well, then, to consider the possibility that war is something for which a moral substitute must be found (as William James memorably put it in 1898), rather than something whose roots must simply be destroyed. "The impulse to danger and adventure is deeply ingrained in human nature, and no society which ignores it can long be stable," Bertrand Russell concluded. There is abundant evidence that the impulse to fight and die in some holy cause still exists, transferred now to the streets, or to the jungles of some more "backward" society where the game of war can still be played. Violence, needless to say, is still with us, in the streets and home, as murder, rape, senseless destruction, terrorism.

After reading this selection, consider these questions:

1. Why does the author think it a mistake to blame the intellectual atmosphere as a cause of World War I?
2. How do you explain the enthusiasm that swept Germany and France at the start of the war?
3. Why can war become exciting for some people?

SELECTION 4:

All Quiet on the Western Front

*O*nce *the war of the trenches began, the misery of war spread among the men in the armies. No better description has been written of these years than that by Erich Maria Remarque in* All Quiet on the Western Front *(excerpted in the following selection). Remarque was drafted at eighteen into the German army and was wounded. These memories would be used later to develop his novel and its main character, recruit Paul Bäumer, who is killed on the eve of the armistice. As this passage opens, Bäumer is speaking.*

Although we need reinforcement, the recruits give us almost more trouble than they are worth.

Erich Maria Remarque, *All Quiet on the Western Front*, trans. A.W. Wheen (New York: Fawcett Crest, 1958), pp. 116–17, 119–21.

They are helpless in this grim fighting area, they fall like flies. Modern trench-warfare demands knowledge and experience; a man must have a feeling for the contours of the ground, an ear for the sound and character of the shells, must be able to decide beforehand where they will drop, how they will burst, and how to shelter from them.

The young recruits of course know none of these things. They get killed simply because they hardly can tell shrapnel from high-explosive, they are mown down because they are listening anxiously to the roar of the big coal-boxes falling in the rear, and miss the light, piping whistle of the low spreading daisy-cutters. They flock together like sheep instead of scattering, and even the wounded are shot down like hares by the airmen.

Their pale turnip faces, their pitiful clenched hands, the fine courage of these poor devils, the desperate charges and attacks made by the poor brave wretches, who are so terrified that they dare not cry out loudly, but with battered chests, with torn bellies, arms and legs only whimper softly for their mothers and cease as soon as one looks at them.

Their sharp, downy, dead faces have the awful expressionlessness of dead children.

It brings a lump into the throat to see how they go over, and run and fall. A man would like to spank them, they are so stupid, and to take them by the arm and lead them away from here where they have no business to be. They wear grey coats and trousers and boots, but for most of them the uniform is far too big, it hangs on their limbs, their shoulders are too narrow, their bodies too slight; no uniform was ever made to these childish measurements.

Between five and ten recruits fall to every old hand. . . .

Bombardment, barrage, curtain-fire, mines, gas, tanks, machine-guns, hand-grenades—words, words, but they hold the horror of the world.

Our faces are encrusted, our thoughts are devastated, we are weary to death; when the attack comes we shall have to strike many of the men with our fists to waken them and make them come with us—our eyes are burnt, our hands are torn, our knees bleed, our elbows are raw.

How long has it been? Weeks—months—years? Only days. We see time pass in the colorless faces of the dying, we cram food into us, we run, we throw, we shoot, we kill, we lie about, we are feeble and spent, and nothing supports us but the knowledge that there are still feebler, still more spent, still more helpless ones there who, with staring eyes, look upon us as gods that escape death many times. . . .

We show them [new recruits] how to take cover from aircraft, how to simulate a dead man when one is overrun in an attack, how to time hand-grenades so that they explode half a second before hitting the ground; we teach them to fling themselves into holes as quick as lightning before the shells with instantaneous fuses; we show them how to clean up a trench with a handful of bombs; we explain the difference between the fuse-length of the enemy bombs and our own; we put them wise to the sound of gas shells;—show them all the tricks that can save them from death.

They listen, they are docile—but when it begins again, in their excitement they do everything wrong.

Haie Westhus drags off with a great wound in his back through which the lung pulses at every breath. I can only press his hand; "It's all up, Paul," he groans and he bites his arm because of the pain.

We see men living with their skulls blown open; we see soldiers run with their two feet cut off, they stagger on their splintered stumps into the next shell-hole; a lance-corporal crawls a mile and a half on his hands dragging his smashed knee after him; another goes to the dressing station and over his clasped hands bulge his intestines; we see men without mouths, without jaws, without faces; we find one man who has held the artery of his arm in his teeth for two hours in order not to bleed to death. The sun goes down, night comes, the shells whine, life is at an end.

Still the little piece of convulsed earth in which we lie is held. We have yielded no more than a few hundred yards of it as a prize to the enemy. But on every yard there lies a dead man.

After reading this selection, consider these questions:

1. What have the years of war taught the veterans?
2. Why are the new recruits of such little help?
3. What has happened to the enthusiasm for the war?

SELECTION 5:

The Home Front

In the following selection, a description of life in Berlin during the conflict comes from the pen of Princess Evelyn Blücher, an English wife of a German officer, in the winter of 1917.

In a small town near here, a sad little ceremony took place the other day. The ancient church bell, which had rung the people from the cradle to the grave for 300 years and more, was requisitioned by the military authorities. The grief felt by the inhabitants was so great that they determined to do their ancient friend all the honor that they could; and after having performed the regular funeral service for the dead over it, a procession was formed, headed by the priest in his vestments, with his acolytes swinging their incense, and the inhabitants following the bell, which was covered with wreaths and flowers and handed over to the military authorities under tears and protestations.

As coffee and tea have entirely run out, all sorts of berries and leaves are being used as a surrogate. Chestnuts are used for feeding the deer, and it is interesting to see the children, who are not old enough to work otherwise, busy plucking and collecting the different things.

Nothing seems to be left unused—salad-oil being extracted from every kind of fruit-stone, and an excellent oil for greasing machinery is being pressed from the seeds of sunflowers. It is marvelous how much has been produced in this way, and it is only a pity we cannot use the latter for cooking and eating purposes too.

The difficulty of getting butter is increasing daily, and one has to use all one's power of persuasion to be able to entice a miserable quarter of a pound of it, after having begged in vain at quite a number of small peasants' houses. . . .

Lighting will prove a great problem this winter, as there is almost no petroleum or methylated spirits to be had; gas-light is next to impossible, on account of the small quantity allowed, and electric-light is also limited. I am surprised that people in the country do not attempt the old way of lighting by means of pine torches. True, they give more smoke than light, but it would be preferable to the gloom of the unlighted houses in the country.

This darkness is especially unpleasant for the people in the town who have to wait for the vegetables and fruit coming in from the country. Our gardener, who goes in daily, tells me that they stand for hours and hours patiently waiting to get but a pound of cabbage, onions, etc., which are all very scarce indeed. Luckily for the purchasers, maximum prices have been settled on all eatables, or it would be impossible for the poorer classes to get anything at all. . . .

The food question is always the most important topic of the day. The less there is of it, the more do we talk of it. The Austrians have already eaten up their stores, and are grumbling and turning to Germany for fresh supplies. It is rather like turning from a sandy desert to a rocky mountain for nourishment. And there is unfortunately no Moses to show us the way to a promising future.

We ourselves have little to eat but smoked meat and dried peas and beans, but in the towns they are considerably worse off. The potatoes have come to a premature end, and in Berlin the population have now a portion of 1 lb. per head a week, and these even are bad. The cold winds of this wintry June have retarded the growth of vegetables, and there is almost nothing to be had. We

Evelyn Blücher, *An English Wife in Berlin* (New York: E.P. Dutton, 1920), pp. 183–84, 231.

are all waiting hungrily for the harvest and the prospect of at least more bread and flour.

After reading this selection, consider these questions:

1. How has the war affected people at home?
2. Why is food running out?
3. What emotions in this reading tell of the weariness caused by the conflict?

SELECTION 6:

The Treaty of Versailles

At the conclusion of the war, German delegates came to Paris expecting to negotiate with the Allies the shape of the peace. Instead they discovered that there would be no discussion; the heads of states of the victors would unilaterally make up the treaty. Thus the Peace Conference ended with the Germans given a document, the Treaty of Versailles, to sign that required them to agree to all its many provisions (excerpted below). The peace was dictated, not negotiated, and the Germans received it with great bitterness.

Article 42. Germany is forbidden to maintain or construct any fortifications either on the left bank of the Rhine or on the right bank to the west of a line drawn 50 kilometres to the east of the Rhine. . . .

Article 45. As compensation for the destruction of the coal-mines in the north of France and as part payment towards the total reparation due from Germany for the damage resulting from the war, Germany cedes to France in full and absolute possession, with exclusive rights of exploitation, unencumbered and free from all debts and charges of any kind, the coal-mines situated in the Saar Basin. . . .

Article 49. Germany renounces in favour of the League of Nations, in the capacity of trustee, the government of the territory defined above. At the end of fifteen years from the coming into force of the present Treaty the inhabitants of the said territory shall be called upon to indicate the sover-

eignty under which they desire to be placed. . . .

Article 51. The territories which were ceded to Germany in accordance with the Preliminaries of Peace signed at Versailles on February 26, 1871 and the Treaty of Frankfort of May 10, 1871, are restored to French sovereignty as from the date of the Armistice of November 11, 1918.

The provisions of the Treaties establishing the delimitation of the frontiers before 1871 shall be restored. . . .

Article 87. Germany, in conformity with the action already taken by the Allied and Associated Powers, recognizes the complete independence of Poland. . . .

Article 159. The German military forces shall be demobilized and reduced as prescribed hereinafter. . . .

Article 160. By a date which must not be later than March 31, 1920, the German Army must not comprise more than seven divisions of infantry and three divisions of cavalry.

After that date the total number of effectives in the Army of the States constituting Germany must not exceed one hundred thousand men, including officers and establishments of depots.

Papers Relating to the Foreign Relations of the United States: The Paris Peace Conference, 1919 (Washington, DC: Government Printing Office, 1947), pp. 159, 162, 166, 183, 208, 319, 320, 413.

The Army shall be devoted exclusively to the maintenance of order within the territory and to the control of the frontiers.

The total effective strength of officers, including the personnel of staffs, whatever their composition, must not exceed four thousand. . . .

The Great Germany General Staff and all similar organisations shall be dissolved and may not be reconstituted in any form. . . .

Article 231. The Allied and Associated Governments affirm and Germany accepts the responsibility of Germany and her Allies for causing all the loss and damage to which the Allied and Associated Governments and their nationals have been subjected as a consequence of the war imposed upon them by the aggression of Germany and her allies.

After reading this selection, consider these questions:

1. What articles sought to keep Germany from ever making war again?
2. Do you think the demand for reparations was a fair request?
3. Was it realistic to expect Germany to disarm permanently?

CHAPTER 16
The Russian Revolution:
How Did Communism Affect Russia?

One of the key moments in early-twentieth-century Europe occurred when the Bolshevik Party came to power in Russia in 1917. This revolution transformed that nation and the other regions of the tsarist territories into the Union of Soviet Socialist Republics.

In chapter 12 we saw how Karl Marx and Friedrich Engels believed that a workers' revolution was bound to overthrow the capitalist system and its institutions. They thought that the revolt would happen in the highly industrialized countries of Germany and Great Britain, but history had another plan. It was in Russia, a nation still overwhelmingly agricultural, that a party following Marx's theories first achieved success.

This party called itself Bolshevik, which in Russian means "the majority." It was called that because another Marxist party offered it competition. Its members received the name Mensheviks, "the minority," despite the fact the Bolsheviks were actually the smaller of the two.

SELECTION 1:

The Bolshevik Revolution

At the head of the Bolsheviks was Vladimir Ilich Ulyanov, who took the name Lenin, a custom among Marxists to disguise their identity from the Russian police. Born in 1870, he became a Marxist at nineteen years of age and began propaganda activities that caused him to be arrested in 1895 and sent two years later into Siberian exile. Once freed, Lenin moved to western Europe, where he began editing and publishing revolutionary journals. In April 1917 he returned to Petrograd, the renamed Russian capital, where he took charge of the revolutionary movement after World War I had sapped the strength of both the tsarist and provisional governments that followed the resignation of Tsar Nicholas II. His aide was Leon Trotsky, who later wrote an appreciation of Lenin's leadership. There were many Marxists who believed that conditions for the proletarian revolution were not yet present. Lenin, on the other hand, urged action. Working through soviets, the assemblies of revolutionary workers and soldiers, he was able to prevail. Trotsky, who was a gifted writer, explains this in his strongly biased account that appears as the selection below.

Finally on October 24, Lenin wrote: "It is as clear as daylight that it is death now to postpone the revolution." And further on, "History will never forgive the procrastination of revolutionists, who could (and certainly would) win today but who chose to run the risk of losing much tomorrow—the risk of perhaps losing everything."

All these letters, every sentence of which was forged on the anvil of revolution, are of exceptional value in that they serve both to characterize Lenin and provide an estimate of the situation at the time. The basic and all-pervasive thought expressed in them is—anger, protest and indignation against a fatalistic, temporizing, social democratic, Menshevik attitude to revolution, as if the latter were an endless film. If time is, generally speaking, a prime factor in politics, then the importance of time increases one hundred-fold in war and in revolution. It is not at all possible to

accomplish on the morrow everything that can be done today. To rise in arms, to overwhelm the enemy, to seize power, may be possible today, but tomorrow may be impossible. But to seize power is to change the course of history.

Is it really true that such a historic event can hinge upon an interval of twenty-four hours? Yes, it can. When things have reached the point of an armed insurrection, events are to be measured not by the long yard of politics, but the short yard of war. To lose several weeks, several days, and sometimes even a single day is tantamount under certain conditions to the surrender of the revolution, to capitulation. Had not Lenin sounded the alarm, had not there been all this pressure and criticism on his part, had it not been for his intense and passionate revolutionary mistrust, the party would have probably failed to align its front at the decisive moment, for the opposition among the party tops was very strong, and the staff plays a major role in all wars, including civil wars.

At the same time, however, it is quite clear that to prepare the insurrection and to carry it out

Leon Trotsky, "The October Insurrection and Soviet 'Legality,'" in *Lessons of October*, trans. John G. Wright (New York: Pioneer, 1937), pp. 82–83.

under the cover of preparing for the Second Soviet Congress [the convention of Marxists] land under the slogan of defending it, was of inestimable advantage to us. From the moment when we, as the Petrograd Soviet, invalidated Kerensky's [Aleksandr Kerensky headed the Provisional Government] order transferring two-thirds of the garrison to the front, we had actually entered a state of armed insurrection. Lenin, who was not in Petrograd, could not appraise the full significance of this fact. So far as I remember, there is not a mention of it in all his letters during this period. Yet, the outcome of the insurrection of October 25 was at least three-quarters settled, if not more, the moment that we opposed the transfer of the Petrograd garrison; created the Military Revolutionary Committee (October 16); appointed our own Commissars in all army divisions and institutions, and thereby completely isolated not only the General Staff of the Petrograd zone, but also the Government. As a matter of fact, we had here an armed insurrection—an armed though bloodless insurrection of the Petrograd regiments against the Provisional Government—under the leadership of the Military Revolutionary Committee and under the slogan of preparing the defense of the Second Soviet Congress, which would decide the ultimate fate of the state power.

After reading this selection, consider these questions:

1. Why do you think that there was no agreement among the Marxists on when to begin the revolution?
2. Why does Trotsky contend that the revolution had already commenced when the order to move the Petrograd garrison to the front was ignored?
3. What is the role that Lenin played in urging action?

SELECTION 2:

The Bolsheviks Take Power

In the following selection, the American historian John Thompson has recreated the scene describing the last hours of the provisional government in Petrograd's Winter Palace. Its capture was a melancholy event, hardly a heroic scene.

Several things were happening at once, none of them quite believable yet each reflecting an aspect of the virtually silent, almost bloodless transfer of power that was to transform modern history. It was late evening on Wednesday, November 7. Mists rose from the Neva River in Petrograd. The night was dark, the moon obscured by clouds. It drizzled occasionally. For hundreds of yards along the river stretched the impressive buildings of the Winter Palace, the headquarters of the Provisional government.

Across the river a few Bolsheviks scampered along the parapets of the immense Peter and Paul Fortress. To signal the launching of the final attack on the Provisional government, a red lantern was to be displayed at the top of the Fortress. This would indicate that its guns were ready to shell the Winter Palace. But as if in some farce, no one could find a suitable lantern and the guns had to be oiled before they could be fired. Soon, however, Bolshevik leaders made sure a lantern was procured and the guns readied. Following a

John M. Thompson, *Revolutionary Russia, 1917* (New York: Charles Scribner's Sons, 1981), pp. 128–30.

blank shot from the cruiser *Aurora*, anchored downstream under revolutionary command, the shelling began. It inflicted little damage on the Winter Palace and affected the struggle for control of the Russian government hardly at all.

On the opposite side of the river, in the center of the city restaurants were open and the opera *Don Carlos* was playing to an enthusiastic audience. In the meeting room of the Petrograd City Duma [the city council], its leaders expressed dismay and anger at news that the ministers of the Provisional government were besieged in the Winter Palace. After some exhortatory statements, they decided to adjourn their session and march peacefully to the Palace to share the fate of their friends and political colleagues there. Bolshevik members of the Duma ridiculed the idea and refused to go along. With a mixture of dignity and bravado, several hundred Duma deputies and their supporters moved four abreast slowly down the main street of Petrograd toward the Winter Palace. Before long a Bolshevik patrol of sailors halted them. The demands of the Duma deputies to be let through were laconically refused. One sailor threatened to spank them; others urged them to go back quietly, which they soon did.

In the Palace itself the situation was confused and eerie. Bolshevik besiegers slipped through gates and windows, climbed over walls, and sneaked in through underground basements and corridors. At first most were apprehended and disarmed. But as the resolve of the few student officers, Cossacks, and members of the Women's Battalion protecting the government weakened and their ranks thinned through desertion, the tables were turned. The Bolshevik infiltrators began to capture the defenders or to talk them into surrendering. Later, at 2:45 A.M., the insurgents finally reached an inner room in the center of the Palace where the leaders of the Provisional government had been meeting off and on for many hours.

The cabinet ministers, determined to perform their last act in authority with dignity, seated themselves around the meeting table. The guards outside the door offered to resist the revolutionaries, but the ministers ordered them to avoid bloodshed and surrender peacefully. The door burst open and a slight, bespectacled man walked up to the table and said, "You are all under arrest." This was Vladimir Antonov-Ovseenko, one of the planners of the Bolshevik insurrection. Despite demands from some of his more aggressive and rowdy followers that the ministers be lynched, he formally registered his prisoners and then conducted them to imprisonment in the same Peter and Paul Fortress from which the delayed signal for attack had originally come.

The astonishing ease of the overthrow of the Provisional government has led to several different interpretations of this climactic moment in the Russian Revolution. Some have seen it as a skillful conspiracy by Lenin and his cohorts, planned and calculated as the final step in a fanatical drive for power. Others have argued that the Bolsheviks "lucked" into office, assisted by a series of fortuitous accidents and the unexpected and extensive ineptitude of their opponents. Still others have concluded that the Bolsheviks came to power because of their tactical and organizational flexibility and their ability to reflect and articulate the masses' fundamental aspirations. As so often in history, elements of each of these explanations ring true. The Bolshevik leaders, pushed by a determined Lenin, did organize and plan the insurrection. Good fortune and their opponents' weakness certainly helped them succeed. And for the brief period between mid-September and early December 1917, the Bolsheviks probably did speak for the majority of the politically aware population of Russia.

After reading this selection, consider these questions:
1. How do you explain the ease of the Bolshevik success?
2. What were the factors that caused the Winter Palace defense to be so weak?
3. Do you see any way that the provisional government could have remained in office?

SELECTION 3:

The Significance of the Russian Revolution

All Marxists believed that the theories for revolution as outlined by Marx and Engels were to be followed exactly. They had written the script. Now all that was necessary was for everyone to play his or her part. History was on the side of a revolutionary movement that would sweep the world. Once in power the Bolsheviks changed their name to Communists. Robert C. Tucker, a prominent American analyst of Marxism and of Soviet history, explains in the selection below.

Classical Marxism—the thought of Marx and Engels—projected the communist revolution as a universal phenomenon. The goal it foresaw for *Weltgeschichte* [world history] was a planetary communist society wherein man would realize his essential creative nature, having overcome by the socialization of private property the alienation endured in the course of history. Although the arenas of proletarian communist revolution would be national, the revolutionary movement would not and could not be confined to one or a few major nations but would overflow national boundaries, owing to the emergence of large-scale machine industry and a world market linking all countries in the bourgeois period.

Thus the *Communist Manifesto* spoke of the communist revolution as occurring initially in "the leading civilized countries at least." In a first draft of the document, Engels had written that "the communist revolution will not be national only but will take place simultaneously in all civilized countries, i.e., at any rate in Britain, America, France and Germany." The communist revolution would be no less universal than its historical predecessor, the bourgeois revolution, for the

world that the proletarians had to win was one that capitalism itself was fast transforming into a socioeconomic unit. . . .

The Russian communist mind held tenaciously to the view that the October Revolution was no mere national event but represented the beginning of a world revolution. "This first victory *is not yet the final victory*," declared Lenin in an address on the fourth anniversary of October. "We have made a start. When, at what date and time, and the proletarians of which nation will complete this process is not a matter of importance. The important thing is that the ice has been broken; the road is open and the path has been blazed." Even in his last essay, written in March, 1923, in the shadow of approaching death, Lenin optimistically maintained that "the whole world is now passing into a movement which must give rise to a world socialist revolution." Significantly, however, what then sustained his confidence in the final outcome was not the immediate prospect of a communist revolution in "the counter-revolutionary imperialist West" but developments in "the revolutionary and nationalist East." In the last analysis, he wrote, the upshot of the struggle would be determined by the fact that Russia, India, China, etc., accounted for the overwhelming majority of the population of the globe: "And it is precisely this majority that, during the past few years, has been drawn into the struggle for

Robert C. Tucker, "Paths of Communist Revolution, 1917–67," in *The Soviet Union: A Half Century of Communism*, ed. Kurt London (Baltimore: Johns Hopkins Press, 1968), pp. 3–5.

emancipation with extraordinary rapidity, so that in this respect there cannot be the slightest shadow of doubt what the final outcome of the world struggle will be. In this sense, the complete victory of socialism is fully and absolutely assured."

After reading this selection, consider these questions:

1. Why would Marx and Engels think revolution would happen all over the world?
2. How does Lenin regard the Bolshevik win in Russia?
3. Why do you suppose Lenin was wrong about the future of world revolution in 1923?

SELECTION 4:

Stalin vs. Trotsky

Once Lenin was incapacitated by a series of strokes, a contest began over who would succeed him as the leader of the Soviet Union. There were two major contenders: Leon Trotsky and Joseph Stalin. Stalin outmaneuvered his opponent and in 1927 even expelled Trotsky from the Communist Party.
Stalin's ability was in organization and in promoting the argument that socialism could succeed in one country. Trotsky's goal remained international revolution. The following selection by a pro-Trotskyist British historian explains.

Now the operative part of Stalin's thesis, the thing that was really new and striking in it, was the assertion of the self-sufficiency of the Russian revolution. All the rest was a repetition of traditional Bolshevik truisms, some of which had become meaningless and others embarrassing, but all of which had to be repeated, because they had the flavor of doctrinal respectability. The thing that was new in Stalin's argument represented a radical revision of the party's attitude. But the revision was undertaken in a manner that seemed to deny the very fact of revision and to represent it as a straight continuation of an orthodox line of thought, a method familiar from the history of many a doctrine. We shall not lead the reader further into the thick of this dogmatic battle. Suffice it to say that Stalin did his best to

graft his formula on to the body of doctrine he had inherited from Lenin.

More important than the dogmatic intricacies is the fact that now, in the seventh and eighth years of the revolution, a very large section of the party, probably its majority, vaguely and yet very definitely felt the need for ideological stocktaking and revision. The need was emotional rather than intellectual; and those who felt it were by no means desirous of any open break with Bolshevik orthodoxy. No revolutionary party can remain in power seven years without profound changes in its outlook. The Bolsheviks had by now grown accustomed to running an enormous state, "one-sixth of the world." They gradually acquired the self-confidence and the sense of self-importance that come from the privileges and responsibilities of power.

The doctrines and notions that had been peculiarly theirs when they themselves had been the party of the underdog did not suit their present

Isaac Deutscher, *Stalin: A Political Biography* (New York and London: Oxford University Press, 1949), pp. 288–89, 91.

outlook well. They needed an idea or a slogan that would fully express their newly won self-confidence. "Socialism in one country" did it. It relieved them, to a decisive extent, of a sense of their dependence on happenings in the five-sixths of the world that were beyond their control. It gave them the soothing theoretical conviction that, barring war, nothing could shake their mastery over Russia: the property-loving peasantry, the industrial weakness of the nation, its low productivity and even lower standard of living, all these implied no threat of a restoration of the *ancien régime* [the former government]. . . .

The truly tragic feature of Russian society in the twenties was its longing for stability, a longing which was only natural after its recent experiences. The future had little stability in store for any country, but least of all for Russia. Yet the desire at least for a long, very long, respite from risky endeavors came to be the dominant motive of Russian politics. Socialism in one country, as it was practically interpreted until the late twenties, held out the promise of stability. On the other hand, the very name of Trotsky's theory, "permanent revolution," sounded like an ominous

warning to a tired generation that it should expect no Peace and Quiet in its lifetime. The warning was to come true, though not in the way its author expected; but it could hardly have been heeded.

In his argument against Trotsky, Stalin appealed directly to the horror of risk and uncertainty that had taken possession of many Bolsheviks. He depicted Trotsky as an adventurer, habitually playing at revolution. The charge, it need hardly be said, was baseless. At all crucial moments—in 1905, 1917, and 1920—Trotsky had proved himself the most serious strategist of the revolution, showing no proneness to light-minded adventure. Nor did he ever urge his party to stage any *coup* in any foreign country, which cannot be said of Stalin.

After reading this selection, consider these questions:

1. Why did Stalin's slogan of socialism in one country sound attractive?
2. Why did Lenin have so much influence long after his death?
3. How does coming to power change a revolutionary party?

SELECTION 5:

The Five-Year Plan

In 1929 the first Five-Year Plan went into effect. Stalin, who now was virtual dictator of the Soviet Union, had decided that the economy of the country must be based on rapid industrialization. All of the energies of the nation were put into gear to secure that end.

To provide the capital for this rush toward heavy industry, the private farms of the Soviet Union were to be extinguished and the peasants herded onto collective or state farms. Rather than give up their property, millions of peasant farmers resisted. They burned their crops and slaughtered their livestock. In 1932 and 1933 over 6 million people died of starvation.

The following selection gives Stalin's comment on the Five-Year Plan. Nothing, of course, was said of the terrible human cost.

What is the Five-Year Plan?

What was the fundamental task of the Five-Year Plan?

The fundamental task of the Five-Year Plan was to transfer our country, with its backward, and in part medieval, technique, to the lines of new, modern technique.

The fundamental task of the Five-Year Plan was to convert the U.S.S.R. from an agrarian and weak country, dependent upon the caprices of the capitalist countries, into an industrial and powerful country, fully self-reliant and independent of the caprices of world capitalism.

The fundamental task of the Five-Year Plan was, in converting the U.S.S.R. into an industrial country, fully to eliminate the capitalist elements, to widen the front of socialist forms of economy, and to create the economic base for the abolition of classes in the U.S.S.R., for the construction of socialist society.

The fundamental task of the Five-Year Plan was to create such an industry in our country as would be able to re-equip and reorganize, not only the whole of industry, but also transport and agriculture—on the basis of socialism.

The fundamental task of the Five-Year Plan was to transfer small and scattered agriculture to the lines of large-scale collective farming, so as to ensure the economic base for socialism in the rural districts and thus to eliminate the possibility of the restoration of capitalism in the U.S.S.R.

Finally, the task of the Five-Year Plan was to create in the country all the necessary technical and economic prerequisites for increasing to the utmost the defensive capacity of the country, to enable it to organize determined resistance to any and every attempt at military intervention from outside, to any and every attempt at military attack from without.

What dictated this fundamental task of the Five-Year Plan; what were the grounds for it?

The necessity of putting an end to the technical and economic backwardness of the Soviet Union, which doomed it to an unenviable existence; the necessity of creating in the country such prerequisites as would enable it not only to overtake but in time to outstrip, economically and technically, the advanced capitalist countries.

Consideration of the fact that the Soviet power could not maintain itself for long on the basis of a backward industry; that a modern large-scale industry alone, one that is not only equal to but would in time excel the industries of capitalist countries, can serve as a real and reliable foundation for the Soviet power.

Consideration of the fact that the Soviet government could not for long rest upon two opposite foundations: on large-scale socialist industry, which *destroys* the capitalist elements, and on small, individual peasant farming, which *engenders* capitalist elements.

Consideration of the fact that until agriculture was placed on the basis of large-scale production, until the small peasant farms were united into large collective farms, the danger of the restoration of capitalism in the U.S.S.R. would be the most real of all possible dangers. . . .

What was the main link in the Five-Year Plan?

The main link in the Five-Year Plan was heavy industry, with machine building as its core. For only heavy industry is capable of reconstructing industry as a whole, as well as the transport system and agriculture, and of putting them on their feet. It was necessary to start the realization of the Five-Year Plan from heavy industry. Hence, the restoration of heavy industry had to be made the basis of the fulfillment of the Five-Year Plan.

After reading this selection, consider these questions:

1. What was necessary in the Five-Year Plan to construct a socialist society?
2. Why were private farms a threat to socialism?
3. In Stalin's opinion, what gave building a base of heavy industry priority over all other considerations?

Joseph Stalin, "Results of First Five-Year Plan," in *Selected Writings* (Westport, CT: Greenwood Press, 1942), pp. 242–44.

SELECTION 6:

Admission of Treason

In the late 1930s a paranoid Stalin decided to be done with all opposition. Old Bolsheviks who had fought through the revolution and had loyally served both Lenin and Stalin were brought to trial and accused of treason. It was hard for observers in foreign countries to imagine what was happening. Could so many people around Stalin have been ready to betray him? A major sign of guilt was the confessions of these men that they had, indeed, been foreign agents.

American political scientist Robert Conquest examines, in the following selection, the confessions submitted by the defendants during these trials.

The question naturally arises, not only why the accused made the confessions, but also why the prosecution wanted them. In the public trials, indeed, as Radek [Karl Radek, editor of the Soviet newspaper *Izveztiya,* was arrested in 1937] pointed out in the dock, there was no other evidence. A case in which there was no evidence against the accused, who denied the charges, would clearly be rather a weak one by any standards.

In fact, confession is the logical thing to go for when the accused are not guilty and there is no genuine evidence. For in these circumstances, it is difficult to make people appear guilty unless they themselves admit it. And it is easier to stage-manage a trial of this sort if one can be sure that no awkward defendant is going to speak up at unpredictable intervals.

In general, moreover, in the public trials of Zinoviev [Grigorii Zinoviev was tried and executed for plotting a murder in 1934] and the others, the confession method can be easily accounted for. Stalin wanted, not merely to kill his old opponents, but to destroy them morally and politically. It would have been difficult simply to announce the secret execution of Zinoviev. It would have been equally difficult to try him publicly,

without any evidence, on charges which he could vigorously and effectively deny.

Even if confessions seem highly implausible, they may have some effect on skeptics, on the principles that there is no smoke without fire and that mud sticks. Even if the confession is disbelieved, a defendant who humbly confesses and admits that his opponents were right is to some extent discredited politically—certainly more than if, publicly, he had put up a stout fight. Even if the confession is disbelieved, it is striking demonstration of the power of the State over its opponents. It is more in accordance with totalitarian ideologies that a defendant should confess, even under duress: it is better discipline and a good example to all ranks. (Those who would not confess properly in court were sometimes provided with posthumous confessions, to keep up the standards, as with the Bulgarian Kostov [Taicho Kostov, deputy prime minister, was accused of treason] in 1949.)

These are rational considerations. But it is also clear that the principle of confession in all cases, even from ordinary victims tried in secret, was insisted on. In fact, the major effort of the whole vast police organization throughout the country went into obtaining such confessions. When we read, in cases of no particular importance, and ones never to be made public, of the use of the "conveyor" system tying down team after team of

Robert Conquest, *The Great Terror: A Reassessment* (New York and Oxford: Oxford University Press, 1990), pp. 130–31.

police investigators for days on end, the impression one gets is not simply of vicious cruelty, but of insane preoccupation with a pointless formality. The accused could perfectly well, it seems, have been shot or sentenced without this frightful rigamarole.

But the extraordinary, contorted legalism of the whole operation remained to the end. It would have been possible simply to have deported thousands or millions of people on suspicion. Yet perhaps 100,000 examiners and other officials spent months interrogating and guarding prisoners who did not, during that time, even provide the State with any labor. One explanation advanced in the prisons was that, apart from a hypocritical wish to preserve the façade, the absence of confessions would have made it much more difficult to find fresh inculpations.

It is also clear that the confession system, involving one single type of evidence, was easier to stereotype down the whole line of investigators than were more substantial methods of faking. When evidence of actual objects was involved, there was often trouble. In the Ukraine, a group of Social Revolutionaries confessed to having a secret arms cache, at the instance of an inexperienced interrogator. The first "conspirator" confessed to having put it in charge of another man. The second man, under torture, said that he had passed the weapons on to another member. They went through eleven hands until, after a discussion in his cell, the last consignee was urged to think of someone who had died whom he knew

well. He could only remember his former geography master, a completely nonpolitical character who had just died, but maintained that the examiner would never believe him to have been a conspirator. He was finally persuaded that all the examiner wanted was to get rid of the arms somehow, so he made the confession as suggested, and the examiner was so delighted that he gave him a good meal and some tobacco. . . .

Beyond all this, one forms the impression of a determination to break the idea of the truth, to impose on everyone the acceptance of official falsehood. In fact, over and above the rational motives for the extraction of confession, one seems to sense an almost metaphysical preference for it.

As early as 1918 Dzerzhinsky [Feliks Dzerzhinsky, founder of the Soviet secret police] had remarked, of enemies of the Soviet government, "When confronted with evidence, criminals in almost every case confess; and what argument can have greater weight than a criminal's own confession?"

After reading this selection, consider these questions:

1. What was the reason for seeking confessions?
2. How do you suppose the trials strengthened Stalin's position?
3. What do the interrogations say about the security system of the Soviet Union?

CHAPTER 17
World War II: What Were Its Origins and Its Impact on World Events?

After only twenty years of peace Europe plunged into a second world war that soon spread to Asia and Africa. The origins of this war grew out of the peace settlement of World War I. Versailles left the German people resentful over a treaty that blamed them alone for beginning World War I and demanded reparations that they believed were impossible to meet.

In the 1920s after a currency collapse had been weathered, the Weimar Republic in Germany took some very positive steps to repair the damage. Then the Great Depression struck and all the progress that had been achieved was lost. In times of crisis people turn to extremes, and the German population had two choices: On the Left were the Communists and on the Right, the National Socialist Party, or the Nazis, led by Adolf Hitler.

In Italy, a country on the winning side of the First World War, there was a similar feeling of depression. Few gains and a host of problems came Italy's way. The prewar politicians seemed to offer no help, so many people turned to the Right, embodied in the Fascist Party of Benito Mussolini. Mussolini promised a better future through the concentration of all power in the state. The ambition of Mussolini and Hitler to expand their nations' territories led to World War II.

SELECTION 1:

Fundamentals of Fascism

Mussolini announced his program in a document published by the Fascists (excerpted in the following selection).

Against individualism, the Fascist conception is for the State; and it is for the individual in so far as he coincides with the State, which is the conscience and universal will of man in his historical existence. It is opposed to classical liberalism, which arose from the necessity of reacting against absolutism, and which brought its historical purpose to an end when the State was transformed into the conscience and will of the people. Liberalism denied the State in the interests of the particular individual; Fascism reaffirms the State as the true reality of the individual. And if liberty is to be the attribute of the real man, and not of that abstract puppet envisaged by individualist liberalism, Fascism is for liberty.

And for the only liberty which can be a real thing, the liberty of the State and of the individual within the State. Therefore, for the Fascist, everything is in the State, and nothing human or spiritual exists, much less has value, outside the State. In this sense Fascism is totalitarian, and the Fascist State, the synthesis and unity of all values, interprets, develops and gives strength to the whole life of the people.

Outside the State there can be neither individuals nor groups (political parties, associations, syndicates, classes). Therefore Fascism is opposed to Socialism, which confines the movement of history within the class struggle and ignores the unity of classes established in one economic and moral reality in the State; and analogously it is opposed to class syndicalism. Fascism recognizes the real exigencies for which the socialist and syndicalist movement arose, but while recognizing them wishes to bring them under the control of the State and give them a purpose within the corporative system of interests reconciled within the unity of the State.

Individuals form classes according to the similarity of their interests, they form syndicates according to differentiated economic activities within these interests; but they form first, and above all, the State, which is not to be thought of numerically as the sum-total of individuals forming the majority of a nation. And consequently Fascism is opposed to democracy, which equates the nation to the majority, lowering it to the level of that majority; nevertheless it is the purest form of democracy if the nation is conceived, as it should be, qualitatively and not quantitatively, as the most powerful idea (most powerful because most moral, most coherent, most true) which acts within the nation as the conscience and the will of a few, even of One, which ideal tends to become active within the conscience and the will of all—that is to say, of all those who rightly constitute a nation by reason of nature, history or race, and have set out upon the same line of development and spiritual formation as one conscience and one sole will. Not a race, nor a geographically determined region, but as a community historically perpetuating itself, a multitude unified by a single idea, which is the will to existence and to power: consciousness in itself, personality.

After reading this selection, consider these questions:

1. In Fascist ideology, why is the state all important?

Benito Mussolini, *The Doctrine of Fascism*, in Michael Oakeshott, *The Social and Political Doctrines of Contemporary Europe* (Cambridge: Cambridge University Press, 1939), pp. 166–67.

2. How does this ideology prepare the way for a dictator?

3. What happens to personal liberties under Fascism?

SELECTION 2:

March to Totalitarianism

The ruthlessness and willingness to use violence against their opponents marked both Mussolini's Fascists and Hitler's Nazis. Both kept paramilitary organizations whose functions were to carry out, with unquestioning loyalty, the leader's every whim. No element of society was to be left to enjoy any independent status. In the following selection, a modern historian, F.L. Carsten, discusses the rise of the totalitarianism of Nazi Germany. First the trade unions, then the political parties, were outlawed.

It was then enacted that the National Socialist Party was the only political party in the country; any attempt to maintain or to form another party became punishable by penal servitude or imprisonment. Germany was a one-party state.

The same process was carried through in every field of national activity. Cultural life was controlled by the setting up of a National Chamber of Culture, with subordinate chambers for fine arts, music, theater, literature, radio, films, and the press. Anyone working in any of these fields was obliged to join the chamber in question, from which all Jews and opponents of the régime were excluded, thus depriving them of their livelihood. Even earlier the books of all authors obnoxious to the régime—whether Jewish, or left-wing, or simply "decadent"—were burnt by crowds of enthusiastic students.

The lectures of Jewish and left-wing professors were made impossible by well organized disturbances. The universities and the civil service were purged by a law "for the restitution of professional civil service." Jewish students were excluded from the examinations. Jewish doctors,

lawyers, etc., were in many cases prevented from carrying on their professions. A boycott of all Jewish shops was proclaimed by [Julius] Streicher on a nation-wide scale on 1 April 1933. All clubs and associations, however non-political their purpose, were brought under National Socialist control and their by-laws reframed according to the "leadership principle."

The opposition did not dare to raise its head. People opposed to the régime could only meet clandestinely and in small groups, and even then they risked immediate arrest and a period in a concentration camp. The tales of horror about what happened inside these camps which soon spread were one of the most effective weapons of the dictatorship. Many thousands of opponents of the régime were simply too frightened to do anything. But many thousands of others continued to work for the Communist and Social Democratic parties in spite of all intimidation and persecution; most of them were soon arrested or had to flee the country. After a few years there existed only minute remnants of the proud German working-class movement. . . .

The purge of 30 June [1934], by eliminating the enemies and the potential enemies of the régime, completed the National Socialist "revolution." Adolf Hitler was in complete and undis-

F.L. Carsten, *The Rise of Fascism* (Berkeley and Los Angeles: University of California Press, 1967), pp. 156–59.

puted control of the whole country.

His amazing success was, above all, due to the economic crisis which drove millions of desperate Germans into his camp, a crisis such as had not occurred in Italy ten years before. It was also due to the expert organization and the propaganda efforts of the National Socialists which no other party could rival, to their violence, dynamism and unscrupulousness in attacking the system and its representatives, in mobilizing the masses and rousing the rabble. There still remains the question how a great nation and many of its leaders could have been taken in and won over by such methods and such aims. Undoubtedly, it was Hitler's nationalism that helped to win many who deeply resented the Treaty of Versailles and desired to restore Germany's position in the world; and it was his anti-Semitism that attracted those looking for a convenient scapegoat for all the ills of Germany. It has to be remembered that a fervent nationalism and a strong anti-Semitism had been endemic in Germany since the nineteenth century, although in less violent forms.

While Socialist or Communist propaganda in favor of the class struggle and international solidarity never influenced people outside the working classes, National Socialist propaganda always used themes which evoked a sympathetic echo in millions of people, and adapted itself with great skill to different audiences. In the conditions of the great crisis it played successfully on middle-class fears of Communism and on their dislike of the republican régime. Not particularly attractive to anyone, the republic was burdened with the acceptance of the Treaty of Versailles and with the inflation of the mark, which largely expropriated the middle and lower middle classes, with the signing of the Dawes and Young plans which, in nationalist eyes, perpetuated Germany's "enslavement" and could be made responsible for the economic decline. Thus the republic found few determined defenders. There was no frontal assault, but its foundations were undermined and sapped by a process of attrition. It was an irony of history that the constitutional guardianship of the republic in the decisive hour was entrusted to the ancient paladin of the House of Hohenzollern. Thus the fortress surrendered without a shot being fired, exactly as Rome had surrendered to Mussolini ten years before.

After reading this selection, consider these questions:

1. What is meant by totalitarianism?
2. Why was there so little opposition to Hitler?
3. How did German nationalism play into Hitler's hands?

SELECTION 3:

A View of the German Future

Hitler was never a person who hid his intentions. He was convinced that his Nazis alone had the key to German greatness and the spread of the nation's culture and population to the East. Nazism had a virulent streak of racism not found in Italian fascism. His appeal to self-interest was a major factor in his coming to power.

Hitler's goals for Germany were outlined in his book, Mein Kampf (My Struggle), which he dictated to his secretary, Rudolf Hess, and published in 1927. The following selection is a representative excerpt from this long and turgid diatribe.

Assuredly at a certain time the whole of humanity will be compelled, in consequence of the impossibility of making the fertility of the soil keep pace with the continuous increase in population, to halt the increase of the human race and either let Nature again decide, or, by self-help if possible, create the necessary balance, though, to be sure, in a more correct way than is done today. But then this will strike all peoples, while today only those races are stricken with such suffering which no longer possess the force and strength to secure for themselves the necessary territories in this world. For as matters stand there are at this present time on this earth immense areas of unused soil, only waiting for the men to till them. But it is equally true that Nature as such has not reserved this soil for the future possession of any particular nation or race; on the contrary, this soil exists for the people which possesses the force to take it and the industry to cultivate it.

Nature knows no political boundaries. First, she puts living creatures on this globe and watches the free play of forces. She then confers the master's right on her favorite child, the strongest in courage and industry.

When a people limits itself to internal colonization because other races are clinging fast to greater and greater surfaces of this earth, it will be forced to have recourse to self-limitation at a time when the other peoples are still continuing to increase. Some day this situation will arise, and the smaller the living space at the disposal of the people, the sooner it will happen. Since in general, unfortunately, the best nations, or, even more correctly, the only truly cultured races, the standard-bearers of all human progress, all too frequently resolve in their pacifistic blindness to renounce new acquisitions of soil and content themselves with "internal" colonization, while the inferior races know how to secure immense living areas in this world for themselves—this would lead to the following final result:

The culturally superior, but less ruthless races, would in consequence of their limited soil, have to limit their increase at a time when the culturally inferior but more brutal and more natural peoples, in consequence of their greater living areas, would still be in a position to increase without limit. In other words: some day the world will thus come into possession of the culturally inferior but more active men.

Then, though in a perhaps very distant future, there will be but two possibilities: either the world will be governed according to the ideas of our modern democracy, and then the weight of any decision will result in the favor of the numerically stronger races, or the world will be dominated in accordance with the laws of the natural order of force, and then it is the peoples of brutal will who will conquer, and consequently once again not the nation of self-restriction.

No one can doubt that this world will some day be exposed to the severest struggles for the existence of mankind. In the end, only the urge for self-preservation can conquer. Beneath its so-called humanity, the expression of a mixture of stupidity, cowardice, and know-it-all conceit, will melt like snow in the March sun. Mankind has grown great in eternal struggle, and only in eternal peace does it perish. . . .

The size of the area inhabited by a people constitutes in itself an essential factor for determining its outward security. The greater the quantity of space at the disposal of a people, the greater its natural protection; for military decisions against peoples living in a small restricted area have always been obtained more quickly and hence more easily, and in particular more effectively and completely, than can, conversely, be possible against territorially extensive states. In the size of a state's territory there always lies a certain protection against frivolous attacks, since success can be achieved only after hard struggles, and therefore the risk of a rash assault will seem too great unless there are quite exceptional grounds for it. Hence the very size of a state offers in itself a basis for more easily preserving the freedom and independence of a people, while, conversely, the smallness of such a formation is a positive invitation to seizure.

Adolf Hitler, *Mein Kampf*, trans. Ralph Manheim (Boston: Houghton Mifflin, 1971), pp. 134–37.

After reading this selection, consider these questions:

1. Do you see a connection between Hitler's ideas and those of Malthus? (See chapter 12, selection 1)
2. How did Hitler's views fit in with German expansion?
3. Why did Hitler consider Jews the great enemy of the Germans?

SELECTION 4:

Hitler's War Plans

In 1935 Hitler announced that Germany would no longer be bound by the Treaty of Versailles. He also told the world that the country intended to rearm. The generals in the German army were appalled at his daring for they feared a war that in 1935 there was no hope of winning. However, neither France nor Great Britain threatened to resist. Hitler's boldness convinced him that he was a diplomatic genius. A modern historian explains in the selection below.

Hitler's superiority over his generals lay in his intuitive understanding of crowds and of peoples. He was convinced that France would not move, and he was right. The *Wehrmacht* [the German army] contingents that occupied the demilitarized zone in March 1936 had orders to retire if the French army crossed the frontiers of the Reich. The Führer was obliged to make that concession to G.H.Q. [the army's General Headquarters], but he had accurately gauged the French state of mind. In 1938, General [Ludwig] Beck resigned when Hitler revealed his projects in regard to Austria and Czechoslovakia. Such projects, declared the old-style generals, would inevitably lead to a world war. They were nationalists, but they were also Christians, and feared for Germany especially, but also for European civilization.

At Munich in 1938, Hitler judged correctly and achieved a peaceful success for the last time. Events had belied the fears of his professional advisers and had justified the amateur's optimism. The Führer believed more than ever in his mis-

sion and his manifest destiny. He went on to make his fatal mistake. The generals' objections seemed to be contradicted by the facts in September 1938, again in March 1939, and even in September 1939 and June 1940. The military victories of 1939 and 1940 exceeded the always cautious anticipations of the experts. But their pessimism as to the ultimate outcome was well founded. Peaceful triumphs and lightning victories made inevitable a war to the uttermost, in a chain of events which Hitler had refused to foresee and refused almost up to the end to recognize.

When he ordered his troops to cross the Polish frontier, he had no doubt that the result would be an Anglo-French declaration of war. But he did not think that their symbolic gesture implied fierce determination to fight to the bitter end and destroy the Third Reich. After the Polish campaign and during the campaign in France, Hitler seems still to have been unconvinced that the British would prove irreconcilable. It may be that he spared the British army at Dunkirk by holding up his armored divisions for forty-eight hours so as not to offend the *amour-propre* of the British and to leave open the opportunity of negotiating with them.

From that point onward, one searches in vain for

Raymond Aron, *The Century of Total War* (Boston: Beacon Press, 1954), pp. 46–49.

any trace in Hitler's successive decisions of a plan elaborated in advance. For several months, without any strong conviction, he played with the idea of a landing in England; but the defeat of his aircraft led him to renounce the attempt, for which the general staffs were unenthusiastic, and in which he himself had been unable to put faith. He thought of attacking Gibraltar, and of sending his armored divisions to Alexandria and Suez. Finally, in the autumn of 1940, after the interview with [Soviet prime minister Vyacheslav] Molotov, he decided on Operation Barbarossa—the invasion of Russia.

There is no lack of historical precedent to suggest that this decision followed inevitably in the wake of conquests in the West and the Battle of Britain. Hitler, like Napoleon, was pursuing the elusive Albion into the snows of Russia. For how could he strike a mortal blow at the British Commonwealth so long as the Russian army and air force were intact, compelling him to keep part of the *Luftwaffe* [the air force] and the *Wehrmacht* in the East, or at least in reserve? If the war of attrition continued in the West for years, would not the Soviet Union inevitably become the arbiter of the situation? Such arguments are easily mustered—as are those to the contrary.

The Soviet Union was carrying out the clauses of the Russo-German Pact with scrupulous loyalty; it delivered all the promised supplies, and offered still more. There had been nothing to suggest that it would have, in the near future, to turn against the Third Reich. Thus, in concentrating its forces against the British Commonwealth in 1941, had not Germany a chance of weakening England to the point of inducing her not to capitulate, but to negotiate? During the first months of 1941, Great Britain was losing 500,000 tons of merchant shipping every month. If the submarine war had been accompanied by the bombing of ports, and if the German army had utilized some of its "unemployed" divisions against Gibraltar and Suez, it is questionable whether [Franklin D.] Roosevelt would have been able to bring about American intervention before Great Britain had been overcome by discouragement. . . .

Improvisation and amateurishness mark the last phase of Hitler's adventure. His fundamental mistake was the counterpart of the accurate intuitions of the first phase. He refused to admit that, in spite of his theories, he had repeated the Kaiser's error in launching a war on two fronts, against the Russians and the Anglo-Saxons. When he could no longer deny the facts, he clung to an argument that seemed to him unanswerable: How could the capitalist democracies and the Soviet empire cooperate to the extent of jointly crushing Germany? Would it not be the height of folly for the British and Americans to lend a hand in the destruction of the only barrier that could protect Europe from the Communist flood? It may have been folly, but it was a folly that he himself had led the Anglo-Saxons to commit.

After reading this selection, consider these questions:
1. What explains the reluctance of the French and British to challenge Hitler?
2. Why were the German generals fearful of Hitler's leadership?
3. Is it possible that Hitler expected to negotiate peace with Great Britain?

SELECTION 5:
The Warsaw Deportation

One of the war's most tragic dimensions was the Holocaust. Hitler's hatred for Jews was so intense that he intended to wipe all of them off the earth.

With the German occupation of Poland, the country with the largest Jewish population in all Europe, Hitler had a greater opportunity to put his plans into effect. The following selection, from Yisrael Gutman's Jews of Warsaw, *describes the deportation from that city and their massacre.*

The mass deportation, or "resettlement," of the Jews of Warsaw began on Wednesday, July 22, 1942—the eve of the Ninth of Av—and continued, with occasional short pauses, until September 12, 1942. During those seven weeks, some 265,000 Jews were uprooted from Warsaw, transported to the Treblinka death camp, and murdered in the gas chambers.

The deportation from Warsaw was part of "The Final Solution of the Jewish Problem"—a comprehensive plan to annihilate the Jews of Europe. In the spring of 1942, forces of the SS [*SchutzStaffel*, the Nazi security force] and the police initiated a campaign of sudden roundups and mass deportations to the death camps within the General-government. These deportations and killings were implemented in the framework of *Aktion Reinhardt* ("Operation Reinhardt") by the units of the *Einsatz Reinhardt*, which were under the command of the *S.S.-und Polizeiführer* of Lublin District, General Odilo Globocnik. The operation shifted into high gear on July 19, 1942, when [Heinrich] Himmler informed the Higher SS and Police Leader of the General-government, Friedrich Krieger, that the evacuation of the entire Jewish population of the General-government must be completed by December 31, 1942. . . .

Globocnik tried to carry out his mission with speed and decisiveness, for he believed that as time went on there was a chance that difficulties might slow down the extermination process. Methodical preparations were made for implementing the extermination program, and during the first half of 1942 the Belzec, Sobibor, and Treblinka death camps were put into operation. All the deportees to these camps—with the exception of a small staff that was maintained for handling necessary skilled jobs and unloading and sorting the belongings left behind by the victims—were

murdered in the gas chambers that had been installed in permanent buildings. In the summer of 1942, construction of the Majdanek camp near Lublin was completed. Like Auschwitz, Majdanek served as both a concentration and extermination camp. Most of the Jews transported there—and particularly children, women, and the elderly—were immediately sent to the gas chambers, while a certain percentage that met the standards of the *Selektion* were assigned to the concentration camp.

In the course of time, Operation Reinhardt was extended to include: (1) siege operations within the ghettos and deportations to extermination camps; (2) supervising the means and rate of extermination in the death camps; (3) exploiting the labor of Jewish prisoners in the forced-labor and concentration camps run by the SS; and (4) the confiscation of Jewish property, be it in the form of money, jewelry, movables, or immovables.

Himmler's above-mentioned order of July 19 stated that at the end of 1942 no Jews were to be left in the General-government, other than laborers who had been concentrated in assembly camps in Warsaw, Cracow, Czestochowa, Radom, and Lublin. The civilian authorities of the General-government not only supported the extermination campaign but encouraged and abetted the liquidation process. Dr. Josef Bühler, a representative of Frank's regime [Hans Frank was the governor of the General-government of occupied Poland] at the Wannsee Conference, promised the administration's full support in implementing the "Final Solution" and proclaimed that "the General-government will be delighted if the solution to the question will commence in the General-government."

On December 16, 1941, shortly before the Wannsee Conference, Frank stated at a meeting of the General-government administration:

As a veteran National Socialist, I must state that if the Jewish tribe were to survive this war while we sacrifice our finest blood

Yisrael Gutman, *The Jews of Warsaw, 1939–1943* (Bloomington: Indiana University Press, 1982), pp. 197–98.

to save Europe, the victory in this war would only be a partial achievement. For that reason, my outlook toward the Jews is based on the hope that they will cease to exist. It is necessary to remove them . . . but what should be done with them? Do you suppose we will resettle them in settlers' villages in Ostland? In Berlin they said to us: What is all the great fuss about? There is nothing to be done with them in Ostland or in the *Reichskommissariat*. Do away with them yourselves.

After reading this selection, consider these questions:
1. Why did the Warsaw ghetto deportation take place?
2. How would you have reacted if you received orders to be deported?
3. Was there anything that foreign states should have done to prevent the Holocaust?

SELECTION 6:

Reflections on Pearl Harbor

While Hitler was pursuing his war in Europe against both Great Britain and the Soviet Union, a dramatic new development took place. This was the Japanese bombing of Pearl Harbor on December 7, 1941.

The Japanese military leaders, with no checks upon them from civilian politicians, decided on this attack. They believed that the U.S. economic embargo placed on Japan, because of its invasion of China, would, in time, strangle the Japanese economy. If Japan were to gain the oil fields of the Dutch East Indies, essential for its war effort, then the United States would have to be dealt with through the bombing of its fleet in Hawaii. In the following selection, Harry Wray looks at the diplomatic situation as December 1941 approached.

The rise of Chinese communism, especially after the mid-1930s, created the fear that unless Japan performed preemptory surgery there another neighbor would become communist. (Ironically, perhaps no factor was more important than the accelerated penetration of China by Japan for causing that country to accept the Chinese Communist party and communism.) Simultaneously, the rise of an increasingly militant Chinese nationalism during the 1920s and 1930s agitated for an immediate end to all foreign investments and concessions. That movement put Japan and China on a collision course. On all of these issues Japan expected sympathy and understanding. The American and British governments saw correctly, however, that much of the Japanese argument was mere casuistry to cloak Japanese territorial ambitions. Japanese sincerity seemed most insincere.

From the Japanese perspective the American attitude toward China was frustrating because of America's vacillating interpretation of the Open Door policy [U.S. foreign policy toward China that allowed all nations entry]. More to the point,

Harry Wray, "Japanese-American Relations and Perceptions, 1900–1940," in *Pearl Harbor Reexamined*, ed. Hilary Conroy and Harry Wray (Honolulu: University of Hawaii Press, 1990), pp. 9–11.

the Japanese resented it and the Americans' assumption that they could proclaim it in Japan's backyard. . . . Japan was determined "to achieve autonomy" and to solve the China question in her own way. The United States was just as determined to contain Japan, to uphold its historic Open Door policy in China, and to check the Japanese by economic actions in concert with its allies. War was imminent.

China became Japan's historical parallel to America's Vietnam. Unwittingly the army and navy found themselves tied down in China despite the fact that their primary potential enemies were the Soviet Union and the United States, respectively. The more Japan struggled, however, the more she became mired in the vast expanses of Chinese quicksand. By 1940 Japan needed desperately to end the war in China, but Chiang Kai-shek, trading space for time, retreated one thousand miles into the interior. He sought—successfully—to tie the United States even more tightly to his sagging government. Although American assistance to China was severely limited and never became more than minimal, its psychological significance to the nationalist government was enormous. The Japanese government could not see that the way to end the war was to achieve a negotiated settlement with Chiang Kai-shek. Instead they reasoned that if the Americans would discontinue aid to the nationalist government the latter would be forced to negotiate a settlement. That may have been true, but the Japanese government was really counting on a situation in which the discontinuation of American support would force Chiang Kai-shek into a negotiated settlement that would recognize some type of Japanese territorial gains in China.

All three parties understood the Japanese rationale clearly; the United States refused to cooperate with the Japanese plan. Each month that the Sino-Japanese War continued the Japanese military became more desperate. In the meantime, the Americans interpreted the Japanese signing of the Tripartite Pact of 1940 with Germany and Italy as directed toward the United States. The three nations appeared to have reached a decision to carve up the world among them. Japan's occupation of all of French Indochina seemed to confirm that suspicion.

The Japanese quest for economic self-sufficiency and empire was met by increased economic sanctions by the United States. The Japanese leadership developed a siege mentality that led to the argument that the only solution to the American, British, and Dutch oil blockade was war. They saw no other options. When Nazi Germany attacked their traditional foe, the Soviet Union, and seemed the inevitable victor in the late fall of 1941, Japan took the opportunity to eliminate U.S. interference in the Pacific.

But was the Pacific War inevitable? Was there no way out of these escalating antagonisms in the diplomacy of the last two or three years before the outbreak of the war? Did some Japanese leaders sincerely seek to avoid war? Did the United States and its Allies miss opportunities to heal the breach and assume incorrectly that the militarists were in such control that there was no way out of the impasse? Was there no way for the Americans to help the advocates of peace within the Japanese government? Had America become a prisoner of its Chinese ally's objectives? In short, despite the Japanese expansion into China, and later into French Indochina, could Japanese and American diplomats have extricated themselves from the impending tragedy?

After reading this selection, consider these questions:

1. How did the United States and Great Britain react when Japan clashed with Chinese nationalists and Communists in the 1930s?
2. Do you think that Chiang Kai-shek was justified in his strategy of retreating deep into China's interior and refusing to negotiate with the Japanese?
3. Why did Japan attack the United States in December 1941?

CHAPTER 18
The Cold War: What Explains the Conflict Between the Communist Nations and the West After World War II?

There were high hopes that at the end of World War II the world would enter an era of peace. The formation of the United Nations, with stronger powers than the League of Nations ever held and with the participation of the United States, promised international cooperation to secure the peace. However, this was not to be.

On the one side of the wartime alliance were the democratic countries, on the other the Soviet Union and those nations of Eastern Europe where its occupation forces installed puppet governments. Following the end of the conflict, China, North Korea, and North Vietnam were added to the list of communist nations. Cooperation between the democratic countries and those with Marxist regimes proved impossible. Both felt threatened that the other side would gain the advantage and both feared a first strike that would catch the other off guard. At first only the United States had nuclear weapons, but both the Soviet Union and China soon discovered the secret of making these terrifying weapons of destruction. The fact that nuclear bombs could be launched and delivered to enemy targets in a matter of minutes poised the world on the brink of catastrophe.

That peace survived this threat was due to the realization by political leaders that even the winner in a nuclear war would suffer immense destruction. Therefore, what developed was a cold war, where surrogate armies in a variety of African, Asian, and Latin American countries battled with conventional weapons. The United Nations provided an assembly for accusations and counteraccusations. This chapter will survey a number of responses to the cold war.

SELECTION 1:

The Novikov Telegram

About a year following the end of hostilities, the Soviet ambassador to the United States, Nikolay Novikov, sent the following telegram to Moscow to his superior, Vyacheslav Molotov, then serving as foreign minister. Molotov took very seriously what he saw contained in the report, under-lining certain sections of it. Novikov's analysis became a starting point for Soviet dealings with the United States. Note the Marxist tenor of Ambassador Novikov's dispatch.

The foreign policy of the United States, which reflects the imperialist tendencies of American monopolistic capital, is characterized in the post-war period by a striving for world supremacy. This is the real meaning of the many statements by President Truman and other representatives of American ruling circles: that the United States has the right to lead the world. All the forces of American diplomacy—the army, the air force, the navy, industry, and science—are enlisted in the service of this foreign policy. For this purpose broad plans for expansion have been developed and are being implemented through diplomacy and the establishment of a system of naval and air bases stretching far beyond the boundaries of the United States, through the arms race, and through the creation of ever newer types of weapons.

The foreign policy of the United States is con-ducted now in a situation that differs greatly from the one that existed in the prewar period. This sit-uation does not fully conform to the calculations of those reactionary circles which hoped that dur-ing the Second World War they would succeed in avoiding, at least for a long time, the main battles in Europe and Asia. They calculated that the United States of America, if it was unsuccessful in completely avoiding direct participation in the war, would enter it only at the last minute, when it could easily affect the outcome of the war, completely ensuring its interests.

In this regard, it was thought that the main competitors of the United States would be crushed or greatly weakened in the war, and the United States by virtue of this circumstance would assume the role of the most powerful fac-tor in resolving the fundamental questions of the postwar world. These calculations were also based on the assumption, which was very wide-spread in the United States in the initial stages of the war, that the Soviet Union, which had been subjected to the attack of German Fascism in June 1941, would also be exhausted or even com-pletely destroyed as a result of the war.

Reality did not bear out the calculations of the American imperialists. . . .

The foreign policy of the United States is not determined at present by the circles in the Demo-cratic party that (as was the case during [Franklin] Roosevelt's lifetime) strive to strengthen the co-operation of the three great powers that constitut-ed the basis of the anti-Hitler coalition during the war. The ascendance to power of President Tru-man, a politically unstable person but with certain conservative tendencies, and the subsequent ap-pointment of [James] Byrnes as Secretary of State meant a strengthening of the . . . .maintenance of high military potential. It was in this very atmos-phere that the law on universal military service in peacetime was passed by Congress, that the huge military budget was adopted, and that plans are

"The Novikov Telegram, Washington, September 27, 1946," in *Origins of the Cold War*, ed. Kenneth M. Jensen, rev. ed. (Washington, DC: U.S. Institute of Peace Press, 1993), pp. 3–6.

being worked out for the construction of an extensive system of naval and air bases.

Of course, all of these measures for maintaining a high military potential are not goals in themselves. They are only intended to prepare the conditions for winning world supremacy in a new war, the date for which, to be sure, cannot be determined now by anyone, but which is contemplated by the most bellicose circles of American imperialism.

Careful note should be taken of the fact that the preparation by the United States for a future war is being conducted with the prospect of war against the Soviet Union, which in the eyes of American imperialists is the main obstacle in the path of the United States to world domination. This is indicated by facts such as the tactical training of the American army for war with the Soviet Union as the future opponent, the siting of American strategic bases in regions from which it is possible to launch strikes on Soviet territory,

intensified training and strengthening of Arctic regions as close approaches to the USSR, and attempts to prepare Germany and Japan to use those countries in a war against the USSR.

After reading this selection, consider these questions:

1. According to Novikov, who determined U.S. foreign policy after World War II, and why had that policy changed after Franklin D. Roosevelt's death?
2. Imagine that you are Stalin and are reading Novikov's dispatch. Would you agree with him? What policy would you adopt on the basis of what Novikov says?
3. Do you think that Novikov actually expected that the United States would attack the U.S.S.R.?

SELECTION 2:

Creating the Soviet Empire

The Soviet victory in World War II meant that Stalin now held all of Eastern Europe in his grasp. At the Yalta Conference Winston Churchill, Roosevelt, and Stalin had agreed that "free and unfettered" elections should take place in Eastern Europe once Hitler was defeated. Stalin, however, had no illusions about the popularity either of the Russians or of communism in that region. As a result, the cold war intensified.

The selection below comes from a Western viewpoint on Stalin's steps toward the establishment of an empire in Eastern Europe.

In bringing the war against Nazi Germany to a victorious end, Stalin created the Soviet empire as a by-product. He had not originally sought a military conquest of the whole area he won. He

would have preferred to advance his power and influence there, as elsewhere, by less risky and more subtle means, although he never ruled out resorting to force if the conditions were right; in this respect, his approach differed from that of his successors less than it may seem. But Stalin was unable (contrary to his hopes) to satisfactorily project his power abroad except by force of

Vojtech Mastny, *Russia's Road to the Cold War* (New York: Columbia University Press, 1979), pp. 308–309.

arms and to maintain it except by putting in charge vassal Communist regimes; as a result, he saddled his country with a cluster of sullen dependencies whose possession proved a mixed blessing in the long run.

Far from providing the ultimate protective shield, the empire enlarged the area whose integrity the Russians had to uphold and also diluted its internal cohesion. In coping with the ensuing challenges, the Soviet leaders since Stalin have greatly refined the art of penetrating other countries without outright conquest and of controlling those previously conquered without excessive resort to force. Despite the refinements, however, the fundamental dilemmas of imperialism they inherited from him are still very much with them, with no resolution in sight. The recurrent Soviet setbacks in uncommitted countries and the smoldering discontent throughout eastern Europe suggest a disconcerting lack of alternatives to force.

In masterminding Russia's ascent during World War II and its aftermath, Stalin proved an accomplished practitioner of the strategy of minimum and maximum aims, a strategy his heirs then continued to pursue with variable success. Apt at both exploiting the existing opportunities and creating new ones, he let his aspirations grow until he realized that he had misjudged the complacency of his Anglo-American partners—as they had misjudged his moderation. So he plunged his country into a confrontation with the West that he had neither desired nor thought inevitable. Not without reason were tributes to his diplomatic proficiency con-

spicuously missing among the accolades that he afterward stage-managed to impress his subjects by the multiple facets of his presumed genius.

Since Stalin, in pursuing his rising aspirations, took into close account the actual and anticipated Western attitudes, his coalition partners contributed their inseparable share to a development that they soon judged was detrimental to their own vital interests. If the Soviet ruler did not rate nearly so high as a diplomat as his reputation suggested, his American and British opposite numbers surely rated even lower. The great war leaders, Roosevelt and Churchill, failed not so much in their perceptions as in their negligence to prepare themselves and their peoples for the disheartening likelihood of a breakdown of the wartime alliance. The British Prime Minister, whose perceptions were keener, is that much more open to criticism than the American President. In any case, by their reluctance (however understandable) to anticipate worse things to come, the Western statesmen let matters worsen until the hour of reckoning was at hand.

After reading this selection, consider these questions:

1. Does the author believe that Stalin intended to establish an empire in Eastern Europe?
2. What was necessary to keep the Soviet satellites linked to Moscow?
3. Why does the author fault Churchill and Roosevelt for their dealings with Stalin?

SELECTION 3:

A Prime Minister Forced from Office

An example of the Soviet purge of democratic leadership in Eastern Europe comes from the pen of Ferenc Nagy, prime minister of Hungary after *the war. Nagy, once a leader in the Smallholders, the peasant party of the nation, soon discovered Soviet intentions for his country. In the following selection Nagy recalls the events of his ouster while on a visit to Switzerland. The ousting of democratic leaders took place throughout Eastern Europe, wherever the Soviet army and the secret police were to be found.*

After a sleepless night, the dawn of May 30 broke. Minister Gordon was at my hotel by nine o'clock to report that Stephen Balogh had telephoned from Budapest at five that unbearable pressure was being exerted for my resignation. He had told Balogh that I insisted upon returning to Budapest at all costs, and asked whether I could reach Budapest unmolested. After a long silence, Balogh had answered stammeringly:

"It is possible that the Prime Minister could reach Budapest, but it is also possible that some misfortune might happen en route."

It was clear what type of misfortune Balogh had in mind. From the Enns Bridge in Austria through Vienna all the way to the Hungarian border, the road passed through the Soviet-occupied zone, and Soviet occupation of Hungary began at the Hungarian border. This was even worse than the Austrian occupation because the occupying Soviet military was supplemented by the Hungarian Communist border guard commanded by Pálfi-Oesterreicher. Various misfortunes could be arranged: the car might be involved in an "accident," or it could simply disappear, its passengers reappearing later somewhere in Russia. Or the Russians might arrest me, just as they had arrested Béla Kovács [another Smallholder official], knowing that this would have no serious consequences for them. Finally, Pálfi-Oesterreicher's Communist police might arrest me as a "dangerous conspirator," disregarding my immunities as Prime Minister and deputy.

Soon afterward, other messages from friends I could trust indicated that the situation was out of hand, and that the Russians would arrest me before I reached Budapest.

At two in the afternoon, I received a telephone call at the legation from Balogh. He said things had reached a point where my return could do no good; it would be better for me to remain in Swiss territory and resign from there, at the same time emphasizing my innocence.

"Your resignation from abroad would facilitate a quick solution of the problems the government and the Smallholders are facing, and you would spare the Hungarian people added suffering," said Balogh.

"But why do they want me to resign? Why should I? What is the charge against me?"

"You remember that you requested that Béla Kovács be placed in the hands of the Hungarian authorities," Balogh stammered. "General Sviridov [Russian commander in Hungary] now answers that they cannot surrender Kovács because their investigation is still in progress, but transmit Kovács's confession alleging that you were aware of the conspiracy; as a result, you were under serious attack in the cabinet meeting."

"But this accusation is false, and of all people Kovács knows it best of all. How can I be charged on the basis of this kind of confession?"

"Please understand, that is not the issue. There is no point in discussing it at this time. The general opinion here is that you would help the Hungarian people greatly if you would send your resignation from abroad."

I replied to Balogh: "I believe that all my life I have only wanted to serve the Hungarian people; I want to serve them now too, and if my resignation can help them I am prepared to consider the matter. The present situation is not of my making, and I have little control over it. I have been told that my little boy would be in danger if I did not act promptly. Very well, you can tell them that I will sign and deliver my resignation here under certain conditions: first, that they immediately send my little boy to Switzerland; second, that they release my secretary, Francis Kapocs, and enable him to join me; third, that Henry Hives, the chief of my cabinet, suffer no

Ferenc Nagy, *The Struggle Behind the Iron Curtain*, trans. Stephen K. Swift (New York: Macmillan, 1948), pp. 417–19.

harm on his return to Hungary just because he happened to accompany me on this trip; fourth, that the news, as published in Hungary, cast no reflection on my integrity; further, that my son, on duty with the Washington legation, immediately be given leave; and finally, that there be no confiscation of my few possessions at home as if I were a traitor. I specify no political conditions because at the moment that would appear to make little sense."

"I can promise immediately that your little boy will be sent. I will communicate your other conditions to the 'authorities,'" Balogh replied.

"Tell me," I asked, "does the Hungarian public believe any of this disgusting affair?"

"You know your people. As to that, you can sleep peacefully."

Thus ended my last conversation with Budapest. Now the extortion with my child began. I maintained relations with the Hungarian government only through our envoy in Bern, Francis Gordon. My contact with the people stopped—with the country where alone I felt at home, and whose worries and cares I had accepted sixteen months earlier in order to lead it out of the most dreadful sufferings in its history. In spite of my innocence there could no longer be any question of my returning home. I knew that possible future Hungarian developments made it dangerous to let myself be tossed into prison. History made my decision and made me an exile.

After reading this selection, consider these questions:

1. What would motivate the Soviets to oust the Hungarian prime minister?
2. Why did Nagy fear to return to Hungary?
3. How could the Soviets use family members as hostages to get their way?

SELECTION 4:

A Soviet View of the Cold War

The position of the United States and the Soviet Union, the two major world powers at the conclusion of the war, was dictated by the perception that each must protect its interests while avoiding direct military action. A recent conference in Washington allowed a Soviet general to review how events in the U.S. military were appraised in Moscow during the cold war; the following is an extract from his presentation.

The US concluded that military superiority was to be maintained by the maximum development of air (space) offensive assets to the detriment of its Army and Navy [until the SLBM (submarine-launched ballistic missile) appeared]. These priorities were the foundation of the strategy of "mas-

sive retaliation," with the obvious emphasis on strategic aviation. Strategic nuclear forces [ICBM (intercontinental ballistic missile), SLBM, strategic aviation] were a very important component of all the succeeding strategies of the USA and NATO ("counter-force," "credible deterrence," "direct confrontation," and so forth) in combination with the development of general-purpose forces. These were also aimed at waging local wars and conflicts within the framework of the strategy of "flexible response." . . .

V.A. Zolotarev, "The Cold War: Origins and Lessons," in *International Cold War Military Records and History*, ed. William W. Epley (Washington, DC: Office of the Secretary of Defense, 1996), pp. 15–17.

One of the first crises occurred in Berlin in 1948–49, which was provoked by the Soviet blockade of land routes to West Berlin. The crisis' main cause was introduction by the Western powers of monetary units in the occupied territory of Germany, which was believed to be economically damaging to the Soviet occupation zone. The blockade of air supply routes to West Berlin might have brought military conflict to Europe with unpredictable consequences. Fortunately, a compromise was found on 5 May 1949 during the negotiations among the former allies. The blockade of Berlin was lifted.

The second Berlin crisis and the threat of war appeared in August 1961 in connection with the construction of the "Berlin Wall." As was officially announced, the Wall was built for the purpose of suppressing subversive activities against the GDR (German Democratic Republic) from West Berlin. But such actions were an open violation by the USSR and the GDR of international legislation and inter-allied agreements on the status of Berlin, where U.S., British, and French troops were located. An armed confrontation appeared inevitable but was eased as a result of various contacts between [Nikita] Khrushchev and [John F.] Kennedy. An informal agreement was reached about free access to Berlin for Allied servicemen and citizens. Judgment about the events of the confrontation can now be made because the USA has just declassified correspondence between the governments of the two countries on this matter.

Later a much more difficult decision was reached by Khrushchev and Kennedy in one of the most dramatic episodes of the "Cold War"— the Caribbean Crisis. Now that the USA has declassified the personal correspondence between Khrushchev and Kennedy during the time of the crisis, it becomes clear that Americans themselves unintentionally provoked the USSR to place missiles on Cuba.

The point is that at the end of the 1950s, when the US and the USSR possessed ICBMs, the two countries were holding equal positions, determined by the time of flight of missiles between both sides (approximately 30 minutes). The level of missile detection capabilities was also equal (15 minutes). In order to gain an advantage in case of war, in early 1962 the USA installed the medium-ranged missiles "Thor" and "Jupiter" in Europe (in Turkey, Italy, and England), which were capable of striking the USSR in 10–12 minutes. To equalize the threat, the Soviet Union in October 1962 secretly introduced into Cuba the medium-ranged "R-12" missiles capable of destroying objects 2000 kilometers inland in the US and began their installation.

The USSR's action was a response in kind, but also dissimilar because the US, according to NATO decisions, had installed its missiles in Europe openly. The USSR was doing it secretly, and even its own people and the international organizations did not know it. When the secret was disclosed, the USSR explained that its desire was to protect Cuba against American aggression. The secret delivery of Russian missiles to Cuba was disclosed by the USA, and it was the main reason for the "missile crisis." As a result of Russian-American talks, the Russian missiles were removed from Cuba and the American missiles were removed from Turkey and Europe.

The Caribbean crisis was considered by world public opinion as an extremely dangerous precedent. Such events could result in a global nuclear war. After 1962, the USA and the USSR stopped threatening each other with nuclear weapons and avoided creating conflicts. The main lesson of the crisis was that even under conditions of military-political contradictions and mutual suspicions, a strong desire for talks indicated the possibility of achieving compromise. Later in the "Cold War" there were other military and political crises which were also capable of transforming themselves into global conflict (the wars in Vietnam, Korea, Afghanistan).

After reading this selection, consider these questions:

1. How did the military prepare themselves for a nuclear war?
2. What made it possible for so many crises to be defused by the leaders of the United States and the Soviet Union?
3. Do you believe it was possible for either nation to be judged a winner in a nuclear war?

SELECTION 5:

The Chinese Revolution Defined

Having defeated the Japanese, the United States counted on an Asian ally in nationalist China. Here Chiang Kai-shek had emerged as the leader of the war effort and his army was expected to disarm the Japanese occupation forces in his country. Chiang, however, was not the only leader in China with an army.

The Chinese Communists' Red Army had also participated in the fight against the Japanese. Its guiding spirit was the creation of Mao Zedong, who for years had rallied the peasants and workers of China to join the Communists. Much to the dismay of the United States it was Mao, not Chiang, that seized the initiative at the conclusion of the war. By 1947 his Red Army was victorious and Chiang and his followers were forced to flee into exile in Taiwan.

In the following selection, Mao sketches his Marxist view of Chinese society in one of several works calling for revolution and a communist China.

Imperialism and the feudal landlord class being the chief enemies of the Chinese revolution at this stage, what are the present tasks of the revolution?

Unquestionably, the main tasks are to strike at these two enemies, to carry out a national revolution to overthrow foreign imperialist oppression and a democratic revolution to overthrow feudal landlord oppression, the primary and foremost task being the national revolution to overthrow imperialism.

These two great tasks are interrelated. Unless imperialist rule is overthrown, the rule of the feudal landlord class cannot be terminated, because imperialism is its main support. Conversely, unless help is given to the peasants in their struggle to overthrow the feudal landlord class, it will be impossible to build powerful revolutionary contingents to overthrow imperialist rule, because the feudal landlord class is the main social base of imperialist rule in China and the peasantry is the main force in the Chinese revolution. There-

fore, the two fundamental tasks, the national revolution and the democratic revolution, are at once distinct and united.

In fact, the two revolutionary tasks are already linked, since the main immediate task of the national revolution is to resist the Japanese imperialist invaders and since the democratic revolution must be accomplished in order to win the war. It is wrong to regard the national revolution and the democratic revolution as two entirely different stages of the revolution. . . .

What classes are there in present-day Chinese society? There are the landlord class and the bourgeoisie, the landlord class and the upper stratum of the bourgeoisie constituting the ruling classes in Chinese society. And there are the proletariat, the peasantry, and the different sections of the petty bourgeoisie other than the peasantry, all of which are still the subject classes in vast areas of China.

The attitude and the stand of these classes towards the Chinese revolution are entirely determined by their economic status in society. Thus the motive forces as well as the targets and tasks of the revolution are determined by the nature of

Mao Zedong, "The Chinese Revolution Defined," in *Selected Works of Mao Tse-Tung,* 4 vols. (Peking: Foreign Languages Press, 1965), vol. 2, pp. 318–19.

China's socio-economic system. . . .

The landlord class forms the main social base for imperialist rule in China; it is a class which uses the feudal system to exploit and oppress the peasants, obstructs China's political, economic and cultural development and plays no progressive role whatsoever.

Therefore, the landlords, as a class, are a target and not a motive force of the revolution.

After reading this selection, consider these questions:

1. What does Mao consider the two great enemies of the Chinese revolution?
2. Who does Mao identify as imperialist invaders?
3. Why is Mao so concerned about class structure in China?

SELECTION 6:

China's Social Revolution

Once the Communists began their rule, members of the landlord class, as indicated by Mao's policies in the previous selection, were vigorously dispossessed, put on trial, and thousands, even millions, died as enemies of the new regime. A Western observer describes this in the selection below.

After the hiatus of the united front period, social issues returned to the fore. But now it was no longer a question of exploiting popular issues for propaganda purposes; the order of the day was social war. Social revolution—terrifying, vast, and primitive—exploded throughout rural China. It did not break out everywhere at the same time. Sometimes the first move was made by the large landowners: on returning to a village they had fled seven or eight years before, they had their henchmen murder the peasants who had seized the land in their absence. At other times the peasants took the lead in settling accounts by lynching a village headman who had collaborated with the Japanese or a peasant who had spied on fellow villagers during the war, and perhaps also, for good measure, whoever happened to be collecting the land tax at the time. Sometimes the leaders of the revolution were outdistanced by the masses;

sometimes they left the masses far behind.

In 1945, the peasants' insistence on immediate distribution of land dismayed the Communists, who were not eager, for example, to alienate an anti-Japanese landlord they had made local headman, or to lose the support of liberals who had not yet chosen sides. At other times, tenant farmers paralyzed by timidity and respect for the landed upper class had to be led by the hand to claim what Communist leaders pronounced to be their due.

Little by little, however, the peasants became bolder, the direction of the revolution became clearer, and the social conflict became more intense. As late as the spring of 1946, there were many areas in which the peasants' only concern was to avoid involvement in the warfare; when the Eighth Route Army [the Communists] left, the villagers stayed behind and welcomed the Nationalists. Soon, however, it became clear that the return of the Kuomintang meant the undoing of social and political advances the peasants had thought they could take for granted, the repeal of reforms relating to interest rates, land tax, and land rent that they had presumed to be part of any

Lucien Bianco, *Origins of the Chinese Revolution, 1915–1949,* trans. Muriel Bell (Stanford, CA: Stanford University Press, 1971), pp. 187–89.

postwar government program, and worst of all, a return to the traditional social and political order. In addition, there was the threat of a resurgent White Terror, whose new victims would be former militiamen, local peasant leaders, members of the village Women's Association, and the like.

The term Liberated Areas, by contrast, especially from 1947 on, when the CCP [Chinese Communist Party] instituted an agrarian policy almost as radical as that of the Kiangsi period, became synonymous with the redistribution of land, the indictment of landlords, and the dictatorship of the Poor Peasants Association. During the winter of 1947–48, while many rich peasants were rallying to the side of the large landowners or trailing in the wake of government troops, some of the most wretched of the rural poor— tenant farmers, small proprietors, farm workers—flocked to the Communists. As the true direction of the revolution became clear, the struggle grew pitiless.

When the villagers realized that their hour had come, that they had gone too far to turn back, years of accumulated hatred were unleashed. Landlords guilty of exploiting their tenants were paraded from village to village and slowly chopped to bits along the way by mobs armed with pitchforks, shears, pickaxes, and clubs, which then fought over the flesh of men alleged to have gorged themselves on the flesh of the people, and mutilated their remains. Some landowners hastened the destruction of their class by resorting to the kind of counter-terrorism used by the Algerian *pieds-noirs* in the spring of 1962. Furious and terrified, feeling their world crumbling beneath them, they took to murdering their more recalcitrant tenant farmers, whose numbers increased daily. Some had whole families of tenants buried alive (*huo-mai*), instructing their men to club back down any head that rose above ground level.

"A poor man has no right to speak," says an old Shansi maxim. When the dikes of silence and submission were swept away by revolution, the village square was inundated by a torrent of speeches and complaints. An avid audience attended, or rather participated in, "Speak Bitterness Meetings," meetings called by the Red Army at which individual peasants took turns recounting their woes and relating them to the general plight of the peasantry. The assembled village was at once the priest hearing confession, the chorus repeating and amplifying the complaint, and the avenger whose resolve was stiffened by this strange and simple ritual.

This public airing of grievances, which aroused or heightened the villagers' class-consciousness, is a good example of the originality of the Red Army, an army different from any that had gone before. Equally original was its use of information, not only about the movement of enemy forces but also, and more often, about conditions in a newly occupied village. The Red Army had a way of knowing the amount of taxes people owed, the names of farmers who had been evicted from their land or victimized by arbitrary treatment, even the names of women who were being ill-treated by their mothers-in-law. Such information was extremely useful in building a militia, a Women's Association, or a Poor Peasants Association, and in arriving at appropriate political and social policies.

The Red Army and the many local guerrilla units were not so much an army as a people in arms—a people, that is, from the numberless villages of the Northeast and the North China Plain.

After reading this selection, consider these questions:

1. What caused problems between the landlords and peasants at the close of the war?
2. What won the peasants over to the communist side and away from the nationalists?
3. How did the Speak Bitterness Meetings serve the communist cause? Do you think that the author is an unbiased observer?

CHAPTER 19
Nationalism in Action: How Did It Cause the End of Empire and the Creation of New Countries?

At the close of World War II the European nations holding colonial possessions presumed that they would be able to hold onto their African and Asian empires. According to this scenario European administrators would keep their places as before and the native population would resume their subordinate position.

Colonial officials overlooked two important facts. One was the creation of a native educated class of men and women that had studied in Europe or America. Many of these students became politically active once they returned home. They were not at all willing to allow Europeans to govern their nations, for nationalism could hardly be kept a monopoly of the West.

The second major factor came out of the exhaustion of the British, French, Dutch, and Belgian peoples. Having lost both people and wealth during the long years of their fight with Nazi Germany, most men and women of the former colonial powers rightly judged that holding onto empires was not worth the trouble.

SELECTION 1:

The Force of Passive Resistance

India led the way. Long before World War II the Hindu nationalist leader Mohandas K. Gandhi had taken charge of the nationalist movement, urging the British to leave India. His strategy was to use nonviolence in this endeavor, to employ only moral force to obtain Indian independence. While many Indian men and women suffered under British batons and jail sentences, Gandhi's tactics began to wear away British resolve. One of his most dramatic moments came when, in 1930, he led thousands of people to the ocean to gather salt, rather than buy it. Salt was a government monopoly, and the British gain from the taxation added to its cost.

Gandhi's career began in South Africa, where he was the advocate of the Indian minority in that country. This led him to consider how British colonialism affected India itself. In November 1909, while at sea on a trip from England to South Africa, he took ten days to compose the Hind Swaraj. *This book, written in the form of a dialogue, developed the idea of nonviolence that was to prove so central to his method of achieving Indian independence. In the following selection, Gandhi speaks of the impact of passive resistance to effect change.*

Editor: Passive resistance is a method of securing rights by personal suffering; it is the reverse of resistance by arms. When I refuse to do a thing that is repugnant to my conscience, I use sol-force. For instance, the government of the day has passed a law which is applicable to me. I do not like it. If, by using violence, I force the government to repeal the law, I am employing what may be termed body-force. If I do not obey the law, and accept the penalty for its breach, I use soul-force. It involves sacrifice of self.

Everybody admits that sacrifice of self is infinitely superior to sacrifice of others. Moreover, if this kind of force is used in a cause that is unjust, only the person using it suffers. He does not make others suffer for his mistakes. Men have before now done many things which were subsequently found to have been wrong. No man can claim to be absolutely in the right, or that a particular thing is wrong, because he thinks so, but it is wrong for him so long as that is his deliberate judgement. It is, therefore, meet that he should not do that which he knows to be wrong, and suffer the consequence whatever it may be. This is the key to the use of soul-force. . . .

To use brute force, to use gunpowder is contrary to passive resistance, for it means that we want our opponent to do by force that which we desire but he does not. And, if such a use of force is justifiable, surely he is entitled to do likewise by us. And so we should never come to an agreement. We may simply fancy, like the blind horse moving in a circle round a mill, that we are making progress. Those who believe that they are not bound to obey laws which are repugnant to their conscience have only the remedy of passive resistance open to them. Any other must lead to disaster.

Reader: From what you say, I deduce that passive resistance is a splendid weapon of the

M.K. Gandhi, *Hind Swaraj and Other Writings,* ed. Anthony J. Parel (Cambridge: Cambridge University Press, 1997), pp. 90–93.

weak, but that, when they are strong, they may take up arms.

Editor: This is gross ignorance. Passive resistance, that is, soul-force, is matchless. It is superior to the force of arms. How, then, can it be considered only a weapon of the weak? Physical-force men are strangers to the courage that is requisite in a passive resister. Do you believe that a coward can ever disobey a law that he dislikes? Extremists are considered to be advocates of brute force. Why do they, then, talk about obeying laws? I do not blame them. They can say nothing else. When they succeed in driving out the English, and they themselves become governors, they will want you and me to obey their laws. And that is a fitting thing for their constitution. But a passive resister will say he will not obey a law that is against his conscience, even though he may be blown to pieces at the mouth of a cannon.

What do you think? Wherein is courage required—in blowing others to pieces from behind a cannon or with a smiling face to approach a cannon and to be blown to pieces? Who is the true warrior—he who keeps death away as a bosom-friend or he who controls the death of others? Believe me that a man devoid of courage and manhood can never be a passive resister.

After reading this selection, consider these questions:

1. Why does Gandhi consider the use of soul-force more effective than the use of body-force?

2. What is Gandhi's answer to the charge that passive resistance rather than resistance by force is cowardly? Do you agree?

3. Gandhi's strategy of passive resistance ultimately succeeded against British rule in India. Suppose that Hitler and the Nazis had been occupying India—would passive resistance have succeeded against them? Do you think that passive resistance is a strategy that can be successfully used against any opponent?

SELECTION 2:

A Woman of Accomplishment

What Gandhi and his followers hoped to avoid was a nation divided. Yet the Muslims of India felt threatened if the Hindu majority were to rule the nation. Gandhi protested that there was only one India with two major faiths, but his pleas fell on deaf ears.

When the British viceroy Lord Louis Mountbatten tried to negotiate between the two parties, he was faced with the Muslim determination that they should have their own state, Pakistan, in western India and eastern Bengal, where they were a majority. The Hindus were led by Jawaharal Nehru of the Congress Party, the Muslims by Ali Jinnah. When independence arrived, it came as two nations, India and Pakistan.

In 1966 India chose as its prime minister Indira Gandhi as the second generation of leaders began taking office. She was literally a second-generation leader, for her father was Nehru, the country's first person to hold that office. Gandhi oversaw many new programs in India that caused a se-

rious opposition to develop. In June 1975 she declared a state of emergency allowing her to rule by decree for the two years she had remaining in her term. For a brief time a new government imprisoned her. Her career, however, did not end; in 1980 she made a political comeback and once more headed the Indian government. Four years later she was assassinated. Ever since, her impact on India has been debated. In the following selections, you will see two sides of Indira Gandhi.

A woman so closely tuned to the country, so complex, so skillful, so far-seeing, so capable of an insightful listening, moved by beauty; and yet, at times, so obsessive, ruthless, brittle, even trivial—a woman who refused to be measured, who laid her own ground rules. She loved her country with passion and tenderness, like a tigress guarding her cubs; her antennae would awaken at the slightest threat. She never ceased to regard herself as a guardian of India and its frontiers.

Her courage was epic. She dared, refused to be intimidated. She had made grave mistakes; the intelligentsia never forgave her for the Emergency. In essence they never forgave themselves for their silence and the fear that enveloped them; for their incapacity to act—except for a handful of people—to fight her with the same degree of courage and fearlessness. But if she sinned, "she sinned bravely."

As a woman Prime Minister, she had little advantage. At first her colleagues tried to manipulate her, refused to take her seriously, until she had proved her mastery over the political process and defeated them on their own ground. After that they lost contact with her and relationships were broken.

Her love for the cultures and peoples of tribal India, for the peasant, the artisan, the weaver, her contact with the creative and sensitive elements in the country, gave her strength.

She was open, accessible, and drew energy from them. Her concern for the poor and deprived went far beyond political strategy. She could reach out, touch them and draw them close.

The feudal landlord, the rich, the trading community and the new middle class brought to the surface her supreme arrogance. She froze in their presence, distanced herself from them. They feared her and waited for an opportunity to strike back.

She was ambivalent about bureaucrats; she respected their experience and intelligence but was suspicious of their knowledge of government procedures and ways of circumventing them. She also could sense their insidious capacity to block what she felt was the will of the people.

In international affairs she played a major role in giving strength to the nonaligned. Her poise and dignity, her refusal to treat with the great powers except on terms of equality, gave her and her country a pride and confidence. Her voice was heard with gravity in the international forums of the world. She had one basic concern—to build an India that was free of both major political blocs—an India that took its rightful place in the comity of nations.

In the first few years of her prime ministership, Indira could act with courage and defiance and had the driving force to see that her plans took root in the country. The stronger the opposition, the more supple the sinews of her body and the swifter her insights for political action. It was the period when she was at her most creative. The years that followed, the period of the Emergency and her defeat at the polls, demanded great resilience to survive. When she returned to power in the eighties, there was an edge to her mind in spite of her growing age, and a determination to fulfill many unfinished tasks. She was firmly entrenched in the belief that she and the lineage from which she came were the instruments for the transformation of India. No doubts on this score disturbed her mind.

[Ved Mehta presents another side of this controversial woman.]

Pupul Jayakar, *Indira Gandhi: An Intimate Biography* (New York: Pantheon Books, 1992), pp. 364–65; Ved Mehta, *The New India* (New York: Viking Press, 1978), pp. 95–96.

Mrs. Gandhi, born in 1917, had a lonely and unsettled childhood. Her parents' marriage was seemingly not very happy. Her father was educated at Harrow and at Cambridge; her mother, Kamala, was unsophisticated and sketchily educated. Her father was in and out of British jails; her mother was sick much of the time with tuberculosis, and died when Indira was eighteen. Indira's formal education was inevitably neglected. Soon after her mother's death, she attended Oxford for a few months; she learned to play badminton there but did not put in much time on studies or sit for any examinations.

While she was in England, however, she met a childhood friend, Feroze Gandhi (not related to Mahatma Gandhi), who was studying at the London School of Economics. They were married in 1942 in India, over the objections of the orthodox and the unorthodox alike, the latter including her father; she was a high-caste Kashmiri Brahman, and Feroze was not even a Hindu—he was a Parsi. They settled in Uttar Pradesh, where their sons were born—Rajiv in 1944, and Sanjay in 1946. The marriage proved to be a stormy one. After seven years, Indira left Feroze and went to live with her father in the Prime Minister's residence in Delhi, where she served as official hostess. There was an attempt at reconciliation some years later, during which Feroze also lived in the Prime Minister's residence, but it was unsuccessful. . . .

Although Nehru, despite his aristocratic background and natural inclinations, sought to conduct himself like a democrat, Mrs. Gandhi conducted herself increasingly like a queen. Certainly the politicians around her appeared to be courtiers. Her conduct may have stemmed from Nehru's position in modern India, from megalomania, or from a lack of self-awareness. In any event, following the proclamation of the emergency she set about building herself a personality cult: billboards and buses everywhere were covered with signs and posters displaying her picture and quoting her sayings; the student branch of the Congress Party set to work organizing Indira Study Circles at universities; Congress politicians began widely circulating a new collection of her speeches and articles, entitled "India." (One of the commonest slogans heard in that period was "India is Indira, and Indira is India.") On the radio and in the newspapers, Mrs. Gandhi often compared herself to Joan of Arc; in an article entitled "My Secret of Success," which appeared in a major Hindi magazine in 1975, she revealed that her success was due to her childhood ambition to grow up to be like Joan of Arc.

After reading this selection, consider these questions:

1. How would Indira Gandhi's early life predict her role in politics?
2. What were the characteristics of her personality that aided her as prime minister?
3. Do you think that the two views of Indira Gandhi can be reconciled, or are they the product of their authors?

SELECTION 3:

Declaration for a New South Africa

The African National Congress (ANC) was the black organization that sought to end apartheid, the legal instruments meant to keep whites and blacks segregated in a relationship of master to servant in South Africa. After its victory at the polls in 1948 apartheid became the program of South Africa's Nationalist Party that sought to keep strictly the whites and blacks apart in as many activities as possible. South Africa's large Asian and Coloured (people of mixed ancestry) communities were also stripped of any political voice.

However, the Nationalists eventually encountered the African National Congress. Founded in 1912, its members vigorously resisted all elements of the government's policies. Not surprisingly, the nationalist government refused to recognize the existence of the ANC and jailed many of its leaders. Police brutality often marked the struggle for racial equality.

In 1989 the African National Congress issued a declaration of its vision for a democratic South Africa (excerpted in the following selection).

ANC envisages a united, democratic, non-racial and non-sexist South Africa, a unitary State where a bill of rights guarantees fundamental rights and freedoms for all on an equal basis, where our people live in an open and tolerant society, where the organs of government are representative, competent and fair in their functioning, and where opportunities are progressively and rapidly expanded to ensure that all may live under conditions of dignity and equality.

When we speak of a united South Africa, we have in mind in the first place the territorial unity and constitutional integrity of our country. South Africa must be seen, as recognized by the international community, as a single, non-fragmented entity including Transkei, Bophuthatswana, Venda and Ciskei.

Secondly, we envisage a single citizenship, nation and a common loyalty. We speak many languages, have different origins and varied beliefs, but we are all South Africans.

Thirdly, all apartheid structures must be dismantled and replaced by institutions of government—central, regional and local—that are truly non-racial and democratic. They must form an integrated and coherent whole, be drawn from all the people and be accountable to the whole community.

Fourthly, there must be a single system of fundamental rights guaranteed on an equal basis for all through the length and breadth of the country. Every South African, irrespective of race, color, language, gender, status, sexual orientation or creed should know that his or her basic rights and freedoms are guaranteed by the constitution and enforceable by recourse to law.

Fifthly, the flag, names, public holidays and symbols of our country should encourage a sense of shared South Africaness.

A unified South Africa requires a strong and effective parliament capable of dealing with the great tasks of reconstruction, of overcoming the legacy of apartheid and of nation-building.

We believe that there is a need for a strong and effective central government to handle national tasks, strong and effective regional government to deal with the tasks of the region and strong and effective local government to ensure active local involvement in handling local issues.

All such governmental structures and institutions shall be based on democratic principles, popular participation, accountability and accessibility. A unified South Africa shall not be an overcentralized, impersonal and overbureaucratized country. The precise relationship between central, regional and local governments can be worked out on the basis of acknowledging the overall integrity of South Africa and the existence of fundamental rights for all citizens throughout the land.

The regions should not be devised as a means of perpetuating privilege, ethnic or racial divisions along territorial zones, but should be based

African National Congress, "Constitutional Principles and Structures for a Democratic South Africa" (New York: United Nations Centre Against Apartheid, 1991), pp. 4–5.

upon the distribution of population, availability of economic resources, communications and urban/rural balance.

After reading this selection, consider these questions:

1. What qualities does the declaration foresee for South Africa?
2. What would happen to apartheid if the ANC program would be adopted?
3. Would you expect that the declaration would gain acceptance from both whites and blacks?

SELECTION 4:

South Africa Seeks a Way Out of Apartheid

The jailed leader of the African National Congress was Nelson Mandela. When both world opinion and a United Nations embargo threatened South Africa, the wall of apartheid began to crumble. In 1989 a new president, F.W. de Klerk , proved much more flexible than his predecessors and freed Mandela. In the following selection, Mandela let it be known he was prepared to open talks with the Congress leaders.

In March, after much negotiation within our respective parties, we scheduled our first face-to-face meeting with Mr. de Klerk and the government. These were to be "talks about talks," and the meetings were to begin in early April. But on March 26, in Sebokeng Township, about thirty miles south of Johannesburg, the police opened fire without warning on a crowd of ANC demonstrators, killing twelve and wounding hundreds more, most of them shot in the back as they were fleeing. Police had used live ammunition in dealing with the demonstrators, which was intolerable. The police claimed that their lives were endangered, but many demonstrators were shot in the back and had no weapons. You cannot be in danger from an unarmed man who is running away from you. The right to assemble and demonstrate in support of our just demands was

Nelson Mandela, *Long Walk to Freedom* (Boston: Little, Brown, 1994), pp. 502–505.

not a favor to be granted by the government at its discretion. This sort of action angered me like no other, and I told the press that every white policeman in South Africa regarded every black person as a military target. After consultation with the NEC [the leadership council], I announced the suspension of our talks and warned Mr. de Klerk that he could not "talk about negotiations on the one hand and murder our people on the other."

But despite the suspension of our official talks, with the approval of the leadership, I met privately with Mr. de Klerk in Cape Town in order to keep up the momentum for negotiations. Our discussions centered primarily on a new date, and we agreed on early May. I brought up the appalling behavior at Sebokeng and the police's unequal treatment of blacks and whites; police used live ammunition with black demonstrators, while they never unsheathed their guns at white right-winged protests.

The government was in no great rush to begin negotiations; they were counting on the euphoria that greeted my release to die down. They wanted to allow time for me to fall on my face and show that the former prisoner hailed as a savior was a highly fallible man who had lost touch with the present situation.

Despite his seemingly progressive actions, Mr. de Klerk was by no means the great emancipator. He was a gradualist, a careful pragmatist. He did not make any of his reforms with the intention of putting himself out of power. He made them for precisely the opposite reason: to ensure power for the Afrikaner [South African of European descent] in a new dispensation. He was not yet prepared to negotiate the end of white rule.

His goal was to create a system of power-sharing based on group rights, which would preserve a modified form of minority power in South Africa. He was decidedly opposed to majority rule, or "simple majoritarianism" as he sometimes called it, because that would end white domination in a single stroke. We knew early on that the government was fiercely opposed to a winner-takes-all Westminster parliamentary system, and advocated instead a system of proportional representation with built-in structural guarantees for the white minority. Although he was prepared to allow the black majority to vote and create legislation, he wanted to retain a minority veto. From the start I would have no truck with this plan. I described it to Mr. de Klerk as apartheid in disguise, a "loser-takes-all" system. . . .

The very fact of the talks themselves was a significant milestone in the history of our country; as I pointed out, the meeting represented not only what the ANC had been seeking for so many years, but an end to the master/servant relationship that characterized black and white relations in South Africa. We had not come to the meeting as supplicants or petitioners, but as fellow South Africans who merited an equal place at the table.

The first day was more or less a history lesson. I explained to our counterparts that the ANC from its inception in 1912 had always sought negotiations with the government in power. Mr. de Klerk, for his part, suggested that the system of separate development had been conceived as a benign idea, but had not worked in practice. For that, he said, he was sorry, and hoped the negotiations would make amends. It was not an apology for apartheid, but it went further than any other National Party leader ever had.

The primary issue discussed was the definition of political prisoners and political exiles. The government argued for a narrow definition, wanting to restrict the number of our people who would qualify for an indemnity. We argued for the broadest possible definition and said that any person who was convicted of an offense that was politically motivated should qualify for an indemnity. We could not agree on a mutually satisfactory definition of "politically motivated" crimes, and this would be an issue that would bedevil us for quite a while to come.

At the end of the three-day meeting, we agreed on what became known as the Groote Schuur Minute, pledging both sides to a peaceful process of negotiations and committing the government to lifting the State of Emergency, which they shortly did everywhere except for the violence-ridden province of Natal. We agreed to set up a joint working group to resolve the many obstacles that still stood in our way.

When it came to constitutional issues, we told the government we were demanding an elected constituent assembly to draw up a new constitution; we believed that the men and women creating the constitution should be the choice of the people themselves. But before the election of an assembly, it was necessary to have an interim government that could oversee the transition until a new government was elected. The government could not be both player and referee, as it was now. We advocated the creation of a multiparty negotiating conference to set up the interim government and set out the guiding principles for the functioning of a constituent assembly.

After reading this selection, consider these questions:

1. According to Nelson Mandela, what was President de Klerk's aim in agreeing to negotiate with the ANC?

2. Why was it symbolically important for South Africa's white government

to open negotiations with the ANC?

3. Why was the issue of defining "politi-

cally motivated" crimes particularly difficult to resolve?

SELECTION 5:

Creation of Israel

The nations of Southwest Asia also looked to be freed from colonialism at the close of World War II. At the close of World War I the League of Nations had handed over most of the countries to Great Britain and France to rule through mandates. In theory the mandate powers were there only temporarily, but no set time defined their length of stay.

In Palestine the British soon found they had a serious problem. While well over 90 percent of the population was Arab in 1918, during World War I Sir Arthur Balfour, the British foreign secretary, agreed that the London government would support the creation of a Jewish homeland. Supported by the Zionist organization, Jews began arriving in Palestine in ever greater numbers. Soon violence broke out between Jews and Arabs, with the British caught in the middle.

The United Nations took over the British charge at the end of World War II and recommended partition. On May 14, 1948, Israel's Prime Minister David Ben-Gurion was ready to declare Israel an independent state.

The Land of Israel was the birthplace of the Jewish people. Here their spiritual, religious and national identity was formed. Here they achieved independence and created a culture of national and universal significance. Here they wrote and gave the Bible to the world.

Exiled from Palestine, the Jewish people remained faithful to it in all the countries of their dispersion, never ceasing to pray and hope for their return and the restoration of their national freedom.

Impelled by this historic association, Jews strove throughout the centuries to go back to the land of their fathers and regain their statehood. In recent decades they returned in masses. They re-

claimed the wilderness, revived their language, built cities and villages, and established a vigorous and ever-growing community, with its own economic and cultural life. They sought peace yet were prepared to defend themselves. They brought the blessings of progress to all inhabitants of the country.

In the year 1897 the First Zionist Congress, inspired by Theodor Herzl's vision of the Jewish State, proclaimed the right of the Jewish people to national revival in their own country.

This right was acknowledged by the Balfour Declaration of November 2, 1917, and reaffirmed by the Mandate of the League of Nations, which gave explicit international recognition to the historic connection of the Jewish people with Palestine and their right to reconstitute their National Home.

The Nazi holocaust, which engulfed millions of Jews in Europe, proved anew the urgency of

"Declaration of the State of Israel" in *A Documentary History of the Arab-Israeli Conflict*, ed. Charles L. Geddes (New York: Praeger, 1991), pp. 288–90.

the re-establishment of the Jewish State, which would solve the problem of Jewish homelessness by opening the gates to all Jews and lifting the Jewish people to equality in the family of nations.

The survivors of the European catastrophe, as well as Jews from other lands, proclaiming their right to a life of dignity, freedom and labor, and undeterred by hazards, hardships and obstacles, have tried unceasingly to enter Palestine.

In the Second World War the Jewish people in Palestine made a full contribution in the struggle of the freedom-loving nations against the Nazi evil. The sacrifices of their soldiers and the efforts of their workers gained them title to rank with the peoples who founded the United Nations.

On November 29, 1947, the General Assembly of the United Nations adopted a Resolution for the establishment of an independent Jewish State in Palestine, and called upon the inhabitants of the country to take such steps as may be necessary on their part to put the plan into effect.

This recognition by the United Nations of the right of the Jewish people to establish their independent State may not be revoked. It is, moreover, the self-evident right of the Jewish people to be a nation, as all other nations, in its own sovereign State.

ACCORDINGLY, WE, the members of the National Council, representing the Jewish people in Palestine and the Zionist movement of the world, met together in solemn assembly today, the day of termination of the British Mandate for Palestine, by virtue of the natural and historic right of the Jewish people and of the Resolution of the General Assembly of the United Nations,

HEREBY PROCLAIM the establishment of the Jewish State in Palestine, to be called ISRAEL.

WE HEREBY DECLARE that as from the termination of the Mandate at midnight, this night of the 14th to 15th May, 1948, and until the setting up of the duly elected bodies of the State in accordance with a Constitution, to be drawn up by a Constituent Assembly not later than the first day of October, 1948, the present National Council shall act as the provisional administration, shall constitute the Provisional Government of the State of Israel.

THE STATE OF ISRAEL will be open to the immigration of Jews from all countries of their dispersion; will promote the development of the country for the benefit of all its inhabitants; will be based on the precepts of liberty, justice and peace taught by the Hebrew Prophets; will uphold the full social and political equality of all its citizens, without distinction of race, creed or sex; will guarantee full freedom of conscience, worship, education and culture; will safeguard the sanctity and inviolability of the shrines and Holy Places of all religions; and will dedicate itself to the principles of the Charter of the United Nations.

After reading this selection, consider these questions:

1. What does this document say about Jewish history?
2. Why do the Zionists claim that they have a right to reclaim their homeland?
3. What problems stood in the way for a peaceful restoration of Eretz-Israel?

SELECTION 6:

Palestine

*A*lthough *the world community for the most part gave recognition to Israel, the Arab neighbors of the new country were not about to acknowledge its independence. Instead the armies of the Arab countries crossed*

*its borders with guns firing and the Israelis had to fight for their lives. Is-
rael survived this test in 1948 and in the several wars that followed. However, peace has still not come to the nation.*

*Arab opposition parties founded their own organization, the Palestine
Liberation Organization (PLO), electing Yasser Arafat to lead it. Its mem-
bership spans a large number of interests, but all are agreed that the
Palestinians have the same rights as Jews to a homeland. The selection
below describes the Palestinian declaration of statehood, a proclamation
still ignored by the Israeli government.*

On November 15, 1988, the Palestine National Council, meeting in Algiers in its nineteenth
session and acting in the name of the Palestinian
people, issued a declaration of independence proclaiming the existence of the state of Palestine.
Shortly thereafter, more than 100 governments
recognized the state of Palestine. The Declaration
of Independence was and remains a central Palestinian document. It was through that document
that Palestinian nationalism formally changed its
position on the two-state solution, pronouncing
UN Resolution 181 (the Partition Resolution of
1947, which provided for the establishment of Israel) an operative part of international law. It
thereby reversed the position taken with respect
to Resolution 181 in the PLO Covenant [that
called for Israel's destruction].

In the month that followed the Declaration of
Independence, the PLO succeeded in meeting the
conditions set down by the United States for negotiations with the PLO (acceptance of Resolution 242, renunciation of terrorism, and acceptance of Israel's right to exist). As a result, the
U.S.-PLO dialogue was initiated, with high expectations on the part of the Palestinians. The
United States had earlier, in September 1988,
taken a strong position in opposition to any unilateral declaration of independence, and when the
dialogue opened, put pressure on the PLO to
abandon such unilateral efforts. At the same time,
the United States demonstrated its ability to
thwart PLO diplomatic efforts, succeeding in
blocking admission of the state of Palestine to the

World Health Organization and successfully
pressuring America's European allies not to con-
fer recognition on the state of Palestine.

The PLO largely abandoned its unilateral efforts at state creation, and over the next seven
years Middle East politics went through the collapse of the U.S.-PLO dialogue, the invasion of
Kuwait, the Gulf War, the Madrid Conference,
the Washington negotiations, the Oslo Accord,
and most recently the Oslo-2 accord on redeploy-
ment and Palestinian elections. . . .

The central fact of the Palestinian experience
is dispossession from land seen as their own in
the ordinary way that any land is seen as belong-
ing to its long-standing inhabitants. Moreover,
the Palestinians have lost their effort to recover
this land in full. Conditions of loss, defeat, state-
lessness, and occupation are conditions in which
personal pride and dignity are threatened and
often shattered. Through resistance and struggle
and refusal to accept defeat and injustice, Palestinians have found modes of existing with dignity despite conditions of weakness. . . .

The strategy of unilaterally creating the Palestinian state and protecting it through a peace initiative was radically different from making concessions in the hope that Israel will agree to
negotiate with the PLO and agree to grant Palestinians a state of their own. The Intifada [the uprising of Palestinian youths against Israeli occupation forces] was a process of massive defiance
and self-assertion. It was a way of tying the hands
of the more powerful Israelis and of stripping
them, in the eyes of the world and in their own
eyes, of their possession of the moral high
ground and even of their self-pride. The Declaration of Independence was an extension of this
process of self-affirmation. By proclaiming the

Jerome M. Segal, "The State of Palestine: The Question of Existence," in *Philosophical Perspectives on the Israeli-Palestinian
Conflict*, ed. Tomis Kapitan (Armonk, NY: M.E. Sharpe, 1997), pp.
221, 233–34.

state of Palestine, it created a perspective from which it was finally possible for the Palestinian movement to launch a sustained and clear peace initiative. It transformed the elements of a peace initiative from concessions to acts of self-assertion, ways of protecting the state, of controlling the agenda, of tying the hands of the other party, and even of transforming his outlook.

Had this process been extended, in particular, had a functioning governmental entity emerged in 1989, the evolution of the behavior and perspective of the Palestinian leadership would have been greatly furthered. The Palestinian leadership was then not yet the leadership of a government. But as it takes on that role, as is at present occurring, it encounters a new ethical, psychological, and political reality.

Movements operate within a different logic from that of governments. Within movements, actors and policies are evaluated and critiqued from a point of view that demands rigourous fidelity to ideals, basic goals, and fundamental norms of justice. Resistance movements can survive only by avoiding stances that strip its participants of dignity. Pragmatic compromise in the face of injustice is extremely difficult for movements. Governments, in contrast, have different primary responsibilities. Their role is to protect and preserve. They bear extended responsibility for the well-being of the populations they claim as citizenry. Moreover, their ability to continue to maintain the generalized obedience necessary for their very existence as governments depends on how adequately they are perceived to be carrying out these functions. Put in a different idiom, one might say that the professional ethics of leaders of a movement are different from that of leaders of a government. A governmental leader who sacrifices vital interests out of pride is judged unfit for high responsibility. The leader of a movement who does the same thing may be viewed as having refused to betray the ideals of the movement.

After reading this selection, consider these questions:

1. Why does this author believe a Palestinian state exists although the Israeli government refuses to recognize its existence?

2. Do you see any comparisons between the Palestinian Liberation Organization and the African National Congress?

3. What makes a settlement in the Arab-Israeli conflict so difficult to obtain?

CHAPTER 20
The Collapse of Communism in the Soviet Union and Eastern Europe and Its Survival in China: What Other Forces Now Shape the Modern World?

The Soviet system created by Joseph Stalin was built upon fear and violence. No one has captured the terror of those years better than the novelist Aleksandr Solzhenitsyn, himself a victim of the system.

In Eastern Europe despite all efforts to repress opposition, the satellite states of Europe had to allow small expressions of dissent. In Czechoslovakia and Poland organizations began to form with the goal of modifying the system. Few people expected that a total collapse of communism was imminent.

In 1985, when the post of general secretary of the Soviet Union's Communist Party came open, the electors of the politburo, the policy-making council, chose Mikhail Gorbachev. It was evident that new ideas were needed to direct the fortunes of the Soviet Union. Most of the collective farms were losing money, and were unable to meet their assigned quotas of food deliveries. Antiquated machinery in industry, corruption among government officials, an unbending party bureaucracy, and an authoritarian system that stifled all efforts to make improvements challenged the new Soviet leader.

He announced a policy of "openness" (*glasnost*) and "restructuring" (*perestroika*) that once begun could not be stopped. The momentum for reform built within the Soviet Union and in Eastern Europe, and soon communism had collapsed.

A different scenario played out in communist China. A series of reforms took place in that country as the influence of Chairman Mao Zedong began to fade. In 1976 Mao died, leaving the leadership in the hands of Deng Xiaoping. Deng permitted others to hold official positions in the government and party, but managed affairs from behind the scene. The growing economic freedom in the country caused a movement for democracy to sweep the nation, especially among the student population. In 1989 Deng and the party hierarchy were confronted by a demonstration of 100,000 reformers in Tiananmen Square in Beijing demanding change. Instead the party officials ordered the tanks to roll, dispersing the protesters and assuring that the party should remain in unchallenged power.

SELECTION 1:

The Knock on the Door

*T*he following selection gives Solzhenitsyn's view of the Stalinist years of terror. Reading it should help you understand why people wanted change.

Arrest is an instantaneous, shattering thrust, expulsion, somersault from one state into another.

We have been happily borne—or perhaps have unhappily dragged our weary way—down the long and crooked streets of our lives, past all kinds of walls and fences made of rotting wood, rammed earth, brick, concrete, iron railings. We have never given a thought to what lies behind them. We have never tried to penetrate them with our vision or our understanding. But there is where the *Gulag* country begins, right next to us, two yards away from us. In addition, we have failed to notice an enormous number of closely fitted, well-disguised doors and gates in these fences. All those gates were prepared for us, every last one! And all of a sudden the fateful gate swings quickly open, and four white male hands, unaccustomed to physical labor but nonetheless strong and tenacious, grab us by the leg, arm, collar, cap, ear, and drag us in like a sack, and the gate behind us, the gate to our past life, is slammed shut once and for all.

That's all there is to it! You are arrested!

And you'll find nothing better to respond with than a lamblike bleat: "Me? What for?"

That's what arrest is: it's a blinding flash and a blow which shifts the present instantly into the past and the impossible into omnipotent actuality.

That's all. And neither for the first hour nor for the first day will you be able to grasp anything else.

Except that in your desperation the fake circus moon will blink at you: "It's a mistake! They'll

set things right!"

And everything which is by now comprised in the traditional, even literary, image of an arrest will pile up and take shape, not in your own disordered memory, but in what your family and your neighbors in your apartment remember: The sharp nighttime ring or the rude knock at the door. The insolent entrance of the unwiped jackboots of the unsleeping State Security operatives. The frightened and cowed civilian witness at their backs. (And what function does this civilian witness serve? The victim doesn't even dare think about it and the operatives don't remember, but that's what the regulations call for, and so he has to sit there all night long and sign in the morning. For the witness, jerked from his bed, it is torture too—to go out night after night to help arrest his own neighbors and acquaintances.)

The traditional image of arrest is also trembling hands packing for the victim—a change of underwear, a piece of soap, something to eat; and no one knows what is needed, what is permitted, what clothes are best to wear; and the Security agents keep interrupting and hurrying you:

"You don't need anything. They'll feed you there. It's warm there." (It's all lies. They keep hurrying you to frighten you.)

The traditional image of arrest is also what happens afterward, when the poor victim has been taken away. It is an alien, brutal, and crushing force totally dominating the apartment for hours on end, a breaking, ripping open, pulling from the walls, emptying things from wardrobes and desks onto the floor, shaking, dumping out, and ripping apart—piling up mountains of litter on the floor—and the crunch of things being trampled beneath jackboots. And nothing is sa-

Aleksandr I. Solzhenitsyn, *The Gulag Archipelago, 1918–1956,* trans. Thomas P. Whitney (New York: Harper and Row, 1973), pp. 4–6.

cred in a search! During the arrest of the locomotive engineer Inoshin, a tiny coffin stood in his room containing the body of his newly dead child. The "*jurists*" dumped the child's body out of the coffin and searched it. They shake sick people out of their sickbeds, and they unwind bandages to search beneath them. . . .

For those left behind after the arrest there is the long tail end of a wrecked and devastated life. And the attempts to go and deliver food parcels. But from all the windows the answer comes in barking voices: "Nobody here by that name!" "Never heard of him!" Yes, and in the worst days in Leningrad it took five days of standing in crowded lines just to get to that window. And it

may be only after half a year or a year that the arrested person responds at all. Or else the answer is tossed out: "Deprived of the right to correspond." And that means once and for all. "No right to correspondence"—and that almost for certain means: "Has been shot."

After reading this selection, consider these questions:
1. What does Solzhenitsyn recall about the multiple arrests of the KGB, the security secret police?
2. How did the KGB perform its duties?
3. What became of many who were placed under arrest?

SELECTION 2:

Obstacles to Soviet Reform

It was against such a regimen that at last the weary Soviet people found hope in the election of Mikhail Gorbachev. Already after Stalin's death there had been some improvements in safeguarding personal liberties, but it was only when Gorbachev announced reforms of major consequence that major changes occurred.

In his Memoirs, *excerpted below, Gorbachev recalls these events that transformed both Soviet foreign and domestic policy at a meeting with his advisers in early 1986. Here they sought to prepare a report for the Twenty-Seventh Communist Party Congress that would open up the system to reform.*

Of fundamental importance in the report was its stress on the interconnectedness, interdependence and integrity of the world, which had an enormous effect on our own and on world politics. Indeed, if this view is accepted as valid, the division of the world into opposing blocs must be seen as absurd. Thus the report contains the following statements: "The policy of all-out struggle

and military confrontation does not have a future." "The arms race, like nuclear war itself, cannot be won." "We must follow a path of cooperation to create a comprehensive system of international security." Therefore "security is a political problem, and it can be solved only by political means."

We linked the transformation of society to the course of accelerated social and economic development that had been adopted at the April plenum [meeting]. What we had in mind was not a revolution but a specific improvement of the system, which we then believed was possible. We

Mikhail Gorbachev, *Memoirs* (New York: Doubleday, 1996), pp. 185, 187–88.

longed for freedom so much that we thought that if we just gave society a breath of fresh air it would revive. We understood freedom in a broad sense, to include actual, not just rhetorical, control of the land by farmers, and of factories by workers, freedom of enterprise, changes in our investment and structural policies and an emphasis on social development. We were aware—although we did not formulate this idea very specifically—of the need for democratization of society and the state, and for the development of people's self-government.

It was almost a year after the April turnaround. It was obvious that the policy of *perestroika* was seen by many as just another campaign, which would soon run out of steam. We had to eliminate doubts of this kind and convince people of the need for the new course, and so the theme of *glasnost*—"transparency"—came up in the report. "Democracy does not and cannot exist without glasnost." "Glasnost must be made unfailing. It is necessary at the center, but no less and perhaps even more in the provinces, where people live and work."

This "accord" achieved at the XXVIIth Congress set up something of a trap for the new leadership. The process of perestroika was bound to move beyond the decisions of the Congress very quickly. The reformers would then be accused of "revisionism," with predictable consequences. There was one way of avoiding this threat: to employ the authority of the Central Committee. According to Party tradition the Central Committee was the real center of power and could make any decision while making only formal references to the guidelines of the last congress.

The Congress closed on 6 March. I immediately invited the Central Committee Secretaries and government members for a talk about the business in hand. First was the problem of the decentralization of the economy, which was already provoking a hostile reaction from the bureaucratic apparatus. I spotted signs of misunderstanding and dissatisfaction even in the upper echelons of the Party and government leadership. However, I was encouraged by the attitudes of the leaders of economic organizations and enterprises.

After the Congress I met newspaper editors and the heads of television and arts organizations, contacts that became a regular thing. But I was most interested in what was happening in the labor collectives, how the people were taking the decisions of the Congress and what actions the cadres were taking. In early April I left for Kuibyshev, which is today called Samara. I went there because major industry is concentrated in this region. . . .

The visit lasted three days. My first sensation was that a time machine had taken me back exactly a year. The secretaries of the oblast [regional party organization] and city committees glared all the time at their subordinates, defining the "permissible" measure of communication between the General Secretary and the people. They would hold up a hand to stop people who were eager for a frank talk, or they broke off conversations that in their view were "unnecessary." My desire to learn the true state of affairs clearly did not suit the local bosses. My talking directly to the people so upset some of them that they tactlessly tried to break in. I had to publicly put them in their places and say that just then I was not interested in talking to them. Their faces would turn red with indignation.

I was glad to see the desire of the workers at the auto plant to master the new methods of economic management—it seemed that they succeeded in this better than others. At that time, the program of modernization was being successfully implemented by the local metallurgy plant. The time for fast-moving and enterprising people had come.

Yet such successes were few and far between. Nor was I receiving encouraging reports from colleagues visiting other regions of the country. The general feeling was that everything was slowed by inertia; the policy of perestroika was making no impact on the life of cities and enterprises. There was a stream of letters to the Central Committee, most of them filled with alarm at the lack of action of local officials. A man from Stavropol bitterly reported that when he approached the director of a state farm with plans for improving production, the director had turned him out of his office telling him not to pry—"It is none of your business." "So this is the way it is," the man concluded his letter, "even after the Congress it's still none of my business." I also got a letter from Gorky, from Vasily Mishin, a former fellow-student at Moscow State University and now a doctor of philosophy and head of department: "Keep in mind, Mikhail, nothing is happening in Gorky, not a thing!"

At the 24 April Politburo meeting we discussed the reasons why perestroika was stuck. The feeling was that it had run up against the gigantic Party and state apparatus, which stood like a dam in the path of reforms.

After reading this selection, consider these questions:
1. What was Gorbachev's goal in introducing his report to the Twenty-Seventh Party Congress?
2. Why were the bureaucrats in the party threatened by the reforms?
3. How was it possible that local officials could thwart *perestroika*?

SELECTION 3:

Slogans in a Grocery Store

Václav Havel, an author, was one of communism's major critics within his nation of Czechoslovakia. His pleas for a more just system during the dangerous times of repression merited him the presidency of his country after communism's collapse. He wrote the following selection early in the 1980s, when to speak the truth still had serious risks.

The manager of a fruit and vegetable shop places in his window, among the onions and carrots, the slogan: "Workers of the World, Unite!" Why does he do it? What is he trying to communicate to the world? Is he genuinely enthusiastic about the idea of unity among the workers of the world? Is his enthusiasm so great that he feels an irrepressible impulse to acquaint the public with his ideals? Has he really given more than a moment's thought to how such a unification might occur and what it would mean?

I think it can safely be assumed that the overwhelming majority of shopkeepers never think about the slogans they put in their windows, nor do they use them to express their real opinions. That poster was delivered to our greengrocer from the enterprise headquarters along with the onions and carrots. He put them all into the windows simply because it has been done that way for years, because everyone does it, and because that is the way it has to be. If he were to refuse, there could be trouble. He could be reproached for not having the proper "decoration" in his window; someone might even accuse him of disloyalty. He does it because these things must be done if one is to get along in life. It is one of the thousands of details that guarantee him a relatively tranquil life "in harmony with society," as they say. . . .

Let us now imagine that one day something in our greengrocer snaps and he stops putting up the slogans merely to ingratiate himself. He stops voting in elections he knows are a farce. He begins to say what he really thinks at political meetings. And he even finds the strength in himself to express solidarity with those whom his conscience commands him to support. In this revolt the greengrocer steps out of living within the lie.

Václav Havel et al., *The Power of the Powerless*, ed. John Keane (Armonk, NY: M.E. Sharpe, 1985), pp. 27–28, 39–40.

He rejects the ritual and breaks the rules of the game. He discovers once more his suppressed identity and dignity. He gives his freedom a concrete significance. His revolt is an attempt to *live within the truth.*

The bill is not long in coming. He will be relieved of his post as manager of the shop and transferred to the warehouse. His pay will be reduced. His hopes for a holiday in Bulgaria will evaporate. His children's access to higher education will be threatened. His superiors will harass him and his fellow workers will wonder about him. Most of those who apply these sanctions, however, will not do so from any authentic inner conviction but simply under pressure from conditions, the same conditions that once pressured the greengrocer to display the official slogans. They will persecute the greengrocer either because it is expected of them, or to demonstrate their loyalty, or simply as part of the general panorama, to which belongs an awareness that this is how situations of this sort are dealt with, that this, in fact, is how things are always done, particularly if one is not to become suspect oneself. The executors, therefore, behave essentially like everyone else, to a greater or lesser degree: as components of the post-totalitarian system, as agents of its automatism, as petty instruments of the social auto-totality.

Thus the power structure, through the agency of those who carry out the sanctions, those anonymous components of the system, will spew the greengrocer from its mouth. The system, through its alienating presence in people, will punish him for his rebellion. It must do so because the logic of its automatism and self-defense dictate it. The greengrocer has not committed a simple, individual offense, isolated in its own uniqueness, but something incomparably more serious. By breaking the rules of the game, he has disrupted the game as such. He has exposed it as a mere game. He has shattered the world of appearances, the fundamental pillar of the system. He has upset the power structure by tearing apart what holds it together. He has demonstrated that living a lie is living a lie. He has broken through the exalted façade of the system and exposed the real, base foundation of power.

After reading this selection, consider these questions:

1. Why were slogans delivered along with produce in communist Czechoslovakia?
2. What happens to a person who rejects the slogans?
3. Why does Havel call the communist system a game?

SELECTION 4:

Communism in China

The crackdown in Tiananmen Square alerted the Chinese Communist Party leaders that they needed to improve their image lest they go the way of the Soviets. Their decision was to permit continued liberalization of the economy, but holding the line against any political reforms that would challenge the party's political control of the country. Dissidents who called for political reform ended up in prison or in exile, while asking for economic change was tolerated and even encouraged. The standard of living for most Chinese has improved in the last decade, but has declined in

*Russia and the new states of the former Soviet Union. A Western observer
analyzes this in the selection below.*

The Central Committee's 1989 four-part agenda . . . included the promotion of ideological work and patriotism, the improvement of the Party's image, and the punishment of corruption. The goal was to reduce the latent criticisms of the Party by pushing conformity and patriotism and to purify the Party in order to regain popular legitimacy.

Over the years, endless doctrinal shifts and reversals had infected ideological belief with cynicism. To counter this, the authorities dusted off the old political study meetings in schools and workplaces. They also, predictably, launched a campaign to emulate Lei Feng [a particularly devoted young Communist]. To enhance the image of Party cadres [groups of Party officials] as being close to the masses, they began an image campaign for the Party and army and a program of sending down middle- and junior officials to lower levels. The propagandists also warned against the international "peaceful evolution" conspiracy against China's socialist system. Even sports was enlisted for politics when Beijing hosted the summer 1990 Asian Games, in which China won the lion's share of medals. Other international athletic events were also used to build national pride.

One would think that reducing corruption would have met with immense public applause, but unfortunately, this was not so easy. The new economic system placed Party officials and cadres in the way of great temptation, with the result that corruption reached into the very highest families, who were unlikely to jail their own children. Some much-publicized corruption prosecutions were reported, but those indicted did not include many big fish. A reregistration of Party members was announced, but its purpose was mainly to discipline those who had sided with the Tiananmen students. . . .

Between 1978 and the early 1990s, the world changed dramatically. Most striking was the collapse of the Soviet Union and its satellite system, the fragmentation of Yugoslavia and Czechoslovakia, and the general refutation of socialist central planning. Meanwhile the growth of the "Pacific Rim" economies (Japan, South Korea, Taiwan, Singapore, and Hong Kong) and other Asian countries continued. As the Soviet-American competition ended, global multipolar politics set in. International business continued to leap across national boundaries and to spread technology and popular culture. . . .

As for the women of China, the demise of the communes and control systems that once governed behavior, and the reemergence of traditional and other arrangements, have led to complex results. Although for many women there are new economic opportunities, many others remain on the land while their husbands and brothers seek industrial employment. Bride price, forced abortions, female infanticide, the kidnapping of women for sale, and other abuses are still frequently reported.

In regard to ideology and culture, the reform period has stirred the once-quiescent pot into a roiling soup of contradiction and confusion. Marxism and socialism are hard pressed to retain any integrity, as official ideologies attempt to refashion some of the fundamental building blocks. What, after all, does socialism mean when it must find a place for all kinds of "capitalistic" elements? Calling it "socialism with Chinese characteristics" helps a little, but not much. Furthermore, Marxism's decline has left a cultural vacuum. Consumption, money-making, and Hong Kong fashions cannot define a fully meaningful existence. Traditional practices and folk religion have reappeared in the villages but may also be unable to shape life in a modern contest of mobility, gender demands, and international economics.

Western ideas like freedom, democracy, and individualism flourish among the educated, but not necessarily among ordinary people; because Western societies, the United States in particular, present ambiguous models, the "streets of gold"

Craig Dietrich, *People's China: A Brief History,* 2nd ed. (New York: Oxford University Press, 1994), pp. 310–11, 314.

myths clashing with news reports of drugs, crime, and chaos. Hence the intellectual and cultural challenge: how to fashion on the rubble of Marxism (and while the rulers stubbornly chant their Marxist mantras) a reasonably coherent set of values and social principles.

After reading this selection, consider these questions:

1. Why are there many contradictions in modern Chinese life?
2. Do you see Marxism as still a moving force in the Chinese Communist Party?
3. Would you predict that the party will be able to control China into the future? What exactly will be its role?

SELECTION 5:
The Muslim Future

In regions of the Muslim world a different set of problems exist. Here a movement is emerging among those people who reject the West and its ways and promote a view of a society that is guided by traditional Islam. While called "fundamentalists" in the West, they are better called revivalists, for they look back to a time when Islam shaped all the values of men and women in the regions where Islam was dominant. In the following selection, a scholar of the Islamic world attempts to analyze the movement, pointing out that a romanticized view of the past is not always a good guide for the present.

The history of the Middle East and of the wider Muslim world reveals a variety of institutional situations. The supposed Muslim norm of the integration of state and religious authority, and the identification of state and religious community, actually characterized only a small segment of Middle Eastern and other Muslim populations. Undifferentiated state-religious situations were characteristic of lineage or tribal societies, as in Muhammad's Arabia, North Africa and Morocco, early Safavid Iran, and as in the reformist period of the eighteenth and nineteenth centuries. Even in such cases the conquest of an agriculture-based, urbanized society would start a process of differentiation that broke down the integral con-

nection of state and religion.

Conversely, the historic norm of Middle Eastern agro-urban-imperial societies has been the institutional differentiation of state and religion. Royal households or courts, political élites and the language and cultural style of the ruling classes were different from those of religious élites. In the 'Abbāsid, Saljuq, Ottoman and Safavid empires the central fact is the differentiation of state and religious institutions, and the central problem has been to define the relations of the two. These relations vary across a wide spectrum from a high degree of state control over a centrally managed religious establishment, to a more independent but co-operative relationship (as in the Saljuq case), to full autonomy and even open opposition to state policies. . . .

However, despite the appeal to the unity of state, religion and civil society, there is a consid-

I.M. Lapidus, "State and Religion in Islamic Societies," *Past and Present*, vol. 146–49 (1995), pp. 24–27.

erable uncertainty about the ideal goals of the re-vival movements. The union of state and society envisioned in the neo-Islamic rhetoric is not an institutional arrangement or a commitment to any particular type of state institution, be it monar-chical, representative, democratic, capitalist or socialist. The revivalist movements are not inter-ested in constitutions; they are concerned rather with individual morals and ethical behaviour. To them the state is simply the force that requires the mass of the people to adhere to Islamic laws. The ideal state has no institutional form; it is embod-ied in the leadership of individuals dedicated to Islam who mobilize other individuals to realize religious values.

Thus the revival movements have ambiguous political implications. While some revivalists be-lieve that the control of the state is essential to the success of an Islamic social and moral pro-gramme, in practice it is not always clear that the revival movements give priority to political ob-jectives. Many look upon states as inherently cor-rupt and incapable of realizing Muslim values. The state is not expected to embody transcendent values. Because they do not see the state as a realm of moral fulfillment, they do not expect that it will serve their aspirations for empowerment and economic well-being either. As in the case of their historical predecessors, there is an ambigui-ty in their attitude towards political power which leaves the way open for a renewed separation of political and religio-communal concerns. . . .

This historical orientation provides a template for the construction of modern Middle Eastern states around secular cultural identities and de-velopment goals defined in either capitalist or so-cialist terms. In such states as Turkey, Tunisia, Egypt, Syria, Iraq and Jordan, Islam has been dis-established or the Islamic religious establishment brought under state control. Islam no longer le-gitimates the state and no longer defines its moral or social vision. All of these states have set up secular educational and judicial systems which

actually compete with, and even replace, the pri-mary functions of Islam. Where Muslim religious life has in general become separated from state institutions, it flourishes in a differentiated "civil society." The fact that the mass of the population has Muslim loyalties means that states give spe-cial consideration to Muslim symbols and Mus-lim practices. In recent years, with the rising im-portance of mass Islamic identifications and strong Islamist political movements, state élites have deferred to popular pressure for official recognition of the primacy of Islam and have re-laxed, or even reversed, the earlier demand for secularism; still, this has not led to the disman-tling of secular legal or educational institutions.

In so far as the historic legacy remains an im-portant factor in the contemporary Muslim world, its diversity is the basis of a corresponding diversity in the relations of states and religious communities. Today, as has been true since an-cient times, we still find both integralist religio-political movements, states defined in Islamic terms, a *de facto* institutional differentiation of state and religion, and a great variety of relation-ships between the two. Are the Islamic cases really different from the Christian, or the Middle Eastern cases from the European? Or is it time to abandon the clichés concerning the unity of Islam in favour of a more complex and realistic appreciation of the issues?

After reading this selection, consider these questions:
  1. Does the author argue that there was a single pattern for Islamic states in the past?
  2. Why is it usual to have tension between church and state in all societies?
  3. Why do you think politicians in Islamic countries find it useful to show what fervent Muslims they are?

SELECTION 6:

The Democratic Ideal

The final selection to this book of readings ends with a question: To what degree is democratic government becoming the norm throughout the world? If, as Americans hold, democracy offers people the best form of government, then what obstacles still exist in its exportation to other countries of the world? Can anything be done to encourage its progress? The journalist and diplomat Strobe Talbott asks that question in the selection below.

Many newcomers to the democratic fold qualify only as partly free. In fledgling democracies, especially countries where the wounds of civil war are still raw and the memory of oppressive rule still weighs heavy, politics can be especially volatile. The old regime's surviving elites divide into factions and vie for advantage in the new order, or for the spoils of the new disorder. Newly elected leaders, unsure of their hold on power or too sure of their infallibility and indispensability, use a heavy hand to silence the opposition, loyal and otherwise. . . .

Throughout the post-communist world, especially in the former Soviet Union, relief and a sense of good riddance at the dismantling of the inefficient, top-heavy command system has given way to wide-spread resentment at what often seems to be the capriciousness and inequity of the market, and to insecurity over the absence of a safety net. Without the prospect of broad-based economic development, voters are likely to become disillusioned with politics and politicians, and thus with democracy itself. Newly enfranchised citizens tend to have unrealistically high expectations about what their elected leaders can accomplish, how long it will take, and how much hardship will be involved. When those expectations are disappointed, voters become vulnerable to demagogic purveyors of foolish or dangerous nostrums based on nostalgia or fear.

In short, the third wave has created an undertow in many countries that have embarked on democratization. . . .

While the idea of democracy is potentially viable everywhere, the process of democratization is long and hard, especially for countries where political progress is hostage to economic disadvantage. Poverty, underdevelopment, and stagnation are not alibis for tyranny, but they are obstacles to freedom. In many countries the gap between the poor and the wealthy is widening as the state undergoes a double transition—from authoritarian to democratic politics and from centralized to market economies. Some regions have the added burden of unsustainable population growth. Even with freely elected and well-intentioned leaders, a country where a rising birthrate outpaces economic growth and exhausts natural resources is unlikely to sustain democratic rule. . . .

There are also hard-core holdouts. Cuba is the Western hemisphere's lone authoritarian regime, and North Korea stands in stark contrast to the thriving democracy to its south. In Burma, a junta of military strongmen suppresses the democracy movement; Aung San Suu Kyi, whose party won a resounding electoral victory in 1990, remains under house arrest.

Then there is China, by virtue of its size the most notable exception to the worldwide trend toward democracy. Chinese leaders maintain that

Strobe Talbott, "Democracy and the National Interest," *Foreign Affairs* (November/December 1996), pp. 55–57.

economic development must precede democratization, and they cite the recent history of South Korea, Taiwan, and other "Asian tigers" to support their case for authoritarian rule in China. In fact, the experience of those nations conveys a more complicated lesson: promoting economic growth while monopolizing political power is an almost impossible balancing act over the long term, especially in a world increasingly linked by communications and trade. As people's incomes rise and their horizons broaden, they are more likely to demand the right to participate in government and to enjoy full protection under the rule of law. The pro-democracy demonstrations that culminated in the bloody crackdown by the military in Tiananmen Square in 1989 suggested that China's urban dwellers were impatient with their leaders' timetable for extending political freedoms.

U.S. policy toward the People's Republic is predicated on the conviction that continued economic and cultural engagement is the best way to induce democratization. That approach does not mean giving the Chinese authorities a pass on human rights, but it does mean recognizing how far China has come in the relatively recent past, and taking the long view on the future. The powers that be remain fearful about loosening political controls, but ordinary Chinese are much freer today than when China began opening to the outside world in the 1970s. It is by no means certain that the liberalizing trend will culminate in full democracy, but the prospects would be worse without active American engagement.

After reading this selection, consider these questions:

1. Why are new democracies difficult to sustain?
2. What connection exists between democratization and economic progress?
3. How do you define freedom?

Acknowledgments

UNIT ONE
Chapter 3:
  Selection 4 Reprinted from Richard Rex, "The Crisis of Obedience: God's Word and Henry's Reformation," *Historical Journal,* vol. 39, no. 4 (December 1996): 863–94, by permission of the author and Cambridge University Press.

Chapter 4:
  Selection 1 From *Louis XIV and Twenty Million Frenchmen,* by Pierre Goubert. Copyright © 1966 by Librarie Artheme Fayard. Translation copyright © 1970 by Anne Carter. Reprinted by permission of Pantheon Books, a division of Random House, Inc.

Chapter 8:
  Selection 8 From *Japan and Its World,* by Marius B. Jansen. Copyright © 1980 by Princeton University Press. Reprinted by permission of Princeton University Press.

Chapter 10:
  Selection 5 From Tulio Halperín Donghi, *The Contemporary History of Latin America,* translated by John Charles Chasteen. Copyright 1993, Duke University Press. Reprinted with permission.

UNIT TWO
Chapter 11:
  Selection 2 Reprinted from *Women and the Limits of Citizenship in the French Revolution,* by Olwen H. Hufton, by permission of the University of Toronto Press. Copyright © 1992 Olwen H. Hufton.

UNIT THREE
Chapter 20:
  Selection 5 Reprinted from Ira Lapidus, "State and Religion in Islamic Societies," *Past and Present,* no. 151 (1995): 24–27, by permission of the author and the Past and Present Society.

  Selection 6 Reprinted from Strobe Talbott, "Democracy and the National Interest," *Foreign Affairs,* vol. 75, no. 6 (1996), by permission of *Foreign Affairs.* Copyright 1996 by the Council on Foreign Relations, Inc.

Index

Absolutism, Age of, 60
Africa
  in colonial age, 162–64
  east coast of
    description of, 112
    Portuguese encounters with, 110–11
  Gold Coast of, 21, 22
  obstacles to European expansion in, 18
  West
    growth of kingdoms in, 106–107
    trends in colonial policy in, 163–64
  see also South Africa
African National Congress (ANC), 213
  democratic vision of, 214–15
Akbar, 87–88
Alexander, John T., 67
Alexander VI (pope), 36
Ali, Mustafa, 79
American colonies, 113
  objection to taxation by Britain of, 114–15
Antonov-Ovseenko, Vladimir, 182
apartheid, 213–14
Arafat, Yasser, 219
Aristotle, 60
Aron, Raymond, 194
Aryans
  movement into India of, 84
Ashworth, William, 144
Augustine, Saint, 43
Ayuba Suleiman Diallo (Job ben Solomon), 108
Aztec Empire, 32

Babur the Lion, 87
Bach, Johann Sebastian, 71–72
Balkans
  as flash point for WW I, 169
  under Ottoman rule, 75–77
Barbosa, Duarte, 111
Barbot, John, 105

Beasley, W.G., 164
Belzec death camp, 196
Ben-Gurion, David, 217
Benin, 105–106
Berlin Wall, 205
Bernier, François, 90
Bethmann-Hollweg, Theobald von, 170, 172
Bianco, Lucien, 207
Blanc, Louis, 151
Blücher, Evelyn, 176
Bluett, Thomas, 108
Bolívar, Simon, 120
  resignation of, 121–22
Bolshevik revolution
  as beginning of world revolution, 183
  Stalin's assertion of self-sufficiency of, 184
  Trotsky's account of, 180–81
Bolsheviks, 179
  capture of Winter Palace, 181–82
Book of Dede Korkut, The, 80
Bophuthatswana, 214
bourgeoisie, 142–43
Boyacá, battle of, 120
Bridge, Anthony, 77
British East India Company, 91–93
  mutiny in ranks of, 160
Bühler, Josef, 196
Burke, Edmund
  on French Revolution, 132–33
Byrnes, James, 200
Byzantium
  effect on Ottoman state, 74

caciques, 33
Calvin, John, 44
  views on women in the church, 46
Calvinism, 57
Cambaya, 112
Caribbean Crisis, 205

Carmelite Order, 50

Carsten, F.L., 191

Casa de Contratación, 38

caste system, 84

Catherine of Aragon, 47

Catherine the Great (Russian monarch), 67–69

    criticism of, 70–71

Charles II (king of England), 92

Charles V (Holy Roman emperor), 40, 44

Chiang Kai-shek, 198, 206

Chick, N.A., 160

China

    culture of, under Manchus, 99–100

    decline of Marxism in, 227–28

    and democracy, 230–31

    eating habits in, 98–99

    influence on Japan, 102–103

    Mao's social revolution in, 207–208

    society of

        in eighteenth century, 95–96

        Mao's Marxist view on, 206–207

    Tiananmen Square crackdown, 226

Christianity

    in Japan, 102

    in Ottoman Empire, 76, 77

    and Protestant Reformation, 42

    spread of

        in Africa, 107

        by Dutch, 29

        among European colonies, 158

        hypocrisy of Spanish in, 21, 36

Churchill, Winston, 201

    diplomatic failure of, 202

Ciskei, 214

civil state

    Rousseau's views on, 65–66

Clapham, Sir John, 142

Clive, Robert, 93

Cobo, Bernabe, 41

Colbert, Jean-Baptiste, 54

Cold War, 199

Colombia

    formation of, 120

colonists

    New England, assumptions of, 30–31

Columbus, Christopher, 24

    achievements of, 26–27

and sugar trade, 40

Committee of Public Safety (French Revolution), 131

Common Sense (Paine), 115

communism

    Chinese

        and Japanese aggression, 197

        after Tiananmen Square, 226

        German middle-class fear of, 192

Communist Manifesto (Marx and Engels), 143, 183

Confucianism, 94, 95

    in Japan, 103

Confucius, 94

Conquest, Robert, 187

Copernicus, Nicolaus, 60

Cornwallis, Lord Charles, 92

    view of Indians, 93

Correa, Gasper, 23

Cortés, Hernando, 32

    meeting with Moctezuma, 33–34

Council of the Indies, 37

Council of Trent, 50

Creoles, 113, 119

Cronon, William, 30

Crosby, Alfred W., 40

Crowder, Michael, 162

Cuauhtémoc, 34

Cuba, 157

    missile crisis in, 205

    as post–Cold War holdout, 230

Cuitlahuac, Lord of, 34

Czechoslovakia, 225

da Gama, Vasco, 110

Dahomey

    female army of, 108

d'Almeida (viceroy of India), 110

Dalzel, Archibald, 107

de Klerk, F.W.

    meeting with Nelson Mandela, 215–16

del Castillo, Bernal Díaz, 33

de la Cruz, Juana Inés, 51

de Las Casas, Bartolomé, 25, 35

democracy

    Fascist view of, 190

    obstacles to process of, 230

    in South Africa, ANC vision of, 214–15

    in U.S., de Tocqueville's view of, 118

de Mugaburu, Josephe, 39
Deng Xiaoping, 221
Descartes, René, 163
de Secondat, Charles-Louis, 64
de Sucre, Antonio José, 120
de Tocqueville, Alexis, 118
Deutscher, Isaac, 184
de Zamárraga, Juan, 49–50
Dias, Bartolomeu, 23
Dietrich, Craig, 226
Donghi, Tulio Halperín, 119
Douglass, Jane Dempsey, 45
Doyle, William, 130
Dundas, Henry, 93
du Plessis, Armand-Jean (Cardinal Richelieu), 53
Dutch East India Company, 28–29
Dutch West India Company, 28
Dzerzhinsky, Feliks, 188

Einstein, Albert, 62
Elizabeth Charlotte (Duchess d'Orleans), 55
Elizabeth I (queen of England), 56
Engels, Friedrich, 143
Enlightenment, 63
Essay on the Principle of Population (Malthus), 138
ethnie (national consciousness), 148
Europe
    Eastern, Soviet domination of, 201–202
    expansion into other lands, 18, 156
        limits of, in Africa, 107
    industrialization of, 137

Fage, J.D., 21, 106
Fascism
    fundamentals of, 190
Ferdinand (archduke of Austria), 78
Ferdinand, Franz (Austro-Hungarian archduke), 169
Ferdinand VII (king of Spain), 119
Fernández-Armesto, Felipe, 26
fiesta
    in colonial Lima, 39
First Zionist Congress, 217
Fischer, Fritz, 171
Five-Year Plan, Soviet, 185
    purposes of, 186
Frank, Hans, 196
Frazee, Charles, 75

Frederick the Great, 72
Frederick the Wise, 44
Frederick William IV (king of Prussia), 152
French Revolution, 126
    Documents of 1848, 151
    role of women in, 128–30
    violence of, 131–32

Galileo, 60–61
Gandhi, Indira, 211
    personality cult of, 213
Gandhi, Mohandas K., 210
Gardner, Brian, 92
Garibaldi, Giuseppe, 154
Germany
    life in, during WW I, 176–77
    restraints on, from Versailles treaty, 177–78
    and Tripartite Pact, 198
    war aims of 1914, 171–72
    under Weimar Republic, 189
glasnost (openness), 221, 224
Globocnik, Odilo, 196
Gorbachev, Mikhail, 168, 221, 223
Goubert, Pierre, 54
Great Britain
    American colonies' objection to taxation by, 114–15
    control of India by, 161–62
    development of railroad and steamships in, 144–45
    economic and cultural influence on colonies of, 157–58
    nineteenth-century laborers in, 141–42
    opposition to WW I in, 173
    Paine's view on independence from, 115–16
    relinquishes Mandate for Palestine, 217–18
Groote Schuur Minute, 216
Guinea
    Portuguese in, 21–22
Gutman, Yisrael, 195–97

Hastings, Warren, 93
Havel, Václav, 225
Henderson, W.O., 145
Henry VIII (king of England), 47
Henry the Navigator, Prince, 104
    and Portuguese expeditions, 20
Herzl, Theodor, 217
Hibbert, Christopher, 154
Himmler, Heinrich, 196

Hind Swaraj, 210
Hinduism, 84
   literature of, 85–86
Hitler, Adolf, 168, 192
   racist theories of, 193
   war strategies of, 194–95
Hodgson, Marshall G.S., 74
Holocaust
   and urgency for Jewish homeland, 217–18
Hobsbawm, E.J., 157
Huang, Ray, 96
Hufton, Olwen H., 128
Huguenots, 53
Hungary
   Soviet occupation of, 203

Ibadatkhana, 87, 88
imperialism
   British, 157–58
   European, 18
     effects of, 157–58
     limits of, in Africa, 107
India
   British East India Company in, 91–93
   under British Empire, 161
   Mughal period
     Babur initiates, 87
     economy of, 88–89
     wealth of emperor, 90
   Muslim invasion of, 87
   political unification in, 84
   Portuguese trade with, 23
   Sepoy Rebellion, 160
Indian Civil Service, 162
industrialization
   contribution to international trade, 146
   of Europe, 137
   of Soviet Union under Five-Year Plan, 185–86
   solutions to plight of laborers following, 142
   and steam engine, 144
Ingersoll, Charles, 117
Institutes of the Christian Religion (Calvin), 44
Intifada (Palestinian uprising), 219
Irish potato famine, 41
Isabella (queen of Spain), 25
Islam
   conversion of Balkan nobility to, 74

   fundamentalist/revivalist movement in, 228
   influence on Ottomans, 73
   see also Muslims
Israel, 168
   creation of, 217–18
   PLO acceptance of, 219
Italy
   Garibaldi's attempt to unify, 155
   nationalist movement in, 153–54
   rise of Fascism in, 189

James, William, 174
James I (king of England), 56
   relations with Parliament, 58–59
Janissaries, 74, 75
Japan
   pre–WW II territorial ambitions of, 197
   riding etiquette in, 101–102
   during Tokugawa period
     economy under, 164–65
     isolation of, 102
Jayakur, Pupul, 211
Jensen, Marius B., 102
Jews
   mass deportation from Warsaw of, 196–97
   Nazi exclusion of, 191
Jews of Warsaw, The (Gutman), 196
Jinnah, Ali, 211
Joll, James, 173

Kennedy, John F., 205
Kerensky, Aleksandr, 181
Khrushchev, Nikita, 205
Kilwa, Congo, 110, 111
Kingsnorth, G.W., 110
Kitchener, Lord Horatio, 162
kokugaku (National Studies) movement, 103
Kostov, Taicho, 187
Kovács, Béla, 203
Kriegesgefahr (danger of war), 170

La Concepción Convent, 50
Lal, Muni, 87
Lapidus, I.M., 228
Lavrin, Asunción, 49
Lenin, Vladimir Ilich Ulyanov, 180, 182
Leopold (king of Belgium), 163

Le Tellier, François-Michel, 54

Lima, Peru, 39

Lin Ze Xu, 159

Louis XIV (king of France), 53
    territorial gains under, 54–55

Louis-Phillipe (king of France), 151

luan (social chaos), 95–96

Ludwig III (king of Bavaria), 172

Luther, Martin, 41, 42, 43
    views on women in the church, 46

Macartney, Lord George, 99

Maintenon, Madame de, 55–56

Malabar, 23–24

Malthus, Thomas, 138

Manchus
    relationship with Chinese, 99–100

Mandela, Nelson, 215

Mao Zedong, 168, 221
    Marxist view of Chinese society, 206–207

Marina, Doña, 33

Marsh, Zoë, 110

Martel, Charles, 78

Marx, Karl, 143

Marxism
    decline of, in China, 227

Mary, Queen of Scots, 56

Mastry, Vojtech, 201

Mathematical Principles of Natural Philosophy, The
    (Newton), 62

Mazzini, Giuseppe, 153, 155

McLane, John R., 161

Mehmed II, 74, 75

Mehta, Ved, 211

Mein Kampf (Hitler), 192

Mémoires (Louis XIV), 54

Mensheviks, 179

Mercier, Louis-Sébastien, 130

Metternich, Klemens, 149

Mexico City
    Spanish settling of, 37–38

Mighty Acts of Lord Rama, The (Tulsidas), 85

Military Revolutionary Committee, 181

Milky Way
    Galileo's description of, 61

Mill, James, 91

Miller, Robert Ryal, 37

minorities
    fate of, under nationalism, 147

Miyan (Niazi of Sirhind), 87

Moctezuma
    meeting with Cortés, 33–34

Mombasa, Kenya, 110, 111, 112

Montesquieu, Charles-Louis de Secondat, baron de
    on religion in France, 64–65

Moors, 24–25

Morel, E.D., 163

Morley, Lord John, 162

Morton, Thomas, 31

Mountbatten, Lord Louis, 211

Mozambique
    Portuguese colonization of, 111

Murphey, Rhoads, 87

Muslims
    invasion of India by, 87
    numbers of, in Ottoman-ruled Balkans, 76, 77
    revivalist movements among, 228–29
    as traders in India, 23–24
    see also Islam

Mussolini, Benito, 189
    on fundamentals of Fascism, 190

Nagy, Ferenc, 202, 203

Napoleon Bonaparte
    compares himself with Washington, 135–36
    invasion of Russia by, 133–35
    overthrow of Spanish Bourbon monarch by, 119

Naquin, Susan, 95

Nasreddin Hoja, 82

nationalism
    cultural and social integration under, 148–49
    elements of, 147
    and end of colonialism, 209
    growth of
        in colonized regions, 156
        in nineteenth century, 125
    in Italy, 153–54
    opposition to, 149–50

Nationalist Party (South African), 214

Native Americans
    conversion to Christianity of, 36
    description of, at Columbus's landing, 25–26
    and New England colonists, 31
    treatment of, by Columbus, 27

Nazi party (German National Socialists), 168, 191

Nehru, Jawaharal, 211

Netherlands

    expansion of overseas empire, 28–29

Newton, Isaac, 61–62

Niña (ship), 25

Noonan, John, 82

Norinaga, Motoori, 102

Novikov, Nikolay, 200

October Revolution. *See* Bolshevik revolution

Oliver, Roland, 106

On the Corruption of Morals in Russia (Shcherbatov), 70

Operation Barbarossa, 195

Operation Reinhardt, 196

Opium War, 159

Ottoman Empire, 19, 73, 169

    division of society under, 76

    folktales of, 82–83

    governmental problems of, 79–80

    military nature of, 74–75

    siege of Vienna by, 77–79

Páez, José Antonio, 120, 121

Paine, Thomas, 115

Palestine

    creation of Jewish homeland in, 217

Palestine Liberation Organization (PLO), 219

Palestine National Council

    proclamation of statehood by, 219–20

passive resistance

    Gandhi's view on, 210–11

Paul, Saint

    epistles, 43

peninsulares (Spanish officials), 119

perestroika (restructuring), 221, 224

Persian Letters (Montesquieu), 64

Peru

    Lima, 39

    revolution in, 120

Peter the Great (Russian czar)

    abdication of, 68

Philip IV (king of Spain), 39

Pitt, William, 114

Pizarro, Francisco, 38

PLO, 219

Plymouth colony, 30

Poland

    deportation of Jews from, 196–97

    Hitler's invasion of, 194

population growth

    Malthus on, 138–39

Portuguese, 20

    in East Africa, 110–11

    in India, 23

    in West Africa, 21–22

potatoes, 41

predestination

    Calvin's view of, 45

Primer (English textbook), 48

Princip, Gavrilo, 169

proletariat, 142–43

Protestants. *See* Reformation

Prussian revolution

    failure of liberals during, 152–53

Ptolemy, Claudius, 60

Puritans, 57

Pyrenees, Treaty of the, 39

Radek, Karl, 187

Radicalism of the American Revolution (Wood), 117

railroads

    development of, 144–45

Raj, British, 161

Rawski, Evelyn S., 95

Recopilación de la Leyes de los Reynos de las Indias, 37

Reflections on the French Revolution (Burke), 132–33

Reformation

    in England, 47–49

    see also Luther, Martin

Remarque, Erich Maria, 174

Rex, Richard, 47

Ricci, Matteo, 98

Richelieu, Cardinal, 53

Rodrigues, João, 101

Rolland, Romain, 174

Roosevelt, Franklin D., 201

    failure of, 201

Rousseau, Jean-Jacques, 65, 126, 149

Russell, Bertrand, 174

Russia

    Bolshevik overthrow of provisional government, 181–82

    Napoleon's invasion of, 133–35

    see also Soviet Union

Russo-German Pact, 195

Santander, Francisco de Paula, 120
Sardinia-Piedmont kingdom, 155
Scammell, G.V., 28
Scholarios, George, 75
SchutzStaffel (SS), 196
Scientific Revolution, 60
Segal, Jerome M., 218
Seghrek (Turkish folk hero), 80–82
Sepoy Rebellion, 160
Shcherbatov, M.M., 70
Sheehan, James J., 152
Sheffield Cutlers Bill, 142
Shi'ite Muslims, 77
Sidereal Messenger, The (Galileo), 60
Sieyès, Emmanuel Joseph, 127
Sino-Japanese War, 198
slavery/slave trade, 104
    economic effect in West Africa, 104
    by Portugal, 21
    recollections of a slave, 108–109
Slavs
    German hatred of, 170
Smith, Adam, 139
Smith, Anthony D., 148
Smith, John, 31
Sobibor death camp, 196
Social Contract, The (Rousseau), 65–66
Socinus, Laelius, 64
Sofala, Mozambique, 110, 111
Solomon, Job ben (Ayuba Suleiman Diallo), 108
Solzhenitsyn, Aleksandr, 221, 222
South Africa, 168, 213
    ANC vision of democracy in, 214–15
South African War, 158
South America
    revolutionary movements in, 119–21
Soviet Union
    and Berlin blockade, 205
    confrontation with West under Stalin, 202
    and Cuban missile crisis, 205
    Hitler's invasion of, 195
    industrialization under Five-Year Plan, 185–86
    occupation of Hungary by, 202–203
    Twenty-Seventh Communist Party Congress, 223
Spain

governance of colonies of, 37–38
Spinoza, Baruch, 64
Spirit and the Letter, The (St. Augustine), 43
Stalin, Joseph, 168, 184, 185, 201
    purges under, 187–88
    and Soviet confrontation with West, 202
    terror under, 222–23
steamships, 144–45
Streicher, Julius, 191
Stromberg, Roland N., 173
Stuart, Mary (Queen of Scots), 56
sugar industry
    in colonial New Spain, 40–41
Süleyman the Magnificent, 74, 77
Swahili, 111

Tacuba, Lord of, 33, 34
Talbott, Strobe, 230
taxation
    of American colonies, objection to, 114–15
    in Ottoman Empire, 76
    Voltaire's views on, 67
Taylor, Ronald, 71
Tenochtitlán, 32
    siege of, 35
Teresa of Ávila, 49
Texcoco, Lord of, 33, 34
Third Estate
    role of, in French Revolution, 127–28
Thompson, E.P., 141
Thompson, John, 181
Tiananmen Square crackdown, 231
    effect on Chinese communism, 226
Tokugawa, Ieyasu, 164
Tolstoy, Leo, 134
Tours, battle of, 78
trade
    in Colombia, 120
    contribution of industrialization to, 146
    in Mughal India, 88–89
    Portuguese, 20
        in East Africa, 111, 112
        in India, 23
Transkei, 214
Treblinka death camp, 196
Trew Law of Free Monarchies (James I), 58
Tripartite Pact (1940), 198

Trotsky, Leon, 180, 184
  and theory of permanent revolution, 185
Truman, Harry S., 200
Tuchman, Barbara, 170
Tucker, Robert C., 183
Tudor, Mary, 47
Tulard, Jean, 133
Tulsidas, 85
Turenne, Vicomte de, 54

United Nations, 199
  establishment of Israel by, 219
United States
  Cold War foreign policy of, Soviet view of, 200–201
  de Tocqueville's view of democracy in, 118
  development of railroad and steamships in, 144–45
  military, Soviet assessment of, 204–205
  Open Door policy in China, 197–98
  post–Cold War policy toward China, 231
  strength of middle class in, 117
Uxkull, Boris, 135

Venda, 214
Venezuela
  Bolívar's address at Angostura, 121–22
  revolution in, 120
Versailles, Treaty of
  and Hitler's rise to power, 192, 194
  as origin of WW II, 189
  restraints on Germany in, 177–78
viceroy, in colonial New Spain, 38
Vienna, siege of, 77–79
Voltaire (François-Marie Arouet), 54
  on Parisian life, 66–67
von der Pfalz, Liselotte, 55

Walker, Barbara, 82
Wan Li, 96–97
Warsaw, Poland
  deportation of Jews from, 196–97
Wealth of Nations (Smith), 139
What Is the Third Estate? (Sieyès), 127
William II (German kaiser), 170
Willson, D. Harris, 58
Wilson, Arthur, 56
women
  in China
    after decline in Marxism, 227
    life of, in Forbidden City, 97–98
  in the church, Calvin's and Luther's positions on, 45–47
  religious, in New Spain, 49–50
  role in French Revolution, 128–30
Wood, Gordon, 117
World War I, 168
  German war aims, 171–73
  intellectual responsibility for, 173–74
  view from trenches, 174–75
  see also Versailles, Treaty of
Wray, Harry, 197

Xiao Duan, 95–96

Zahirud-Din Mūhammad (Babur), 87
Zanzibar
  Portuguese contact with, 110
Zinoviev, Grigorii, 187
Zionism, 217
Zolotarev, V.A., 204
Zuckmayer, Carl, 173